Cottonwood, Minnesota:

Celebrating 125 Years

<u>1888-2013</u>

General Editor: Pat Aamodt

Contributing Editor: Dana Yost

Research Editors:

   Greg Isaackson, Steve Lee

125th Anniversary Steering Committee:

   Joel Dahl, Timothy Fruin, Carol Bossuyt

125th Anniversary logo design: Shelly Meyer

125th Anniversary celebration: July 4- 7, 2013

List of City of Cottonwood officials and employees in 2013

Cottonwood City Council Members (term expiration):
Mayor:
Ellen Lenz (12/31/2014)
Council Members:
Dan Louwagie (12/31/2016)
Christopher Dahl (12/31/2016)
Corey Moseng (12/31/2014)
Shawn Myers (12/31/2014)

City Staff:
Kathy Dahl, city clerk-treasurer
Charlie Seipel, community development coordinator
Steve Alm, maintenance manager
Randy Fenger, maintenance employee
Allen Olsen, maintenance employee

Introduction

This book is intended to be a celebration of Cottonwood, the city that many of us have called or still do call home. The place where we went to school, raised our children, found our careers, or settled into retirement. A place that flies strong in the face of rural decline almost everywhere around it — populations in many other small towns have fallen, yet Cottonwood's has risen steadily, reaching a new high of 1,212 in the 2012 Census; it continues to attract new businesses and many existing businesses have had great growth; a new school was built in 2002; and the area remains a strong base of agricultural business. There has been grief, loss and change, but also renewal, a strength of spirit and character, and, always, pride in Cottonwood and those who live in and around it.

This book is published in connection with Cottonwood's 125th anniversary celebration in the summer of 2013. It is not filled with a year-by-year chronology of every year of the city's history, as a reader might find in a centennial history book. Nor does it highlight every major news event of the last 125 years. Indeed, there is a special emphasis on the last 25 years of Cottonwood's history, from 1988-2013, since the official centennial history book did offer a thorough look at the first 100 years.

Yet, this book does not ignore the first 100 years, either — there has been some very thorough research into the businesses and buildings of the town, into city development projects, and the history of our lake. And we include many remembrances of the town's earlier years. The book is perhaps both a supplement to earlier histories of Cottonwood, and also an expansion of them — presented with valuable new information and insights.

In two ways, we hope you will find this book to be the best of both worlds:

• one, in that it offers stories and history about the deep past, and about the last 25 years (including write-ups on nearly every business that existed in 2013);

• two, in that the book is a hybrid of historical lists, charts and chronologies and narrative history that aims to bring the voices and memories of our residents to life, and provide some context and explanation for many aspects of Cottonwood history.

In other words, there is both hard, raw data, and words that analyze, remember, explain, and capture emotions — from sorrow to a sense of accomplishment to wide-open laughter.

We have tried to be as inclusive as possible. We sought input and involvement from every business, institution and organization in and near Cottonwood, and are grateful to all those who replied with information, photos and essays.

Some did not respond, despite repeated requests both verbal and in print. We are sorry for that, because their responses would have made the book more complete. We also apologize in advance for any omissions or mistakes that readers may find in the book. Be assured they are not intentional. We gave our honest, best efforts to be as complete and accurate as possible.

With that, we sincerely hope you enjoy this history of Cottonwood as it celebrates its 125th anniversary.

— *Editors and contributors*

Greetings from Mayor Ellen Lenz

Where can you say there has been real change in the last 25 years? All over Cottonwood.

Cottonwood has been talking about its 125th anniversary for a while, and now here it is. Time goes by so quickly. In the last 25 years, we saw the fall of Communism, attacks on New York and the Pentagon, the Iraq war, Hurricane Katrina and other worldwide happenings that affected small-town living.

Places that were corn and bean fields are now filled with houses and a school. Main Street businesses started to leave empty spaces, and new businesses are starting to take their place. Many businesses have relocated, but stayed in Cottonwood.

Another field has turned into an industrial park, and new water treatment ponds were added because Cottonwood is growing.

As a city, we have cheered and cried with our citizens, welcomed new families, and mourned the loss of those too young. The citizens that have decided they could make a difference have run for city and school offices and sat through meetings and discussion, all in the best interest's of Cottonwood's citizens.

This is my home — not that I was born here, but this is where I chose to call home.

As we come together for this anniversary, new memories will be made, friendships renewed and there will be time to sit and talk about "remember when." Enjoy your time together and come back often, and see the landscape of Cottonwood continue to change.

You're always welcome here, and we hope you join us in looking forward to see what happens on the 150th anniversary. What we will see here in the next 25 years will astound us.

Thank you for being part of this community. Stay, and make your life here.

— *Mayor Ellen Lenz, April 2013*

Table of Contents

OUR CITY

Census Data for City of Cottonwood

Census Year	Population
2012	1,212
2000	1,148
1990	982
1980	924
1970	794
1960	717
1950	709
1940	690
1930	615
1920	813
1910	770
1900	549

A Timeline of Cottonwood City Leadership

DECADE	MAYORS	COUNCIL MEMBERS	CITY CLERKS
1960s	CLARENCE HATLESTAD	KENNETH NELSON	ERWIN SCHWARTZ
	LESLIE LARSON	JAY AGRE	
	TOM COLLINS	OTIS OLSON	
		MARTIN BAHN	
		HOWARD REWERTS	
		MURL ERICKSON	
1970s	TOM COLLINS	GORDON KNUTSON	GREG ISAACKSON
	FR. DENNIS BECKER	GEORGE DAVIS	
	LOREN ERICKSON	GENE DESMET	
		EVERET WILLHITE	
		NORMAN GEIHL	
		ADRIAN GOLBERG	
		AL MARTIN	
		WAYNE PETERSON	
1980s	TORGNY ANDERSON	DAVE SCHOEPF	
	JIM DUNCAN	JOEL DAHL	
		BILL KROGER	
		JAN JOHNSON	

1990s	TIM FRUIN	MEREDITH DOOM	
		RICK REKEDAL	
		KAREN GEIHL	
		MAILEN PRINGLE	
		LONA NEVILLE	
		DEBBIE ANDERSON	
		ALAN SMITH	
		ELLEN LENZ	
2000s	ELLEN LENZ	JOEL DAHL	
		RAFAEL GONZALEZ	
		RYAN FENGER	
		LISA VARPNESS	
		MATTHEW LEE	
		MICHELLE SCHULTZ	
		LEONARD DOOM	
		LINDA MAGNUSON	
2010s	ELLEN LENZ	DAN LOUWAGIE	KATHY DAHL
		COREY MOSENG	
		SHAWN MEYERS	
		CHRISTOPHER DAHL	

Chronology of Developments by City of Cottonwood

Compiled by Greg Isaackson

<u>1963-2013</u>

1963 —

Cottonwood's 75th Anniversary Celebration (Diamond Jubilee) held in August

1967 —

Natural gas service extended into the city

1968 —

Center island constructed on two blocks of Main Street business district for parking in the center of the street

1969 —

New water well constructed on land acquired three miles east of town from Leland Krumrey, along with construction of a water transmission line into the city

City acquired old downtown North Star Insurance building; used initially as Senior Citizens Center

Old Cottonwood Co-op Station acquired from Co-op for remodeling into municipal liquor store

1970 —

New ambulance purchased from Smith's Farm Store, along with organizing the Ambulance Service

Evergreen Park Addition residential plat approved

Lindsay Court plat approved as mobile home court

1971 —

Community TV began cable television system in Cottonwood

Bel-Mar Addition residential plat approved

Schwartz Addition residential plat approved

Sunview Addition residential plat approved

Marshall Millwork began manufacturing operations in old creamery building

1972 —

Cottonwood Housing and Redevelopment Authority formed

1973 —

Lake Improvement Committee formed to study the water quality of Cottonwood Lake

Ritter's Sanitary Service of Marshall entered into agreement with city for providing garbage collection services

Construction of the 30-unit West Prairie Apartments and 10 single-family low-income homes was undertaken by the Cottonwood Housing and Redevelopment Authority

1974—

City Clerk's Office and Library moved to old North Star Insurance building, joining the Senior Citizens as occupants

Street, and curb and gutter improvements made on various streets in the city

1975—

New city maintenance shop constructed

An addition to the fire hall was constructed to house a new fire pumper and new rural fire truck

Lakeview Estate Addition Plat was accepted. Water, sanitary sewer, lift station and street grading improvements were made

1977—

Water and sanitary sewer extensions made to Bel-Mar Addition and Lakeview Estates Addition

1978–

Alan Martin awarded garbage collection contract

City donated land to Mid-Continent Cabinetry and made infrastructure improvements for expansion project

1979—

Comprehensive Plan for guiding future city growth and development adopted

Mink farm property cleaned up

Lakeview Estate Addition and Idso's First Addition plats approved

1980—

Bituminous surfacing of Shoreview Drive and Pass Street completed

Northwood Addition residential plat approved

1981—

City provided industrial revenue bonds to Empire State Bank for construction of new bank building

Wastewater Treatment Project (consisting of ponds, pumping station and outfall line) constructed at a cost of $665,000

Community Center constructed with financial contributions and volunteer labor

East Main Street Bridge replaced by Lyon County

Center island was taken out of the business district portion of Main Street, switching over to diagonal parking

Railroad Depot moved to city's Wastewater Plant site

1982 —

Street, bridge and water and sanitary sewer improvements made to Industrial Area around Mid-Continent Cabinetry building with funding from a Community Development Block Grant

Pagers purchased for fire and ambulance personnel (for the first time)

Cottonwood Industrial Park First Addition Plat approved

Lakeview Park constructed with state grant funds

1983 —

Approval given by city for locating Meal Site in the Community Center

1984 —

Takle Hardware store building burned down by area fire departments as a training drill

1985 —

Downtown Business District Sidewalk replacements made with Tax Increment Financing funding

Window, heating and bathroom improvements made to municipal building with grant funds

Construction of a new water well, pumphouse 2-1/2 miles north of Cottonwood, with a water transmission line, funded with Small Cities Development Program grant funds. The well was put into service in 1986

1986 —

Idso's First Addition and Lakeview Estates Second Addition annexed into the city

Bituminous street surfacing improvements made to the northwestern portion of Shoreview Drive

Construction of a gravel street on Northwood Drive completed

1987 —

A 48-by-36-foot addition to the Fire Hall was constructed

City contracts with Lyon County for law enforcement services

1988 —

Cottonwood's 100th Anniversary Celebration

Rebuilding roof of Municipal Building was completed, funded with grant funds

1989 —

A new 150,000-gallon water tower was constructed in the city's Industrial Area to accommodate an expansion by Mid-Continent Cabinetry, funded with federal EDA and Small Cities Development Program grant funds, and Tax-Increment Financing

1990 —

City's Revolving Loan Fund established, to make fixed-asset loans available to new and expanding businesses

1992 —

City Clerk's Office and Library moved to remodeled facilities at 86 W. Main Street

Village Court was opened as the city's Business Incubator Project

Lindsay Court Second Addition plat approved

1993 —

Evelyn Swenson donated the Norseth/Larsen Historic House to the city, with the Cottonwood Area Historical Society being responsible for the care, maintenance, operation and funding of the house

Storm sewer improvements made along West Second Street from North Star Insurance and Co-op Oil to Cottonwood Lake after heavy summer rains made these properties vulnerable to flooding

1994 —

City received an Economic Recovery Fund grant for loaning to North Star Insurance for its expansion project

Formation of the city's Economic Development Authority for business development and promotion activities was initiated

Idso's Second Addition plat annexed into the city and approved

City approved EDA's purchase of 15.91 acres of land from Andrew Boerboom for business/industrial development purposes

EDA entered into option for purchase of Bahn land between state Highway 23 and County Road 75 for business/industrial development

1995 —

Sanitary sewer extension made to Northwood Drive, and street, curb and gutter improvements to Bel-Mar Addition were completed

1996 —

Bituminous surfacing, and curb and gutter improvements made by Lyon County to Barstad Road

1997—

A 40-by-40-foot game room and storage room was added to the north side of the Liquor Store

1998—

After the extremely difficult winter of 1996-1997, a new front-end loader and snow blower were purchased to handle cleaning city streets more efficiently after heavy snowfalls

The city and Chamber of Commerce hosted WCCO Radio's "Good Morning Show" at the school in July

EDA proceeded with purchasing the remaining 12.46 acres of Bahn land on the northeast corner of town between state Highway 23 and County Road 75

1999—

Final residential plat of Southeast Addition approved

Northwood First Addition annexation and final residential plat approved on the north side of Northwood Drive

Extended Area Service approved by Minnesota Public Utilities Commission for toll-free calls between Cottonwood and Marshall

2000—

Water, sanitary sewer and lift station extension made to Southeast Addition

Street, curb and gutter improvements made to Southeast Addition and Shoreview Circle

Water and sanitary sewer service improvements made to Northwood Drive

Sanitary sewer main rerouted along Barstad Road into the city's main wastewater pumping station

2002—

Northwood Drive bituminous street, and curb and gutter improvements made

2004—

Upgrades to the wastewater treatment facilities were undertaken, including expansion of the pond system by the addition of a fourth settlement pond and manhole rehabilitation improvements

Along with the EDA, the city purchased the old school building and playground site for residential purposes

2005—

Sanitary sewer rerouting and lift station construction around the east side of the industrial plat to accommodate Mid-Continent Cabinetry's expansion project on East Second Street was constructed, funded with city and state grant funds

2006 —

East Main Street reconstructed, along with sidewalk improvements, by Lyon County

Old School Addition plat approved for residential use

Water, sanitary sewer and street improvements made in Old School Addition

2008 —

Various street, curb and gutter and storm drainage improvements made on Juno Lane, Vermillion Street, Westview Circle, Lake Street, Cottonwood Street and West First Street

2009 —

"Welcome to Cottonwood" sign installed at the northern entrance to the city

Pedestrian/bike path construction along Barstad Road, funded in part through the state's Safe Routes to School Program

Agreement was reached for the city's acquisition of the 220 northern feet of the Old Athletic Field from Cottonwood Co-op Oil Company for the trade of the Old Fire Hall to the Co-op, once a new Fire Hall has been built

Because of a lack of profitability, the Liquor Store was put up for bids and sold to private ownership. It was opened in 2010 as a bar and grill named LeRoy's

2010 —

The Norseth/Larsen Historic House was sold to private ownership since the Cottonwood Area Historical Society was unable to provide the personnel and finances for the care and operation of the house

2011 —

After extensive study and discussion on the development of new city facilities (new Fire Hall/Ambulance Garage, City Office/Library, and Maintenance Shop), a special election was held on a $1,905,000 bond issue that resulted in it being defeated by a vote of 93 yes votes and 177 no votes. After the vote, other less-costly options were explored by the city for the development of more affordable facilities

Northwood Second Addition annexed into city and residential plat approved

2012 —

The city maintenance shop was relocated to the property at 300 East Fourth Street North, that the city had acquired, with a portion of the building being leased to Lyon County for its maintenance garage

2013 —

City offices were relocated into the building at 78 West Main Street, that had been remodeled

The Community Library is being remodeled and expanded for occupying all of the building at 86 West Main Street by doubling its size, where the City Offices had previously occupied the front portion

Plans are being developed for construction of a new Fire Hall/Ambulance Garage on the northeast portion of the Old Athletic Field that the City had acquired from the Cottonwood Co-op Oil Company

Village Court closed in March

Cottonwood celebrates its Quasiquicentennial (125th Anniversary) in July

Fishing and relaxing in a pontoon on Cottonwood Lake. (Tri-County News photo)

Cottonwood Fire Department

By Kirk Lovsness

Al Martin served as Fire Chief from 1982 until 2001. Longtime firefighter and assistant chief Paul Geihl stepped up to serve as Chief from 2001 until 2004. Dale Louwagie took over as Chief in 2004 and continues to serve in that capacity.

In 1994 the department replaced the rural pumper and city pumper with one shared pumper truck, which is still in service. In 1999, a combination pumper/emergency response truck was added to serve as a first-response vehicle to rescue calls and auto accidents.

Most recently, in 2013, a new tanker truck was added to replace a unit which had been in service since 1975.

The department has also raised funds to purchase the latest model thermal imaging camera to assist in rescue and firefighting. The department is equipped with Scott self-contained breathing apparatus to allow firefighters to enter smoke-filled environments.

The City of Cottonwood and surrounding townships have strongly supported the Cottonwood Fire Department over the years, providing the funding and volunteers to serve. The Department also has raised funds over the years by hosting a very popular hog roast each summer. Proceeds have been used to help purchase equipment.

The Cottonwood Fire Department, and Cottonwood Ambulance Service, were honored in 2008 with Public Service awards at the North Memorial Public Safety Service Awards ceremony for their roles in responding to the fatal 2008 school bus crash on Feb. 19, 2008, just south of Cottonwood.

Membership averages approximately 25 members. Many dedicated firefighters serve 20 years or longer. New members are always welcome. We'd like to encourage you to consider joining and serving our community.

Cottonwood Ambulance Service

By Kathy Martin

The Ambulance Service was started in 1970 with 39 members who had completed first aid. Kermit Huso was President, Vice President was Joe Derynck, Secretary/Treasurer was Stella Smith, and Andy Viaene was appointed to coordinator.

Andy would also take all the phone calls during the day for ambulance calls.

The first name was Cottonwood Ambulance Service and Rescue Association, and then later in the year we changed the name to Cottonwood Ambulance Service.

The charge for service was $25 for a call and 60 cents per loaded mile.

On Aug. 10, 1970, ambulance was in Springfield, Ohio, and would be ready in eight weeks, a 1970 International (purchased from Smith's Farm Store). Joe Derynck and Joel Dahl flew to Ohio and returned it to Cottonwood.

1974 — 32 runs for the year and service had a new radio installed, rates $40 per call and 75 cents per mile

1980 — Second ambulance purchased and pagers for the crew members to receive the ambulance call from Lyon County dispatch.

1988 — Third ambulance purchased

1995 — Fourth ambulance purchased, Type 3

2004 — Fifth ambulance purchased, Ford Type 3. This ambulance replaced the 1988

2012 — A new 2011 ambulance replaced the 2004 ambulance

In 1976 the EMT training was developed and consisted of 81 hours and CPR. Today's class is now 140 hours and CPR. Also required for today's members are passing a national test and hands-on skills, plus additional training that is required because of special equipment we are able to use. Every two years everyone must have 24 hours of class for recertification.

In June of 1994 the first cardiac defibrillator was purchased for those patients that were in cardiac arrest. The medical director at this time was Darrell Carter.

The Virginia Louwagie memorial scholarship was established in Virginia's memory and for her dedication and time devoted to the ambulance. We have done many fundraisers over the years consisting of dances, pork feed, French toast breakfast, steak fry, hamburger sales, to name a few.

The Cottonwood Ambulance has helped the community with blood drives in the past, and a mock car crash for the high school students to show the effects of drinking/texting while driving.

The Cottonwood Ambulance does a lot of training during each year to keep our skill levels up and ready for the next call, we are always implementing new and better ways of taking care of patients.

In 2003 we started utilizing Advanced Life Support intercepts with Marshall North ambulance and then later with Granite Falls Ambulance and North Ambulance Redwood Falls. This allows us to bring the emergency room to the ambulance out in the field and patients receive the higher level of care instead of waiting to get to the hospital.

In 2009 Cottonwood Ambulance Service started its own part-time Advanced Life Support. We have three paramedics: Scott Boehne, LeAnn Boehne and Dane Meyer, who, when are available, can bring that ER care to patients early to help with a better outcome.

When no paramedic is available we are a Basic Life Support ambulance. Here are skills an EMT Basic can do: CPR, advanced airway , IV's, Aspirin, Nitro, Epi Pens, Albuterol , 12-lead ECG and trauma.

ALS allows the service to provide pain control, 12-lead EKGs to see if patient is having a heart attack, advanced airways, cardiac arrest medication, breathing assistance with medications, trauma, and many other advanced skills.

In 2012 we did 150 calls for service and training for the year. We cover the city of Cottonwood and rural area around Cottonwood, the City of Hanley Falls, Wood Lake and Echo and the surrounding rural area. We take patients to Granite Falls, Marshall, Redwood Falls and Montevideo.

We have 14 members on the Cottonwood Ambulance Service 2013:

Dane Meyer, Director

Ellen Golberg, Co-Director/training officer

Shelly Meyer, Supply Coordinator

Wendy Bossuyt, Training officer

Brian Bossuyt, Vehicle caretaker

Terry Dieken, Vehicle caretaker

Jamie Anderson

Brandon Jeseritz

Jeremy Mead

Dave Nelson

Zack Meyer

Scott Boehne

LeAnn Boehne

Brooke Maxwell

We are in the process of purchasing a new defibrillator with 12-lead capabilities, blood pressure, Pulse OX and many more features. The cost is around $30,000.

There have been many community members who have served on the ambulance since service started in Cottonwood in 1970. There have also been many families that have had multiple family members on at the same time. Many thanks to all who gave precious time from their families to make Cottonwood a safe place to live.

Earlier members of the Cottonwood Ambulance Service:

1970s: James Cole, Tom Collins, Joel Dahl, Sylvia Dahl, Joe DeRynck, Harriet Doom, Floyd Engel, Darrin Erickson, Darold Gniffke, Loris Gniffke, Carol Huso, Kermit Huso, Jerry Husong, David Idso, Nellie Idso, Tom Idso, Georgia Idso, Robert Javens, Bonnie Knutson, Lorraine Lancaster, Lucille Loe, Betty Losvness, Elaine Meyer, Arline Miller, Bruce Mogenson, Arthur Peppersack, Dale Reishus, Donna Mae Reishus, Marguerite Richard, Don Rosa, Marge Seitz, Stella Smith, LaVonne Stoks, Vincent Stoks, Andrew Viaene, Douglas Warnke, Harvey Rasmussen

1976, 81-hour training plan: Terry Dieken, Mary Boll, Pat Laleman, Rick Rekedal, Greg Gniffke, Carol Belling, Bernard Belling, Alan Martin, Steve Stoks, Brad Rosa, Marc Rosa, Ann Dosdall, Dan Dosdall, Beulah Anderson, Char Rekedal, Caryl Bartels

Cottonwood City Office

From the City Clerk's Office and the March 20, 2013, issue of The Tri-County News

In 1993, the Cottonwood City Clerk's Office moved to its location at 86 West Main Street in conjunction with the Cottonwood Library after the building was purchased from Edna Ericksen.

The Clerk's Office was housed in the front portion of the building and the Library was housed in the back. The office housed the City Clerk, the Clerk's Secretary and, for a time, the Community Development Coordinator.

In March of 2013, the City Clerk's Office relocated a few buildings down to 78 West Main Street. The new office provides more room for City Staff and also provides space for the City Council Chambers and committee/board meetings.

"After much consideration and city-wide surveys it was decide that some remodeling would be done in the established building rather than building a new building," Dahl said. "We have more room and are able to have our own office area even though it will basically be one big room. There is a spot for the city council to meet in the new office space, unless it will be a largely attended meeting."

The Cottonwood Library was expanded into the former city office space after renovations at the site at 86 West Main Street.

Starting in 1974, Gregory Isaackson served as the City Clerk-Administrator until the spring of 2011. Mason Schirmer served as the Clerk-Administrator until March of 2012 and Kathy Dahl is currently serving as the City Clerk-Treasurer. Charlie Seipel was hired in November 2006 as the Community Development Coordinator and Peg Hauge was hired in the summer of 2012 as a part-time office assistant.

Village Court

Village Court opened in late 1992 as a result of efforts from the city of Cottonwood and The Cottonwood Economic Development Authority with financial grant assistance from the Southwest Initiative Fund. Village Court was set up to serve as a business incubator in which new businesses would have a space to start and expand out of as they grew. Village Court was housed at 78 West Main Street by purchase of the Seitz Building and 82 West Main Street through donation of a building use from John Murphy.

Village Court hosted a large number of small businesses over the years, some of which have grown to become established Cottonwood businesses, and served as a shopping destination for Downtown Cottonwood. At its beginning, Village Court was overseen by manager Erma Huso. Other retail clerks over the years included Helen Dahl and Bonnie Knutson.

In 2006, Village Court downsized to a single building at 82 West Main Street and the building at 78 West Main Street was used to house the Professional Dental Lab. In March of 2013, the decision was made to close Village Court because of projected operating losses.

Housing and Redevelopment Authority

The Housing and Redevelopment Authority of Cottonwood was organized in 1970 with the following people serving on the first HRA Board of Commissioners: Philip Desilet, Thelma Egeland, Adrian Golberg, Burton Schwerin and Dennis Becker.

In April of 1974 the West Prairie Apartments officially opened their doors for new tenants. The HRA currently consists of 29 units at the West Prairie Apartments, and 10 scattered site family units.

In the last 10 years, the HRA has begun to completely remodel the kitchens and bathrooms at West Prairie and also in its 10 family units. As of this writing only a few units remain to be remodeled.

Our community rooms have also undergone remodeling and a new natural gas generator has been installed for use in case of power outages.

In 1974, Kathy Martin was named as the Executive Director after Ardis Michaelson retired. Kathy is still the Executive Director after 39 years.

Current board members are: Mayor Ellen Lenz, Helen Dahl, Carla Mack, Pat Lange and Dan Louwagie. The caretakers are Norman and Faye Myers, who have also been with the HRA for more than 20 years.

West Prairie Apartments is a busy place, hosting monthly birthday parties, monthly communion services, lots of Christmas activities and many informal coffee conversations.

We encourage our tenants to make use of the services of Senior Dining and home health care, which is provided by agencies in our local area. This enables the elderly to "age in place," and enjoy their beautiful surroundings at West Prairie.

Our family units are always full and provide a much-needed source of affordable housing for families with children, with full basements and great yard space.

Cottonwood Library History

From information found in the Cottonwood Jubilee book, a submitted piece written by Mrs. Leslie (Ruth) Larson states that in 1940 the Cottonwood Study Club became active in organizing a county library. Mrs. Alex Kolhei and Mrs. L.E. Norstad were elected to represent the club, and later Mrs. C.A. Hatlestad was added to the committee. After many meetings with representatives throughout Lyon County, the Marshall-Lyon County Library became a reality in 1942. The piece goes on to state that a "Library Station" was to be established in Cottonwood.

The first location of the Cottonwood Library was in the Cottonwood City Hall, which at that time, could be found in a building west of the water tower and directly behind the first Cottonwood Co-op Oil Company Station, which is now LeRoy's bar and restaurant.

It is unclear as to who the first librarian was, however, two names that have come to be associated with the position were Mildred Wilson and Mary Javens. At a later date, Maxine Dahl became the librarian and the library was relocated to the back part of the Variety Store on Main Street. All this time the connection with the Marshall-Lyon County Library has remained, with the book collection and other materials basically loaned to Cottonwood by the Marshall-Lyon County Library.

Upon Mrs. Dahl's retirement from business, the library was relocated once again, and this time found a home in the basement of what was once the North Star Insurance Building and is now the Senior Citizens Building (40 W. 1st St.). This took place during the first part of the year 1974, with Ann Dosdall becoming the librarian. In 1978, Joy McGuire was hired as the librarian of Cottonwood. She left the library in 1980 to return to her home state of Pennsylvania, at which time Charlotte Rekedal, having been hired as the substitute librarian, was offered the permanent position.

In April of 1992, the library was moved from the basement of the Senior Citizens Building to its new location in the back part of the building occupied by the City Clerk's office, where it remained until April 2013. With the relocation of the City Office to 78 West Main Street, the Cottonwood Library has now taken over the entirely remodeled building at 86 West Main Street as its permanent residence.

The library is open 20 hours a week for its patrons' use and enjoyment. It remains a branch of the Marshall-Lyon County Library and continues to be a part of the Plum Creek Library System of Southwest Minnesota.

(Please note that this information has been respectfully submitted by Gregory Isaackson, former city clerk of Cottonwood; Karen Klein (daughter of Maxine Dahl); and Charlotte Rekedal, Cottonwood librarian.)

County Road 10 Resurfacing

From the April 24, 2013, issue of The Tri-County News

Lyon County Board approves concrete surface for County Road 10 to Cottonwood

The Lyon County board on April 16 approved a low bid from Schafer Contracting Company to put a concrete resurfacing on County Road 10 from U.S. Highway 59 east into West Fifth Street in Cottonwood.

The bid was for $4,388,684.88. Work was expected to start May 13, 2013, and be completed by Aug. 9, 2013.

Other construction began in the summer of 2012 to redo County Road 10 from Cottonwood west to U.S. Highway 59. The angle of the curves 1-1/2 miles west of town have changed to make them driveable at 55 mph.

Area Townships

Information on Lyon County and Yellow Medicine County townships that neighbor the city of Cottonwood.

Lucas Township Board: Sherry Anderson before 1983-1994; Tony Van Uden before 1983-spring 1996; Jerry Aamodt 1977-present; Don Bot 1985-present; Dean Rigge 1995-1998; Allison Vandelanotte 1995-present; Denny Allex 1996-2005; Paul Fenger 2000-present; Steve Boerboom 2006-present.

Normania Township: Since Normania Township was organized in 1872, many of the township's residents have helped to continue this form of grassroots government by serving in different capacities on the Town Board. Current board members are: Supervisors: Gary Geihl (since 1991), Lyle Danielson (since 1995), Richard Jolstad (since 2002); Clerk: Jonnie Danielson (since 1995); and Treasurer: Monica Geihl (since 2009).

Sandnes Township Officers: Chairman: Charles Timm, current. Supervisor: Douglas Gregoire 1992-present, Henry "Bud" Gregoire, until 1992. Supervisor: Elmo Volstad, 2011-present, Tom Locher, 2000-2011, Norman Varpness, until 2000. Treasurer: Wayne Carlson, 2010-present, Marvin Kremin, until 2010. Clerk: Peter Hellie, 1990-present, Harland Rowberg until 1990.

Vallers Township: Supervisors: Alton Huso, 1978-present; Camille Hoflock, 1968-2000; Donald Wyffels, 1988-2011; Ronald Timmerman, 2000-present; Curt Boerboom, 2011-present. Treasurers: John Hovdesven, 1989-1991; Joe Hoff Sr., 1991-1997; Charlotte Hoff, 1997-2003; Wendy Hall, 2003-2005; Melissa Louwagie, 2005-present. Clerks: Carol Kompelien, 1988-1994; Ruth Louwagie, 1994-2012; Derek Louwagie, 2012-present.

PEOPLE

Greg Isaackson

When he finished college, Greg Isaackson was hired in May 1974 as Cottonwood's city clerk-administrator. It was the first job he held.

And the only one he ever had.

Isaackson stayed in the position for 37 years until he retired in May 2011, giving Cottonwood a stable hub of city leadership in the form of a local native whose attachment to his home town only grew stronger with time.

"I tried to look upon myself and approach my work with the City Council as being a tool for them and the community in carrying out the work of the community to address issues and move the community forward," Isaackson said in an interview for this history book. "In this role, I did bring ideas to the City Council and other community groups to help facilitate changes, solving problems and making improvements.

"The position of City Clerk-Administrator placed me in a position where I [had] a lot of opportunity to make a difference. I was fortunate to have a part in the development and growth of the community including development of residential areas, development of businesses, and providing enhanced services to the community, such as playing a role in getting toll-free telephone service for calls between Cottonwood and Marshall. Also, I was involved with the development of a new water well north of town, a new wastewater pond system, a new water tower in the industrial area of town, building of the golf course and community. These things were made possible by having good people on the City Council and civic-minded people in the community."

He said he learned a great deal about himself and the community in his 37 years in the position.

"Over the years I have gained a better understanding of the Cottonwood area and its people," Isaackson said. "I have grown in my attachment to my hometown, and as Clerk-Administrator, I gained a strong sense of responsibility for what occurred in our community.

"I [felt] responsible for making sure that things [went] right, and also a sense of disappointment when things didn't work out."

Isaackson sees much to be proud of as he looks at the last 25 years of Cottonwood's history.

"There have been a lot of changes over the past several years," he said. "There have been disappointments, such as a decline in the downtown business district. It's not what it used to be when I was growing up, and never will be again. It's a sign of the times where people are so much more mobile in where they travel to do their business.

"On the positive side, Cottonwood has experienced steady growth and development from a population of around 800 in the 1970s to a population of 1,212 in the 2010 Census. Growth has occurred because of the increase in the number of homes in town, especially around the lake. People are attracted to Cottonwood because of its excellent school system, employment opportunity, proximity to Marshall as a regional center, and the entrepreneurial spirit and ability of many people who have started and grown jobs and employment opportunities in Cottonwood and its surrounding area."

It's part new physical construction and part a determined attitude that have helped Cottonwood buck the trend of rural decline that's hit so many rural communities.

"We have more than off-set the loss of downtown businesses by increasing the number of service and manufacturing businesses," Isaackson said. "The credit for these successes goes to the positive, can-do attitude of people in the community."

That Isaackson stayed in the clerk-administrator position for 37 years should not be surprising, given his and his family's history.

"As a lifelong Cottonwood area resident, I feel a very close attachment to our community," he said. "My roots run deep in this community, with my great-grandparents having settled here in the 1880s and fourth- and fifth-generation family members having always been here as examples of showing commitment to this community and area.

"Cottonwood is a good community, a good place to live, work and raise a family. I have been fortunate to be a part of that experience."

Cliff Hanson

Cliff Hanson retired in 2001 after 47 years at North Star Insurance, including the last 28 as the company's president. He and his wife, Sue, continue to call Cottonwood home and are proud to do so.

While at North Star, and in retirement, Cliff has been very involved in community life through various organizations, such as the Lions Club, and church activity.

In response to questions for this book, Cliff said "Cottonwood is my hometown and your hometown!," adding that he hopes current residents approach the next 25 years with the same kind of pride and civic engagement that has made the previous 25 years so dynamic and important to Cottonwood's strength as a thriving small city.

He said one factor that's allowed Cottonwood to grow — in population, with the building of the new Lakeview Public School (along with residents of Wood Lake), with a wide range of developments, for example — is the way people pull together.

"Yes, I am proud to call Cottonwood MY HOME TOWN! I hope you do also!," he said. "To me, it has always been a TOGETHER TOWN: *whatever* the project, *whatever* the need, Cottonwoodites respond. What a pleasure it has been to pitch in side-by-side and get the right things done and see them enjoyed."

Cliff continued:

"North Star Mutual has been a great blessing, aside from our attachment to local churches that have served so well. Thanks to [early North Star leaders] Bror Anderson and Mort Egeland for all of the things they taught me...what a privilege. Hats off also to the many, many employees of North Star that have served so well and continue to do so.

"There is something special about Cottonwood: take a look around! We are a small town and yet have a pretty good group of industry firms. It's a great place to live!"

He said the school system — first Cottonwood Public Schools and, later, with the consolidation with Wood Lake, the Lakeview Public Schools, is important. "Let us not forget Cottonwood/Lakeview Schools. Another blessing right here in Cottonwood."

Then, looking forward to the next 25 years and encouraging residents to continue to work to keep the community vital, Cliff added, "Let's 'Keep on Keeping On!'"

Joel Dahl

Joel Dahl's words echo those of one of America's Founding Fathers when he talks about how much Cottonwood means to him.

"I am profoundly PROUD to call Cottonwood my home!!!!" Dahl said in response to interview questions for this history book.

"Even with the changes that occur and a life that might be more fulfilled living elsewhere, I say 'Give me Cottonwood or give me death.' I think that small-town values are still here and will remain for years to come. "

That sentiment is similar to the famous words of Patrick Henry during the Revolutionary War, when Henry said, "give me liberty or give me death." They both signify some strong feelings about a place that's held close to the heart.

Not that Dahl didn't do important things beyond Cottonwood's city limits. He did, and yet managed to stay deeply rooted in his hometown at the same time.

Dahl is a Cottonwood native who attained one of the highest elected offices any Cottonwood resident ever has, when he served as Lyon County Sheriff from 2003 until his retirement in 2008.

He was first elected Sheriff in the fall of 2002, capping a long, successful career in law enforcement.

"I worked in the Sheriff's Office from April 1977 until I was elected Sheriff in the fall election of 2002.," Dahl said. "I served as Sheriff from 2003 until I retired in 2008. I worked for four sheriffs and, in a way, was mentored by all of them as I strived to become an elected Sheriff.

"You will note that I always refer to the Office of Sheriff and not Department. This is in following a historical view that the Sheriff, in an elected position, was responsible solely for that Office, unlike appointed department heads of other county departments — just as the County Attorney (elected) leads the County Attorney's Office but the Highway Engineer is appointed to the County Highway Department.

"I was truly honored to be elected by the voters as Sheriff and always tried to be open and available to their needs and concerns. Dana [Yost, author of this story]: you will also recall that I tried to be as open as possible with the media as well and considered the media an ally."

A lot has changed in Cottonwood over the last 25 years. Dahl, who served on the city council, believes most of the changes have been for the good — helping the community defy demographic trends in many other rural Minnesota cities. Cottonwood's population has continued to rise, while a lot of rural towns its size have lost population.

"A certain change, as a 'lifer,' if you will, notes that Cottonwood is a growing and diverse town," he said. "I can't name the number of times or people who have said 'I used to know who lived in every house' and 'now I don't even know everyone that lives in my neighborhood.' The local roots seem to be changing and in a way, sadly, the historical interest is so it seems waning."

But while ties to the city's history may not be as strong for many newcomers, those new residents have helped make its current situation solid by bolstering the work force, school-enrollment numbers and bringing in people who have filled important leadership roles.

"As far as the last 25 years in Cottonwood, I think that the city has continued to stay strong and progressive with the appropriate industries and a strong farming view," Dahl said. "The ability of towns to come together to build a K-12 school also shows a needed strength that local people have. When I served on the city council in the 1980s with the expansion of a new water tower and subsequent creative funding of a Revolving Loan Fund, to benefit business expansion, it proved one more positive step to stay strong, and still is working today."

Harold Fratzke

By Pat Aamodt

As a young boy of 7 or 8 years old and responsible for picking up the grass clippings after mowing, Harold Fratzke made himself a removable hayrack that he put in his coaster wagon, which enabled him to carry more grass. When his work was done, he removed the rack and had his regular coaster wagon again.

He became such a good, productive inventor he was inducted into the Minnesota Inventor Hall of Fame in 1994.

Harold started inventing in earnest in about 1972-1973, and continues to do so. His first awards were won at that time.

When asked how he comes up with ideas for his inventions, he replied, "Usually there is a need for a change in how something works. If I'm thinking on an idea when I go to bed, I often have the answer when I wake up."

Often it takes about three prototypes before it's what he wants as a finished unit.

We talked about a few of his inventions.

Why and how he designed the Roto Chopper: Chopping stalks was a dirty job, time-consuming and often required an extra worker. He mounted a router lawn mower underneath the corn head and it worked so well that the following winter he ordered gear boxes and designed one for his six-row corn head. The next fall K & M Manufacturing came out and watched it work in the field, liked what they saw and started manufacturing them. To date most major manufacturers have followed his design and are mass-producing choppers.

The Pick-up Tool Box is a tool box that slides over the edge of the pick-up box for easy access to the tools. It can also be released to make it a portable box to carry where it's needed.

The Safe-T-Hitch Pin was designed to lock the hitch pin in place.

Tractor mirrors weren't available in 1984, so Harold designed the first tractor breakaway mirrors for K & M Manufacturing. Later on, he designed mirrors that came with signal lights for left- and right-hand turns, which reach out past the trailers, so the driver behind can see the signals.

In 1988, Harold designed the <u>Self-Hitch</u>. It went on the 3-point of the tractor, and could be lowered to the ground to automatically connect to the trailer hitch pin. Therefore you never had to leave the tractor to hook up.

<u>Sun Visors</u> for your tractor cab or combine. Why not?

In 1984, he invented what he considers to be his most successful invention, the <u>Hydra-Covers</u>, which are manufactured by K & M Manufacturing. When tractors came out with hydraulics, they had a rubber plug that had to be put in the hydraulic ports to keep the dirt out. He invented an automatic closing cover over the hydraulic ports to keep the dirt out. Now all major manufacturers have copied that design.

The <u>Convert-A-Lift</u> is designed to lift riding lawn mowers to make it easier to change blades and clean underneath the mowers. You can also remove the lift forks and install a box for yard work.

The Step-Up, for which he won a gold prize, allows you to walk up into your pick-up box with the tail gate either open or closed.

Harold has also invented some changes for bicycles. One is a two-wheel-drive bicycle. Why a two-wheel-drive bicycle, you might ask. His answer is: You've got two arms and two legs, so why not use both? You can use just the foot pedals or just the hand pedals, or both. In the winter, it can go in the basement and be used as an exercise bike.

Another (four-wheeled) bike for children is powered by the hands and steered by the feet.

Harold designed a side car for bicycles, used for transporting children. It's safer than a pull-behind, because the side car is on the right-hand side, away from oncoming traffic.

Some of Harold's inventions have made him wonder why he hadn't thought of them sooner.

Throughout the years there have been at least three different manufacturers, K & M Manufacturing of Renville, Metro Hydraulics of Minneapolis, and Tebben Manufacturers of Clara City, that have made the different items.

Many of Harold's inventions have won awards, from gold to bronze, at the Minnesota Inventors Congress, which is held each year in Redwood Falls.

In 1994, Harold was inducted into the Minnesota Inventor Hall of Fame. A plaque that hangs on the wall in his home reads that, at that time, he had 27 or more economically significant inventions or innovations on agricultural, sports, recreational and transportation equipment and tools. There have been another five or six since that time.

Harold and his son Kent have also spent time together over the years restoring many tractors.

Tim Fruin

By Dana Yost

From the time he was a child, Cottonwood has been Tim Fruin's home. And, in part because of his memories of his childhood, Fruin has long felt a sense of duty to keep Cottonwood a vibrant place to live and raise a family — even as that means adjusting to changing times, or seeing some of his favorite childhood places close or disappear, or finding the courage to lead the city into investing in serious development needed for the future.

While some of those changes mean Cottonwood is no longer like the place Fruin grew up in, they also have meant growth — new residents, a new school, expansion of large local employers, and other steps that have kept Cottonwood a growing community on the prairie. And, with some of those steps, Fruin had a direct hand in helping them take shape: he was Cottonwood's mayor from 1990-2000.

"[Former elevator manager] Jim Duncan was the mayor before me, and I always had an interest in local government," Fruin said in an interview for the 125th anniversary history book. "And he and I used to talk whenever we got the chance. We were talking one night, and he said he was not going to run for mayor again. He encouraged me to run.

"Growing up in Cottonwood, I felt like I should give back to the community. And I felt this was a way I could do some public service."

Fruin earned a degree in government from St. John's University, so it was a good fit — putting his education and loyalty to the community to work for the same purpose.

"When I think about growing up in Cottonwood, I always say it was an idyllic childhood," Fruin said.

The definition of idyllic is "extremely happy, peaceful or picturesque," and Fruin fondly recalls the freedoms and security of a quiet small town.

"We spent all our time playing in the lake, playing baseball, playing football," he said. "It was just idyllic. It leaves you with a real appreciation for Cottonwood, the place you grew up. I am one of those people who enjoys Cottonwood, who knows a lot of people and enjoys visiting with them."

Another part of the definition of idyllic is something that is "unsustainable," meaning a good, happy place doesn't stay the same forever. Cottonwood isn't the same, yet that doesn't mean it isn't good or happy.

"There has been change, as far as I'm concerned, a huge change," Fruin said about the last 25 years of Cottonwood.

"Back when I was growing up, we had a strong downtown. There were guys — and yes, they were guys, no women, unfortunately, but guys who were good leaders: Dick Lynne, Jim Duncan and Tom Collins at the elevator, Cliff Hanson.

"It's hard now to have a retail-[heavy] downtown district. Fortunately, the business climate is still good — North Star and the elevator have had to get bigger to succeed. But I don't know how you do retail in a small town anymore, with the Wal-Marts and places like that. I know that some people don't mind [the Wal-Marts] but I miss what we had downtown. But you can lament that, but the fact remains that it is reality."

Some small towns have collapsed when faced with that reality. Fruin, as mayor, drew lessons from his good friend, the late Paul Larson, who was the longtime mayor of nearby Minneota. Larson often took an upbeat approach to small-town life, believing, like Fruin, that the best and brightest — those who were given a good education by the small town's schools — sometimes had to give back to the town that had nurtured them. They had to emphasize and build on the good qualities of the town to make it stronger, keep it going, Larson would say.

"Paul Larson gave me a lot of guidance," Fruin said. "He understood the challenge of small, rural Minnesota towns, and what they needed to do if they wanted to continue to live and prosper."

What was needed?

Good leadership that was open-minded, worked to make "the right decisions," and was not afraid to invest in infrastructure and new development — if you invested, that meant you believed in the future of your town.

The approach is working: Cottonwood's population reached an all-time high in 2010, and the Lakeview Public Schools enrollment has been increasing since the new school opened in September 2002.

Fruin said that means two things — one, that Cottonwood residents who commute to jobs in Marshall have managed to keep a sense of belonging to community in Cottonwood, and Cottonwood itself continues to be a good provider of jobs.

"Those two things [population and enrollment] are directly related to jobs in the community," he said. "An example that started when I was mayor is Extreme Panel. [Terry and Linda] Dieken started that business on their farm, but they moved to town in 1992, and we [as a city] helped facilitate that. And they keep growing.

"I think a good example of how local government can make investments in the future is what happened out at Northwood Drive. Fortunately, we had Greg [Isaackson], who had 30-plus years experience as city administrator. I couldn't have been the mayor without Greg."

At the time, in the early 1990s, Northwood was not nearly as developed as it has become. There were mainly only houses on the lake side of the street, and the road itself was gravel.

If there was to be more development, it would require a costly new sanitary sewer system and paving of the street. Residents there at the time faced what could possibly have been extremely high property assessments to pay for the improvements. But Fruin and Isaackson negotiated an agreement that called for residents on the lake side of Northwood to be assessed for the sewer project and residents on the north side of the street — most of whom were not even there yet — to eventually be assessed for the costs of street improvements.

"We struggled for a couple years with that project," Fruin said. "The sewer system was really expensive — how do you assess [the costs]? Only one side of the street was developed and annexed to the city. So we came up with this solution where we assessed the sewer costs to property on the lake side of the street, and the paved road to the north side, when they built. And they built faster than I ever expected.

"It comes back to making the right decisions, and it helps to have good people like Greg, Kathy [Dahl] and Steve [Alm] on your city staff. We're pretty lucky with the city employees we have. For most small cities like us in southwest Minnesota, it's hard to keep those good employees. So often, places like us are a training ground for young people starting their careers. They move on pretty quickly. We have had good people choose to stay here working for the city."

Throughout Fruin's decade as mayor, the city took many steps to foster business growth and community development — helping projects in the 1990s, but also laying groundwork and establishing a vision for what would come.

Among the steps: starting the Village Court in 1992 as a business-incubator project; making storm sewer improvements along West Second Street in 1993 to stave off future flood damage; getting an Economy Recovery Fund grant in 1994 to help North Star with an expansion project; forming a city Economic Development Authority, annexing or purchasing several pieces of land adjacent to city limits, much of which has become land for new business and industrial development.

Fruin said the city also was able to convince Minneota hardware store owner Virgil Gislason to buy Cottonwood's hardware store when Glenn Gniffke retired in 1991. The Gislason family ran it for two years before it was sold to the Farmers Coop Elevator, which has continued to make investments in and operate the busy store on Main Street.

"With Gissie coming over, that saved the hardware store," Fruin said. "And now it's still there, and it's still thriving."

Fruin said he learned a lot about the community and himself in his decade as mayor.

"One of the things I learned is that I think everybody looks at a job like the mayor and has some preconceived notions about it — that it's easy to do and that 'I can do that,'" he said. "It's only after you are there, in the role, and see all the competing stakeholders in any issue, see what is all at stake do you realize what it is like.

"At the time, we were discussing a cut to the city's funding to Senior Dining. It wasn't a big cut, something like 10 cents [a meal] a day. But I tell you, that was the only time in my 10 years as mayor that we absolutely filled the council room up for a meeting — and it was all the senior citizens who had come. Needless to say, there wasn't any cutting.

"[The support for Senior Dining] goes back to the sense of identification as a community, especially with that generation, with all the challenges they faced in their lifetimes — the Depression, World War II. They were used to doing things as a group to get results.

"For me, personally, I developed more of an appreciation for all sides of an issue. To be willing to sit back and listen and learn. Sometimes, we enter these things with a little arrogance and thinking you know everything, and then you find out there are many different sides to every issue. That was a learning experience for me."

Cottonwood may no longer be the place of Fruin's youth, but it is still home.

He sees much in the community that makes him happy — including the fact that its young residents and its new residents are embracing the notion of community, and what it takes to sustain not just a town but the things that make a town home.

"I don't know everybody in town like I used to," Fruin said with a laugh. "But I meet a lot of people who are new to town, and I like visiting with them, getting to know them.

"The other thing I find encouraging about Cottonwood is that a lot of young people are taking an interest in the community, serving on boards, active in organizations. I am glad to see that kind of commitment. When the new school was built, you saw all these things all kind of intertwined in making a community a good, safe place to live and raise a family."

Fruin continues to give back to Cottonwood, serving with Joel Dahl and Carol Bossuyt on the steering committee for the 125th Anniversary celebration. In that role, too, he has seen things that keep him convinced the sense of community is strong.

"A lot of young people are starting to step up, saying 'I'll volunteer to do this,' or 'I'll volunteer to do that,'" he said. "When our committee was formed about a year ago, I was a little worried we were not going to have enough people to do everything. It looks like it's not going to be a problem now.

"Back in 1988 for the Centennial, they could get more volunteers because there were a lot more who lived in town working right in town, so it was easier," he said. Now, more residents commute to jobs in places like Marshall or Granite Falls. But even those who commute are joining in, including Fruin himself, who has commuted to work in Marshall most of his adult life. He now works at Turkey Valley Farms in Marshall.

"When I was growing up, it was Cottonwood. There is still that sense of community among a lot of people I talk to," he said.

"It's even kind of funny at work. I work at Turkey Valley and [Daryl] Heidebrink works there, too. And we're identified as the Cottonwood guys. We do have that identity no matter were you're at — you're from Cottonwood."

Torgny Anderson

By Pat Aamodt

With the passing of Torgny Anderson on April 7, 2002, Cottonwood lost a man who played an important role in its history.

He was the first to push to get a Cottonwood Area Historical Society formed. With the help of several other interested community members, that became a reality on Dec. 16, 1991, with the signing of the Articles of Incorporation.

Torgny was also instrumental in keeping alive the history of the Anderson family and the Cottonwood community with his work with "The Little Red School House," which is located on the west edge of Cottonwood. This school house was originally the District 15 school, which, in 1878, was located 1-1/2 miles west of Cottonwood, near where the first curve on Lyon County Road 10 is now.

In 1970, Torgny researched and gathered information from throughout Lyon County for his publication of *The Centennial History of Lyon Co., Minnesota.*

For many years, Torgy wrote a column for the Cottonwood Current, titled "The Real McCoy." Many of these articles included stories that he remembered hearing from his dad, "Old Tom," as he often referred to him, and contained a lot of Cottonwood history.

Torgny was a Lyon County Commissioner during that time, so some of his articles also included things that were going on in the county.

Torgny and his wife Bertha are buried in the St. Mary's Catholic Cemetery in Cottonwood.

Lowell W. Fenger

By Kathy Dahl

He served as the last local Cottonwood police chief, for 21 years, from 1964-1985. During that time, he was a special deputy for the Lyon County Sheriff's Department, a member of the Southwest Police & Peace Officers Association, and Tri-State Police Officers Association. Officers who served under Lowell were Al Martin, Joel Dahl, Doug Buysse, Scott Kuester and Brian Gniffke.

Edwin and Gertrude Chambers

The last time Cottonwood celebrated a major historical milestone, Edwin and Gertrude Chambers played an important role.

The husband and wife wrote an illustrated history of Cottonwood for its 100th anniversary celebration in 1988, called *A Centennial History of the Cottonwood Community 1888-1998.*

Ed Chambers grew up in Kulm, N.D., graduated from what is now North Dakota State University and taught industrial arts in Verndale, Minn., where he met Gertrude, who was a Cottonwood native.

Ed served as a machinist and trainer during World War II. After the war, he worked as an industrial engineer for Western Electric in St. Paul and later near Chicago. He, Gertrude and their family lived near Chicago, in Clarendon Hills, Ill., for more than 30 years.

When Ed retired in 1982, they moved to Cottonwood and he quickly adjusted to their new home. His obituary said that although "Ed's ancestors came from Germany, Scotland and Ireland, he became an honorary Norwegian. He learned Norwegian hymns and became one of the few non-Norwegians to seriously appreciate lutefisk."

In 1991, Ed and Gert moved to Northfield, Minnesota, where their daughter Jo lived. Ed died at the age of 90 on Jan. 26, 2009, in Northfield.

Their initial Cottonwood connection came through Gertrude, who was born Feb. 8, 1920, in Cottonwood and died Feb. 19, 2002, in Northfield.

Gertrude's parents were Nora and Adolph Mossige. Nora Mossige was born Sept. 12, 1891, in rural Clarkfield to Nicholai and Gustava (Lende) Peterson.

Gert was one of three children of Nora and Adolph Mossige, according to the website www.familytree.geneaology.com. Her brother Erling Mossige was also born in Cottonwood and her brother Norman Mossige was born in Hamilton, Mo.

Centenarians

Eight Cottonwood residents or former residents who lived to the age of 100 died between 1988 and 2013:

Mabel Aamodt lived to 100: She was born March 19, 1894, in Vallers Township, Lyon County, to Erik and Ann (Nelson) Roti. She died Tuesday, Sept. 13, 1994, at the Clarkfield Care Center. She and George Aamodt were married Oct. 18, 1922.

Mayme Reishus lived to 101: She was born Aug. 18, 1902, in Echo to Sever and Betsy (Anderson) Gullickson. She died March 1, 2004, at the Minneota Manor. She and Clarence Reishus were married Oct. 30, 1938.

Myrtle Buysse lived to 101: She was born March 8, 1905, in Echo Township, Yellow Medicine County, Thomas Allan and Mary (Falkingham) Miller. She died Sept. 6, 2006, in Glacial Ridge Hospital in Glenwood. She and Ernest Buysse were married Feb. 4, 1929. She lived in Cottonwood from 1937-2004.

Selma Rosvold lived to 103: She was born Feb. 26, 1903, in Camp Township, Renville County to Samuel M. and Minnie Amanda (Jacobson) Lee. She died Sept. 7, 2006, at Avera Marshall Medical Center in Marshall. She and Wilhelm E. Rosvold were married in June 1927. After being a widow for several years, she married Oliver Rosvold in April 1959.

Thelma Egeland lived to 100: She was born Aug. 18, 1907, in Dawson to Alfred and Annie Foss. She died April 4, 2008, at Friendship Village in Bloomington. She and Morton Egeland were married in 1942.

Leona Peterson lived to 102: She was born Jan. 29, 1908, to Joseph and Matty (Samuelson) Garry. She died Feb. 19, 2010, at Morningside Heights Care Center in Marshall. She and Hjalmer Peterson were married Sept. 1, 1937.

Orville Kompelien lived to 103: He was born May 8, 1908, in Normania Township, Yellow Medicine County, to Theodore and Louise (Hanson) Kompelien. He died July 12, 2011, at the Minneota Manor. He and Glenda Arneson were married Oct. 22, 1937.

Lila Viola (Lien) Roti lived to 102: She was born Dec. 30, 1908, in rural Cottonwood to Anton and Ronoug Lien. She died Aug. 28, 2011, at Maple Lawn Nursing Home in Fulda. She and Walter Roti were married June 24, 1929.

OUR BUSINESSES

Tracing The History of Building Sites and Businesses in Them as Closely as Possible

Compiled by Pat Aamodt

SITE		BEGINNING	ENDING	INFORMATION FOUND	BUILDING OWNER		
MAIN STREET - NORTH SIDE - WEST TO EAST							
COTTONWOOD FARM SERVICE	15 W 2nd St N				Doug Winn		
Doug Winn		abt. 2005		Info from Doug Winn	Doug Winn		
Doug Kerkvliet - Consolidated Ag Services		Feb. 1996	about 1997	City News Letter & Teresa Hoff	Doug Kerkvliet		
Doug Kerkvliet - Cotton. Welding & Machine (South)		1982	1995	City News Letter & Teresa Hoff	Doug Kerkvliet		
Rob Hoff - Performance Center Garage (NorthSide)		Nov. 1990	Feb. 1996	Teresa Hoff	Robert & Teresa Hoff		
Smith Farm Store	(North Side)						
Feed Grinding Store	(South Side?)						
CPA	190 W Main St				Robert & Teresa Hoff		
Teresa Hoff - CPA	(West Side)	Jan.1, 1988		Teresa Hoff	Robert & Teresa Hoff		
Residence	(West Side)				Robert & Teresa Hoff		
ART'S REPAIR	190 W Main				Robert & Teresa Hoff		
Art Milner - Vehicle Repair	(East Side)	4-May-09		May 20, 2009 Tri Co News	Robert & Teresa Hoff		
Vacant					Robert & Teresa Hoff		
Robert Hoff - Performance Center Garage (East Side)		Sep. 1996	Dec. 2005	(Back in business) Teresa Hoff	Robert & Teresa Hoff		
Robert Hoff - Performance Center Garage (East Side)		Oct. 1986	Aug. 1995	Aug. 9, 1995 TC N & Teresa Hoff	Robert & Teresa Hoff		
Torke Schulze - Garage							
Mike Wood - Garage							
Ed Newberry - Garage / Repair Shop		Jul. 1980		July 24, 1980 Cottonwood Paper	Ed Newberry		
Gary Miller - Gary's Auto Service / Garage		Apr. 1975	1980	May 1,1975 Cottonwood Paper	Gary Miller		
Matt & Eva Macheledt - Matt's Auto Sales / Garage			Apr. 1975	May 1,1975 Cottonwood Paper	Matt Macheledt		
Carl Boedigheimer - Garage							
Ted Bergeron - Garage				Sonny Olson	Ted Bergeron		
Wesley Olson - Garage				Sonny Olson	Ted Bergeron		
Ralph Olson & Sons - Garage		1963		Sonny Olson	Ted Bergeron		
Ted Bergeron - Garage (built east half)				Sonny Olson	Ted Bergeron		
Sever Gullickson - Station		by 1938		ad in 1938 Cott. Hist.	second location		
" "				second station			
Martin Hatlestad - Station							
North Star - Implement Co							
Wellen Bazaar							
VACANT LOT					Robert & Teresa Hoff		
Residence - Ed Harmening Family				Bldg. removed			
Molly Kise - Dime Store / Candy Shop							
Dr. Clarence Dahl - Office							

SITE	BEGINNING	ENDING	INFO FOUND	BLDG OWNER		
MaCKs SALON & JULIES MASSAGE THERAPY {WEST}				Neil Kroger		
158 W Main St						
Shari Wee - MaCKs Salon (West Front)	Jan. 1, 2010		Shari & 3-20-2013 TCN Progress			
Julie Long - Julie's Massage Therapy (West Rear)	Oct. 2005					
Jessica (Enger) Citrowske - Hair Stylin (West Front)	Jan. 2007	2009	Jan. 24, 2007 Tri Co News			
Deb Ness - Hair Styling (West Front)	Oct. 1, 2005	Jan. 2007	Nov. 2, 2005 & Jan. 24, 2007 TCN			
Ellen Kroger - Interior Decorating (West)	Jan. 1, 1991	2005	Feb. 27, 1991 Tri Co News			
Faye Myer - Interior Decorating (West)		Dec. 31, 1990				
CRYSTAL SMITH PHOTOGRAPHY {EAST} 158 W Main St				Neil Kroger		
Crystal Smith - Photography (East Front)	Oct. 2009					
Neil Kroger - Neil's Plumbing & Heating (East)	Jan. 1991	Jan. 1, 2007	Feb 5, 2007 Marshall Ind			
Norm Myer - Norm's Plumbing & Heating (East)	Sep. 1980	Jan. 1991	2-27- 1991 & 9-25-80 Tri Co News	Norm Myer		
" " "			moved fr. Old harness shop			
American Legion - Club Rooms						
Wally Olson - Hatchery	1943					
Kise Hatchery		1943	Pg. 110 Cent. Hist.			
Jim Sullivan -Jimmy's Bakery	1940		after fire in 1st bldg. across street			
Alfred Julian-bakery?			may have just worked at Jimmy's			
Custer - Blacksmith Shop						
UPSTAIRS						
Living Quarters						
COTTONWOOD COMMUNITY CENTER 142 W. Main St			West Side of CCC			
Jay Agre & Art Olson - Produce (here first)	abt 1936 ?	before 1963	then moved to next bldg. east			
Jay Agre - Produce	1930					
Oscar Naab & Herb Kremin - Electrical ?	1929		75th Cottonwood History			
Engum Mattress Factory ?						
Millinary Store	early 1920s		old picture has sign			
COTTONWOOD COMMUNITY CENTER 142 W. Main St			East Side of CCC			
Cottonwood Community Center	16-May-81		Chronology of City 1963-2013			
" " "			also Pg. 167 Cent. Hist.			
Meal Site	1983		2013 History article			
Tae Kwon Do	abt 1991					
Cleared for future CCC	Sep. 1980		Sep. 25, 1980 Cotton. Paper			
Norm Meyer - Plumbing (here first)	abt 1970	Sep. 1980	Sep. 25, 1980 Cotton. Paper			
" "			moved to Legion Hall			
Art Olson - Produce		early 1970s	Art's obit.			
Jay Agre & Art Olson - Produce (here second)	by 1963	1960s	moved here fr. next bldg. west			
			Oct. 15, 1986 Cotton . Paper (obit)			
			1963 business directory			

SITE	BEGINNING	ENDING	INFO FOUND	BLDG OWNER	
Harold Hill - Shoe Repair ?					
Monge - Shoe Shop (same time as Egeland)		still in 1938 ad	ad in 1938 Cott. Hist.		
Martin Egeland - Harness Shop (same time as Monge)	There in 1918	still in 1938 ad	Cent. Hist. - ad - P. 73		
Wall & Egeland - Harness Shop	by Oct. 25, 1907		Pg 52 Cent. Hist. - pg. fr. C.Curr.		
Charlie Wall - Harness Shop	Before 1893		Apr. 24, 1980 Cottonwood paper		
" " " "			& picture of Harness Shop		
" " " "	Before 1893		Cent. Hist. - Picture - P 34		
TNT GIFT SHOP **134 W Main St**					
Vacant				Glenda VanLerberghe	
Glenda Vanlerberghe -TNT Plus -Gifts,Tanning,Video,Cafe		Aug. 2011	Glenda	Glenda VanLerberghe	
Glenda Vanlerberghe -TNT Plus -Gift Shop & Video	Jan. 1, 2002		Glenda	Glenda VanLerberghe	
Julie Long - Massage Therapy	May. 1, 2003	Oct. 2005	Apr. 16, 2003 & Nov. 2, 2005 TCN	Glenda VanLerberghe	
Todd & Tammy French - T&T Video Rentals & Fitness	Dec. 1997		Dec. 3, 1997 TCN	Vanlerberghe's & French's	
Todd & Tammy French - T&T Video Rentals	Abt 1995		City News Letter	Vanlerberghe's & French's	
Swan Lake Church Fellowship Hall	1985	Nov. 1994	Swan Lake History	Swan Lake Church	
Y-Knot Shop	Nov. 1982		Nov. 17, 1982 Cottonwood Paper	Loren & Edna Ericksen	
Loren & Edna Ericksen - Ericksen's Furniture	11-May-05	1982	1963 business directory	Loren & Edna Ericksen	
Clarence Hatlestad - Furniture			Cent. Hist. Pg. 118		
Roy Neal - Hatchery	in 1950s				
Walt LeMon - LeMon John Deere		1940s	built new shop across street		
Paul Lange - John Deere					
Anton Engum - Tailer					
Sheggeby - Tailer					
"Bicycle Olson's" Repair Shop	by 1893		on pict. Of Harness Shop	pg 34 in Cent. Hist.	
" "			pg 34 in Centennial History		
" "			see "Real McCoy" Apr. 24, 1980		
UPSTAIRS					
Apartments	1996 - 1997				
Furniture display and storage					
POST OFFICE **106 W Main St**					
Post Office	Dec. 1933		Pg 106 Cent. History	Jim Munson	
Louie Sechrist - Furniture & Funeral Parlor					
Ben Foss - Furniture & Funeral Parlor	There in 1917		Cent. Hist. - Ad - P. 73		
Joe Anderson - Furniture & Funeral Parlor					
UPSTAIRS					
Living Quarters					

SITE		BEGINNING	ENDING	INFO FOUND	BLDG OWNER
COTTONWOOD GROCERY	104 W Main St				
Jim Munson - Cottonwood Grocery		Jun. 2, 1997		Jim Munson, Jun 4, 1997 TCN	Jim & Sandy Munson
Gene DeSmet - Star Market Grocery		Aug. 1, 1977	Jun. 2, 1997	Jim Munson & Carol DeSmet	Gene & Carol DeSmet
Martin Bahn - Star Market Grocery		1958	Apr. 1977	Jun. 9, 1977 - TCN, Jim Munson	Martin Bahn
				1963 business directory	
Clarence Runholt - Grocery Store		1957	1958	Jim Munson	
Alf Ristvedt - Grocery Store				Jim Munson	
Ristvedt & Johnson - Grocery Store		by 1936	1938	Jim Munson, Nov. 13, 1936 C.Curr.	
J.T. Knutson - Grocery Store		1918		Jim Munson	
Kolhei - Merchantile			1918	Jim Munson	Kolhei
Eischen & Kolhei - Merchantile		1911		Jim Munson	Eischen & Kolhei
Eischen - Merchantile		1910	1911	Jim Munson	Eischen
A.G. Arneson - Merchantile		by 1907	1910	Cent. Hist. - P.56, Jim Munson	A.G. Arneson
Arneson & Olson - Cottonwood Merchantile & Machinery		1891 or 1905 ?	1907	Cent. Hist. - P.55	
" " "				see also Cott. Grocery hist.	
Martin Ness - Hotel & Store (question on this lot)		1888 ?		38 Hist. Pg 4, '63 Hist. Pg 19-22	Martin Ness
" " "				see also Cott. Grocery hist.	
UPSTAIRS					
Living Quarters					
Dr. R. J. Kirwin, Dentist - Office		by Nov. 1936		Nov. 13, 1936 Cottonwood Curr.	
" "				ad in 1938 Cottonwood Hist.	
Dr. Stevens, Dentist - Office					
Dr. Paul G. Schmidt, MD - Office		by Nov. 1936		Nov. 13. 1936 Cottonwood Curr.	
Dr. Henry, MD - Office					
Dr. Clarence Dahl - Chiropractor					
Mae Ristvedt - Beauty Shop					
R.E. Erickson, MD - Office		by 1938		ad in 1938 Cottonwood Hist.	
HOT LOOKS SALON (West Side)	90 W Main St				
Lisa Fratzke & Megan Dieken - Hot Looks Salon					
Megan Dieken - Hot Looks Salon		Mar. 2005			
Carla (Timm) Schlenner - Hot Looks Salon		Jun. 1989	Mar. 2005		
Deb Ness - Hot Looks Salon		Nov. 1986	Jun. 1989		
Lisa Fratzke - Hot Looks Salon		Nov. 1986			
Empire State Bank		Apr. 1965	Nov. 1981	now includes N. Star lot also	
Empire State Bank		Feb. 6, 1933	Nov. 1981	United Southwest time line	
Cottonwood State Bank		late 1920s ?	1931	United Southwest time line	
" " "				1902 plat shows bank here	
" " "				see also Pg 106 - Cent. History	
Bazaar				on picture before 1918	
MIRROR SOLUTION (East Side)	90 W Main St				
Kim Sander - Mirror Solution		Mar. 1, 2011		5-19-11 Monte American News	
" "				Jul 25, 2011 Tri Co News	

SITE		BEGINNING	ENDING	INFO FOUND	BLDG OWNER
Centrol Crop Consulting		Feb. 1983	Dec. 2010	Leo Langer	
Empire State Bank		Apr. 1965	Nov. 1981	Chronological Look of Bank	
" " "				expanded to North Star Lot also	
Bldg. demolished to expand Empire State Bank			1964-1965	Cent. Hist. Pg.106,141,142,91	
Beth Thompson - Beth's Variety Store		Mar. 1963	1964-1965	bought from Ericksen	
Loren Ericksen - Variety Store			Mar. 1963	1963 business directory	
Phil Desilet - Variety Store					
Art Green - Variety Store					
North Star Insurance		1926	1950	Cent. Hist. Pg. 91 & 121	
Sperber - Huntzicker - Hardware Store		abt. 1897	by 1925	Cent. Hist. - P. 29 & 91	
" " "				not on business list in 1925	
Martin Norseth - Hardware Store		1888		Cent. Hist. - P. 29	
LIBRARY	**86 W Main St**	Jun. 2013		Chronology of City 1963-2013	City owns
City Office	(Front)	Apr. 2, 1992	Mar. 2013	Chronology of City 1963-2013	
Library	(Rear)	Apr. 17, 1992		Chronology of City 1963-2013	
John Deering - Midwest Video			1988		Edna Ericksen
Loren Ericksen - Furniture or storage?		Feb. 1977	By 1982	Loren's obit.	Loren & Edna Ericksen
George Lewis - Café		In Jan. 1975 ad			
Ben and Stella Slette - Café (2nd location)			still in 1963	"Real McCoy"	
Krandall Café		1940s/1950s			
Orville Reishus - Grocery Store					
Louis Retrum - Grocery Store		by 1925	still in 1938	pg. 91 Centennial History &	
" " "				ad in 1938 Cottonwood Hist.	
Spencer - Drug Store					
FORMER VILLAGE COURT	**82 W Main St**				John Murphy
JOYCE WARNKE - DOLL CLOTHES	**(Rear)**	Apr. 2013			
INEE LOKE - INEE'S ALTERATIONS	**(Rear)**				
JESS CITROWSKE HAIR STYLIN'	**(Rear)**				
Villiage Court Mall (Incubator Project)		Oct. 1992	Mar. 31, 2013	Oct. 22, 1997 Tri Co News	
Villiage Court Mall (Incubator Project) closed			Mar. 31, 2013		
Joyce Warnke - Doll Clothes		Aug. 1, 2011	Mar. 31, 2013	Joyce	
Charles Seipel - Community Development Office		By Nov. 2006	Mar. 31, 2013	Nov. 22, 2006 Tri Co News	
Jeanette Barber & Debbie Pederson - Dollar Store		By May 2004	Mar. 31, 2013	May 26, 2004 Tri Co News	
Dr. Paul Puetz - Complete Chiropractic Center		Sep. 2000	Oct. 2001	9-27-2000, 10-31-2001 Tri Co	
" " "				moved across the street	
Barb Hubley - Throws & Blankets		By May 2004		May 26, 2004 Tri Co News	
Steve Bartz - Christian Home Material		By May 2004		May 26, 2004 Tri Co News	
Mailen Pringle - Main Street Gallery		By May 2004		May 26, 2004 Tri Co News	
Sharon Verly - Avon		By May 2004		May 26, 2004 Tri Co News	
Sue Hanson - Greeting Cards		By May 2004	Mar. 31, 2013	May 26, 2004 Tri Co News	
Barb Hagen - Cottonwood Floral		By May 2004		May 26, 2004 Tri Co News	

SITE	BEGINNING	ENDING	INFO FOUND	BLDG OWNER
Cindy Lundy - Nearly New clothing	By May 2004		May 26, 2004 Tri Co News	
Jean Goslar - Ceramic Greenware	By May 2004	Mar. 31, 2013	May 26, 2004 Tri Co News	
Cottonwood Senior Citizens - Dish Towel & Hot Pads	By May 2004		May 26, 2004 Tri Co News	
Store Manager - Helen Dahl	By May 2004		May 26, 2004 Tri Co News	
Kraft Korner - Area Students	By Mar. 1999		Mar. 3, 1999 Marshall Ind.	
Helen Dahl - Dahl's Hardanger	By Sep. 1997		Sep. 12, 1997 Marshall Ind.	
Community Based Internet Service	By Sep. 1997	Mar. 31, 2013	Sep. 12, 1997 Marshall Ind.	
Tee Shirts & Souvenirs Promoting Cottonwood	By Sep. 1997	Mar. 31, 2013	Sep. 12, 1997 Marshall Ind.	
Bonnie Knutson - The Flower Nook	By Mar. 1997		Mar. 8, 1997 Marshall Ind.	
Kathy Knutson - The Flower Nook	By Mar. 1997		Mar. 8, 1997 Marshall Ind.	
Mindy Lange - Clothing and More Store	By Oct. 1995		Oct. 23, 1995 Marshall Ind.	
Erma Huso - Villiage Court Manager	Oct. 1992		Oct. 7, 1992 Tri Co News	
Kathy Knutson & Bonnie Knutson - Kid's Korner	Oct. 1992	by Nov. 12, 1994	Dec. 5, 92 & Nov. 12, 94 Marsh Ind	
Laurie Gregoire - Classic Images Photography	Oct.1992	1996	Dec. 5, 1992 Marsh Ind & Laurie	
Mailen Pringle - Main Street Gallery	Oct. 1992		Dec. 5, 1992 Marshall Ind.	
Lorraine Lancaster - Lancaster Crafts and Candles	? 1992		Feb. 27, 1993 Marshall Ind.	
Inee Loke - Inee's Alterations	Oct. 1992		Dec. 5, 1992 Marshall Ind.	
Kim Sanow - Peau Soin International Skin Care	Oct. 1992		Dec. 5, 1992 Marshall Ind.	
Glenda VanLerberghe - G & R Crafts	Oct. 1992		Dec. 5, 1992 Marshall Ind.	
North Star Satellite - Satellite Dish Sales	Oct. 1992		Feb. 27, 1993 Marshall Ind.	
Handprints - Crafts and Wood Crafts	Oct. 1992		Dec. 5, 1992 Marshall Ind.	
Minnesota Wildflowers - Natural Seed and Plants	Oct. 1992		Dec. 5, 1992 Marshall Ind.	
The Tree Top - Mountain Man Nuts and Fruits	Oct. 1992		Dec. 5, 1992 Marshall Ind.	
Rivendell Candles - Hand Dipped Candles	Oct. 1992		Dec. 5, 1992 Marshall Ind.	
Melaleuca - Facial Care	Oct. 1992		Dec. 5, 1992 Marshall Ind.	
Gloria Hagen - Norwegian Gifts, Books, Etc	Oct. 1992		Dec. 5, 1992 Marshall Ind.	
Barb Shemon - Watkins	Oct. 1992		Dec. 5, 1992 Marshall Ind.	
Doris Stevens - Dori's Attic & Stanley Products	Oct. 1992		Dec. 5, 1992 Marshall Ind.	
The Sweat Shop	Oct. 1992		Dec. 5, 1992 Marshall Ind.	
Jean Goslar - D & L Ceramic Greenware	Oct. 1992		Dec. 5, 1992 Marshall Ind.	
G & L Woodcrafts	Oct. 1992		Dec. 5, 1992 Marshall Ind.	
Vacant				
Bill & Joyce Kroger - Short Stop Café & Mini Mall	Nov. 23, 1985		Nov. 27,1985 Cottonwood Paper	
Steve Brockman - Hardware Store	1982	Sep. 25, 1985		
Vince Stokes - Hardware Store				
Clarence Tritz - Coast to Coast Hardware Store	Apr. 1959		May 1, 1959 Cottonwood Current	
Orville Reishus - Coast to Coast Hardware Store		Apr. 1959	May 1, 1959 Cottonwood Current	
Oscar Naab - Hardware Store	by 1938			
Hans Oftedahl - Hardware Store	by1925		Pg. 91 Centennial Hist	
Andrew Rossland - Hardware Store				
Anderson - Hardware Store				
Gus Arneson - Hardware Store				
H.P. Voth - Grocery Store "Dainty Grocery" ?	by 1925	after 1938	P. 91 Cent. Hist. & ad in 1938 Hist	
Forsberg - Barbershop				

SITE		BEGINNING	ENDING	INFO FOUND	BLDG OWNER	
UPSTAIRS						
Living Quarters						
Dr. Paul Schmidt, MD - Office		by Jan. 1936	Nov. 1936	was above Ristvedt Grocery in		
" "				Nov. 1936 as per Nov. 13, 1936 C.C.		
CITY OFFICE	**78 W Main St**	Early Mar. 2013		Mar. 20, 2013 Progress Edition	City owns	
John Lenz & Charles Freiss - Lenz Dental Lab		Sep. 2006	2012	Sep. 13, 2006 Tri Co News		
Randy & Patty Groff - American Express Financial Adv.		Oct. 2003		Oct 1, 2003 Tri Co News		
Terry Lange & Jason Fisher - CJT Claims Service		Mar. 2001		Mar. 7, 2001 Tri Co News		
" " "				insurance adjustments		
Terry Lange & Jason Fischer - Precision Auto		Mar. 2001		Mar. 7, 2001 Tri Co News		
Part Of Villiage Court Incubator Project		Oct. 1992		Aug 13, 1992 Marshall Ind		
Somody Warehouse						
Floyd Pfarr - Used-A-Bit Shop		abt 1974		Sep. 6, 1979 Cottonwood Paper		
" "				on south side in 1979		
Wilson Seitz - Drug Store		1944	Mar. 1974	75th Cottonwood History & Marge		
Clarence Sather - Drug Store		Jun. 1936	1944	75th Cottonwood History &		
" "				Jun. 26, 1936 Cott. Current		
Jones - Drug Store						
Lud Eng - Drug Store		By Oct. 1926		Oct 19, 1926 Cottonwood Current		
Sjostrom - Drug Store						
M.B. Olson - Drug Store						
Alexander B. Peterson - Jeweler		Early 20s	1934	from an E-Mail		
Fredrikson						
Sager						
1st National Bank		1904	maybe 1929	Pg 91, 106 Centennial Hist - see		
" "				also 75th Ann. Chronology		
UPSTAIRS						
Living Quarters						
Dr. Robertson - Office						
Dr. Frank - Office						
Dr. A. F. Nellermoe - Dentist Office		1913	1936	May 14, 1936 Cottonwood Curr.		
Masonic Lodge - Meeting Hall						
MURPH'S COFFEE SHOP / POOL HALL	**74 W Main St**					
John & Neely Murphy - Coffee Shop / Pool Hall		Dec. 2008		Dec. 3, 2008 Tri Co News	John & Neely Murphy	
John & Neely Murphy - New Pool Hall		Dec. 2007		Dec. 5, 2007 Tri Co News	John & Neely Murphy	
Vacant					John & Neely Murphy	
Jeff & Julie Meyer - Tri Co News		Feb. 1993	Sep. 2006	Mar. 3, 1993 & Dec 5, 2007 TCN		
Jeff & Julie Meyer - Lakeside Print & Kountry Keepsakes		Feb. 1993		Mar. 3, 1993 Tri Co News		
Mike Lee - Lee's Tae Kwon Do		by Sep. 1989	Nov. 1990	Info from Suzanne Lee	Adrian Golberg	

SITE		BEGINNING	ENDING	INFO FOUND	BLDG OWNER
Ralph Kroger - Good News Gym		Nov. 4, 1985	Apr. 1989	Nov. 4, 1985 Marshall Ind	
" "				also Apr 12, 1989 Tri Co News	
Owen Ausen - T.V. Store					
Dennis Ozmun - Ozmun's Clothing & Fabric		Jun-73	abt. 1978-79		
Dave & Nellie Idso - Paint Store/Clothing Store		late 1960s	mid-70s	Nellie	
Beth Thompson - Variety Store		1965	late-60s		
Loren Ericksen - Furniture Store		1953?	1958?	1963 business directory	
Clarence Hatelstad - Furniture Store			1953?	1963 business directory	
Clarence Hatelstad - Dairy Store					
George Gunderson - Jewelry Store					
Oscar Naab - Hardware Store					
Sjostrom Drug		Jan. 1912		50th Ann. Pg. 9	
Post Office					
UPSTAIRS					
Living Quarters					
Fred McLennan - Theatre					
Lawrence Madison					
Opera House		Jan. 1912		50th Ann. Pg. 9	
INSURANCE SERVICE AGENCY	**68 W Main St**				
Kirk Lovsness - Insurance		1990		Mar, 7, 2012 Tri Co Progress	
Dennis Vien - Insurance		1972	1990	Mar, 7, 2012 Tri Co Progress	
Eugene Schrader - Tax Service	(Rear)				
Mark Christianson - Lawyer	(West Side)				
Teresa Hoff - Tax Service	(Rear)	Jan. 1982	Jan. 1, 1988	Teresa	
Les Christianson - Lawyer	(West Side)	abt 1977			
Erwin Schwartz - Insurance & Taxes (3rd location)		late 1960s	1972	Mar, 7, 2012 Tri Co Progress	
Charles B. King - Shoe Shop & "The Family Store"		1955		75th Cottonwood History	
Ben & Stella Slette - Café (1st location)		1948		75th Cottonwood History	
Harold & June Gredvig					
Elmer "Slim" & Marietta Jarcho - Café		Feb. 1946	1948	75th Cotton. History & Marietta	
Bill Crandall - Café			Feb. 1946	Marietta Jarcho	
Leslie & Ruth Larson - Café		1939 -1940		Curtis Larson's Book - Pg 133	
Joe & Clara Nelson - Café		in 1938 ad	1939 - 1940	Curtis Larson's Book - Pg 133	1938 Cott. History
Carl Larson - Café		by Apr 1933		P. 102 - Centennial Hist	
John Anderson - Café					
Merl Thompson - Café		by 1925		P. 91 - Centennial Hist	
Liberty Lunch Room		1908-1917 era		see P. 73 Centennial Hist	
" "				destroyed by fire (have photo)	
LIVING QUARTERS	**56 W Main St**				
Carl & Marge Carlson - Living Quarters		1979		info from family	Marge

SITE	BEGINNING	ENDING	INFO FOUND	BLDG OWNER	
Ole J. Johnson - City Meat Market	Oct 30, 1891	Aug. 1897	Court House Record	O.J. Johnson	
Christian S. Orwall		Oct. 30, 1891	Court House Record		
VACANT				John Murphy	
Several Owners - For Playing Cards	2001	Dec. 2007	Feb. 3, 2001 & Dec. 5, 2007 TCN		
Andy Viaene - Poolhall	1966	Jan. 2001	Fran Viene & Jan. 10, 2001 TCN	Andy Viaene	
Martin Bruss - Poolhall					
Floyd Pfarr - Poolhall					
Wynston Boe - Poolhall					
Trygvie Skaaras - Poolhall					
Wm. Arndt - Poolhall					
Henry & Ernie Buysse - Poolhall	by 1938				
Ed Reishus - Poolhall	by Apr. 1933		Pg. 102 Centennial History		
Joe Nelson - Poolhall					
Berg Brothers - Poolhall	1908/1917 era		P. 73 Centennial History		
Kise Brothers - Poolhall					
John H. Anderson	1907		Court House Record	John H. Anderson	
Ole J. Johnson - Dry goods, etc.				Ole. J. Johnson	
Ole J. Johnson - Rental rooms	Dec. 2, 1892		Court House Record	Ole. J. Johnson	
UPSTAIRS					
Vacant					
Barber Shop					
Bowling Alley (Duck Pin Bowling Alley ?)					
VACANT				Bob Haugen	
Dave & Kathy Johnson - Johnson's Meat Market	Jun. 1980	Jul. 1987	6-26-80 & 7-29- 1987 Cott Paper	Dave Johnson	
Joe Johnson - Meat Market	1960	1980	1963 business directory	Joe Johnson	
Wes Olson - Meat Market		1960	1963 business directory		
Gordon Colburn - Meat Market	abt. 1945 ?		Gordy's Obit		
Lende & Kleppe - Meat Market	by 1925				
Lende Bros. - Meat Market					
Keene Bros. - Meat Market					
Tennis Lende - Meat Market	By 1907	after 1917	P. 59, 74 Centennial History		
			on 1917 snow picture		
Andrew O. Lende - Meat Market	Nov. 13, 1902		Court House Record	Andrew O. Lende	
Jacob H. Dahl owned		Nov. 13. 1902	Court House Record	Jacob H. Dahl	
VACANT 32 W Main St					
Karen Isaackson - Karen's Kids Korner	Jul. 1987		Jul. 29, 1987 Cottonwood Paper		
Dave & Kathy Johnson - Johnson's Grocery	Jun. 1980	Jul. 1987	Pg 164 Centennial History, bought		
" " "			4-17-1980, 7-29-1987 Cott.Pap	Dave & Kathy Johnson	

SITE	BEGINNING	ENDING	INFO FOUND	BLDG OWNER	
Marge Carlson - Marge's Beauty Shop (West Side)	1960	1979	info from family		
John Rewerts - Johnny's Barbershop (East Side) 2nd loc.	1960	1994	75th Cottonwood Hist. & Obit.		
Ivan Sechrist - Barbershop	1938		ad in 1938 History		
Keith Sisson - Newspaper					
W.A. Sisson & Son Keith Sisson - Newspaper	By 1938				
W.A. Sisson - Newspaper	By 1929				
Huddleston & W.A. Sisson - Newspaper	By 1905				
C.W. Folsom - Newspaper	By 1904				
W.D. Lovelace - Newspaper & Post Office	Dec. 1898				
W.D. Lovelace - Newspaper	By 1894				
W.H. Deen - Newspaper	By 1893				
J. F. Paige - Newspaper	By 1893				
E.L. Raymond	By 1892				
W.H. Mulhane - Newspaper "The Current"	Feb 6,1892		Jan. 29, 1992 Cottonwood Current		
G.E. Graber - Newspaper "The Leader"	By 1891	Aug. 1891	Jan. 29, 1992 Cottonwood Current		
Brenna	Nov. 4, 1889		Court House - bought from		
"			Charles Tyler & John Schultz		
UPSTAIRS					
Living Quarters					
Marge Rickard - Living Quarters	1960	1979	1963 business directory		
Dr. Borgerson, MD - Office					
Dr. Clark, MD - Office					
Don Juhl - Watch Repair					
VACANT LOT {STORAGE BLDG. IN REAR} 48 W Main St			Aug. 6, 2003 Tri Co News	John Murphy	
			bldg. demolished Aug 4, 2003		
Rick Rekedal - Electric	mid-1960s	abt 1989	Char Rekedal		
Pangrac - T.V. Shop					
Erv Schwartz (2nd location)	1963?	late 1960s	then moved 2 doors west		
Marge Gigstad - Café	mid-1960s	mid-1960s	Marge for about a month		
Dorothy Bjornebo - Café	late 1950s	early 1960s			
Howard & Ollie Rewerts					
Arnold & Ida Johnson					
Shortie Michaelson					
Osmond & Lisa Forgard - Café		late 1950s			
Marie Slette - Café					
H.P. Voth - Dainty Grocery	by 1925	still in 1938	Pg 91 in Centennial History		
			ad in 1938 Cottonwood Hist		
Mel Forsberg - Barbershop	by 1938		ad in 1938 Cott. Hist.		
Liberty Lunch Room ? (In this area of buildings)	1908-1917 era		see Pg. 73 Centennial History		
" " "			destroyed by fire		
Liquor Store					
Fred Hegemeister - City Meat Market	Aug. 1897		Aug. ? 1897 Cottonwood Current		

SITE		BEGINNING	ENDING	INFO FOUND	BLDG OWNER
Kermit Huso - Huso's Market		1958	Apr. 1980	Pg 164 Centennial History	Kermit Huso
Ivan Sechrist - Grocery			1958	Pg 164 Centennial History	
Kay Knudson - Grocery					
Ludwig Dahl - Grocery					
Ludwig Dahl & C.R.Laingen - Grocery		1918		P. 87 Centennial History	
Grieve, Laingen & Co - Grocery		By 1907	1918	P. 87 Centennial History	
Mickie & Grieve - Grocery					
J.H. & Herman Dahl - Grocery					
Dahl & Lieberg - Grocery					
Christian Dahl - Post Office & Grocery		Feb. 15, 1889		Pg 33 Centennial History	
Ingebor O. Reishus - Post Office & Stationary Store		1888	1889	Pg 33 Centennial History	
Jacob H. & Christ Dahl - General Store		1888		Pg 164 Centennial History	
" " "				P 5 1938 Cottonwood History	
UPSTAIRS					
Vacant					
Twins Beauty Shop					
Masonic Lodge & Eastern Star			Apr. 1938	Apr. 1, 1938 Cottonwood Current	
J.V. Mathers - Attorney					
Living Quarters					
TRI CO NEWS	1 N Barstad R	Aug /Sep. 2006		Sep. 6, 2006 Tri Co News	John Murphy
Laurie Gregoire - Classic Images Photography		1996	2003	Laurie	John Murphy
Kacy Idso - Sporting Goods & Small Engine Repair		Jan. 1994		Jan. 5, 1994 Tri Co News	Kacy Idso
Len & Kateri Elliott - TV Repair		1983	Apr. 15, 1992	Apr. 8 & 15, 1992 Cotton Curr.	
Duane Fruin - Trucking Office		1951			
Eugene Schrader - Tax Service					
Norman Earhart - Furniture Stripping					
Municipal Liquor Store		1937		P 103 Centennial Hist	
Schmidt's Bowling Alley					
Notions Shop					
Molly Kise's Store					
Renen - Saloon					
Volkmann - Café		by 1917 ?		1917 storm pict. Has café	
UPSTAIRS					
Living Quarters					

SITE	BEGINNING	ENDING	INFO FOUND	BLDG OWNER		
MAIN STREET - SOUTH SIDE - EAST TO WEST						
LEGION MEMORIAL PARK						
O.J. Johnson - 2nd Great Northeran Hotel	Dec. 1897	Jan. 11, 1918	Pg 7 - 1938 Hist, Pg 87 - 1988 Hist	O.J. Johnson - Court House		
(Must have been managed by Mr & Mrs Fossum)			Dec. 3,1897 Marshall News Mess.	Sep 19, 1903-Cott. Current		
O.E. Gilman - 1st Great Northeran Hotel		1896	Pg 5, 7 - 1938 Hist, burned in 1896	Leased from John Anderson		
John Anderson - 1st Great Northeran Hotel	1888			John Anderson		
LIVING QUARTERS 61 W Main St						
Steve Michelson - Living quarters						
Curt Dahl - Feed						
Art Green - Variety Store						
Oscar Naab - Coast to Coast Hardware						
Poolhalls: (not sure of correct order)						
Ed Keil						
Alfred Brendon						
Andy Viaene - South Side Pool Hall	1958	1966	info from Fran Viaene			
Cyriel Viaene - South Side Pool Hall		1958	info from Fran Viaene			
Leon Davis						
Ed Quelette						
Bert Catton						
Jim Ellis						
Art Miller	by 1938		ad in 1938 Cottonwood Hist			
Bill Ousley						
Tom Kind						
Bill Davis						
Elmer Berg						
LIVING QUARTERS 73 W Main St				Galen & Nancy Prairie		
Dr Paul Puetz - Complete Chiropractic Center	Oct. 2001		Mar. 6, 2002 Tri Co News	Galen & Nancy Prairie		
Nancy Prairie - Beauty Shop	Nov. 1976	2001	info from Nancy	Galen & Nancy Prairie		
Floyd Pfarr - Used-A-Bit-Shop (second location)	1979		Apr. 11, 1974 Cottonwood Paper			
Duffys - Barbershop						
Hovland - Café						
W.C. Schmidt - Café						
J.H. Lynner - Branch of Clarkfield Mortuary	Ma. 1936		May 15, 1936 Cottonwood Current			
Charles Aamodt - Grocery Store						
Bank of Cottonwood						
UPSTAIRS						
Living Quarters						

SITE		BEGINNING	ENDING	INFO FOUND	BLDG OWNER	
NORWEGIAN MUTUAL INSURANCE	**95 W Main St**	Fall, 2012		Jul. 5, 2012 Tri Co News		
Joel & Brenda Krumrey - Snooks Café		Summer 2001	Mar. 14, 2008	8-15- 2001,3-19-2008 Tri Co News	Joel & Brenda Krumrey	
				Demolished Dec. 15, 2011		
Jim Schrupp - Jim's Café		Sep. 1, 2000	Summer 2001	Aug. 30, 2000 & Aug. 15, 2001 TCN	Jim Schrupp	
Nadyn Balding & Leah Christensen - Skillet Café		May. 1, 1997	Aug. 31, 2000	May. 7, 1997 & Aug. 30, 2000 TCN	Nadyne Balding	
Jim Schrupp - Jim's Café		Sep. 1993	Apr. 1997	Sep. 15, 1993 & May 7, 1997 TCN	Jim Schrupp	
Nick Schwartz - Residence						
Lyon Co. Library						
Telephone Office						
Post Office						
Bank						
NORWEGIAN MUTUAL INSURANCE	**95 W Main St**	2012				
Joel & Brenda Krumrey - Snooks Café		Summer 2001	Mar. 14, 2008	Aug. 15, 2001 & Mar. 15, 2008	Joel & Brenda Krumrey	
" " "				Marshall Ind.		
				demolished Dec. 15, 2011		
Jim Schrupp - Jim's Café		Sep. 1, 2000	Summer 2001	Aug. 30, 2000 & Aug. 15, 2001 TCN	Jim Schrupp	
Nadyn Balding & Leah Christensen - Skillit Café		May. 1, 1997	Aug. 31, 2000	May. 7, 1997 & Aug. 30, 2000 TCN	Nadyne Balding	
Jim Schrupp - Jim's Café		Mar. 1, 1990	Apr. 30, 1997	Mar. 7, 1990 Tri Co. Advocate	Jim Schrupp	
Bernice Bossuyt, June Kroger - Grandma's Kitchen			Feb. 1990	Mar. 7, 1990 Tri Co. Advocate		
Merle & Ruth Lange - Lange's Café		Nov. 1975	1981	Info from Ruth Lange		
Ray Fenger - Café						
Ben Steinhouse - Café		1962		1963 business directory		
Herb Steinhouse - Café						
Ed & Avis Kroger - Café						
John & Madeline Kroger - Café			1962	1963 business directory		
Shortie Michelson - Café	(first site)	mid 1940s	after 1956	Mike Michelson		
Howard & Ollie Rewerts						
Forgard's - Café						
Bill Hatlestad - Café						
Werner's - Café						
Dick Picknew - Café						
August Volkmann - Café						
A.G. Nelson & Art Olson - Produce			1936	1963 business directory		
NORWEGIAN MUTUAL INSURANCE	**95 W Main St**	2012				
Popcorn Stand		1920s-1999				
Desiree Wiesen		1997	1999	Dec. 18, 2000 Marshall Ind.		
Delilah Wiesen		1993		Jul. 2, 1997 Tri Co News		
Heidi, Chris, Sonja & Trudy Hanson		1979			Cliff & Sue Hanson	
Todd Lewis		1976				
Jeff Lewis		1973				

SITE	BEGINNING	ENDING	INFO FOUND	BLDG OWNER
Jerry Rekedal	1970			
Steve Rekedal	1967			
Ray & Marge Gigstad	1958			Ray & Marge Gigstad
Lloyd & Ruby Kroger	1956			Lloyd & Ruby Kroger
Harlan & Dori Gniffke	1948		June 19, 1991 Cottonwood Curr.	Harlan & Dori Gniffke
" "			Built last popcorn stand	
Amanda (Nordli) Madison	1934			
Victor Lien	1931		From a cart & then he & Wendall	
" "			Knudson built 1st stand	
Ed Ringsven			Sold from a cart	
George Davis "Popcorn Davis"	1920s		Sold from a cart, Jul. 2, 1997 TCN	
NORWEGIAN MUTUAL INSURANCE 95 W Main St	2012			
Vacant lot			Jun. 5, 1985 Tri Co	
" "			burned for practice May 29, 1985	
Loren Ericksen - Furniture (storage?)	1974		Karen (Dahl) Klein	Loren Ericksen
Maxine Dahl - Variety Store	1968		Karen (Dahl) Klein	Maxine Dahl
Ken Nelson - Hardware Store	1955		Karen (Dahl) Klein	Henry Takle
Henry Takle - Hardware Store	1933	1955	Karen (Dahl) Klein	Henry Takle
Fred McLennan - Hardware Store	by 1925	1933	Pg. 91 Centennial Hist.	Fred McLennan
Judd-Wilbur Lines - Hardware Store	by 1907		Pg. 51 Centennial Hist.	
Sever Gullickson - Hardware Store				
John Mickie - Hardware Store			Pg. 33 Centennial Hist.	
UPSTAIRS				
Living Quarters	1950s			
Mason Meeting Room	Apr. 1938		Apr. 1, 1938 Cottonwood Current	
Wm.J. Tregesen - Attorney	abt 1914		Pg 72 Centennial History	
J. V. Matthews - Attorney	1898 -1907 era?		Pg 52 Ad in Centennial History	
"Syndicate Hall" - First Public Meeting Place	early history		Apr. 1, 1938 Cottonwood Current	
NOTE: The United Southwest Bank current site had been				
3 different businesses: First was the Red Owl on the corner				
& Skogmos to the west & then the Cozy Theater.				
We're not sure which was in which building.				
UNITED SOUTHWEST BANK 111 W Main St	Jan. 1, 1997		from Empire State to US Bank	
Empire State Bank	Nov 10,1981		Bank article in 2013 Hist.	
Vacant			demolished in 1974-see July 18,	
"			1974, Cottonwood paper	
Martin Bahn - Grocery Store		by 1962	moved across street in 1962	
Jim Flor - Red Owl Store	by 1950s		see Karen Klein's art. in 2013 His.	

SITE		BEGINNING	ENDING	INFO FOUND	BLDG OWNER
" "				not on 1963 business list	
Electric Supply		before 1940		Jan. 5, 1940, article about fire	
Co-op Offices		before 1940		Jan. 5, 1940, article about fire	
Post Office			1933-1934	see Post Office art. In 2013 Hist.	
Olson, Bisbee, Roti - Implement		?		here before going to 1st St	
UPSTAIRS					
Living Quarters					
UNITED SOUTHWEST BANK	111 W Main St	Jan. 1, 1997		from Empire State to US Bank	
Empire State Bank		Nov. 10, 1981		Bank article in 2013 Hist.	
Vacant					
Ed & Judy Vermilyea - Skogmo's Store		1950s		see Karen Kleins's art. in 2013 His.	
Hanson - Store					
Charles King - "V" Store					
Central Telephone - Office?					
L.O. Larson - Clothing		by 1918		Ad	
Abrahamson - Clothing & General Merchantile		by 1911		1911 picture	
UPSTAIRS					
Living Quarters					
Modern Woodsmen Lodge Rooms					
UNITED SOUTHWEST BANK	111 W Main St	Jan. 1, 1997		from Empire State to US Bank	
Empire State Bank		Nov. 10, 1981		Bank article in 2013 Hist.	
Empire State Bank (for expansion)				bought theater in 1975 for bank	Empire State Bank
				expansion - Pg. 158 Cent. Hist.	
Wayne & Della Peterson - Dell Theatre		Nov. 1946	Aug. 17, 1975	Pg 111 & 158 Cent. Hist. New bldg	
" " " "				in 1946 see 8-21-1975 Cott. Paper	
" " " "				& Nov. 28, 1974, Cottonwood Paper	
" " " "				demolished July 1, 1980	
" " " "				Jul. 3, 1980 Cottonwood Paper	
Wayne & Della Peterson- Cozy Theatre		1942	1946	tore down to build new theater	
" "				Pg 111 Cent. Hist.	
Wayne & Della Peterson & Richard Peterson - Theater		1938	1942	repaired burned building	Wayne, Della and Richard Peterson
Vacant				(add'l theater info from Audrey	
Lauretson - Cozy Theater		before 1938	before 1940	Hostetler, Helen Dahl, Karen Klein)	
H.J. Larson - Drug Store					
Ness - Furniture		1920s		picture in Jun. 3, 1987 Paper	
ALLEY BETWEEN UNITED SOUTHWEST & HARDWARE HANK					
Jim Sullivan - Jimmy's Bakery		before 1938	Jan. 1, 1940	ad in 1938 History	
" "				burned Jan. 1, 1940: Jan. 5, 1940	

SITE		BEGINNING	ENDING	INFO FOUND	BLDG OWNER
" "	" "			Cottonwood Current article	
Julian - Bakery				may have worked for Sullivan?	
Fratzke-Millinery-Hat Shop?					
HARDWARE HANK	**177 W Main St**	Apr. 1, 1993			Farmers Co-op Elevator
Cottonwood Farmers Elevator Office	(West 1/2)	1993	about 2000 ?		Farmers Co-op Elevator
Don & Barb Rye, Managers - Coast to Coast		1992			Virgil Gislason
Virgil Gislason - Cottonwood Home & Farm		1991			Virgil Gislason
Doug Winn - Cottonwood Farm Service	(in rear)	Apr. 1991	2005	from Doug	
Cottonwood Farm Store			1991		Glenn Gniffke
Gordon Knutson & Bruce Snyder - K & S Implement		1963		John Deere Implements	Gordon & Bruce
Walter LeMon -John Deere Implement		1940s	1963	new bldg. in 1940s	Walter LeMon
Mattress Factory		before 1940			
Pete Dahl - Ford Garage				burned on Jan. 1, 1940:	
				Jan. 5, 1940 Cottonwood Current	
Traggeser - Implement					
Sever Gullickson - Oil Station				first station	
HARDWARE HANK					
Little Building that was next to Le Mon Implement					
Residence - Howard & Ollie Rewerts					
Fratzke-Millinery-Hat shop?					
HARDWARE HANK'S STORAGE LOT					
Bot Warehouse			Jan. 1, 1940	Jan. 5, 1940, Current story on fire	
Harmening - Livery Barn		by 1912		on 1912 picture	
COTTONWOOD FARM SERVICE STORAGE	**215 W Main St**				
Doug Winn - Cottonwood Farm Service Storage		abt 2009			
Casey's			abt 2006		
Vacant Lot					
Part of 1st Golf Course					
DENTAL CLINIC	**231 W Main St**				
Dr. Pat Patel - Dentist (East Side)		May, 1978		Mar. 16 & May 1978 Cotton.pap.	Dr. Pat Patel
Dr. Judd Copeland - Dentist (East Side)		May.1978	mid-2000s	Mar. 16 & May 1978 Cotton.pap.	
Dr. Gregory Strazinsky - Dentist (East Side)		May 1,1974	Jan. 1978	Apr. 13, 1994 & Jan. 12, 1978	
" "	" "			Cottonwood Paper	
Dr. Houg - Dentist (East Side)		Jun. 1972		Jun. 8, 1972 Cottonwood Paper	
Dr. Marvin Perrizo - Dentist (East Side)		1955	Nov. 1971	75th Cottonwood History	
" "	" "			died in car accident - 1971	

SITE		BEGINNING	ENDING	INFO FOUND	BLDG OWNER
Dr. Brad Handeland - Chiropractor	(West Side)	Apr. 25, 2013			
Ashley Potter - The Escape Massage	(West Side)	Nov. 2009	Aug. 2012	City News Letter	
" " "				last ad - Aug. 22, 2012	
Susan Hoff - Wit's End /Counseling	(West Side)	May. 2003		May 7, 2003 Tri County News	
Cottonwood Clinic	(West Side)	Sep. 1, 1992		Aug. 26, 1992 Tri Co News	
Dr. Susan Briones		Sep. 1, 1992		Aug. 26, 1992 Tri Co News	
Dr. Jason Hughes		Oct. 1,1992		Sep. 2, 1992 Tri Co News	
Cottonwood Clinic - Dr. Robert Telste	(West Side)		Jun. 1, 1991		
Cottonwood Clinic - Dr. Leon H. Ewin	(West Side)	1987		Pat's records	
Cottonwood Clinic -Part Time Service	(West Side)	1976		Pg 150 Centennial History	
Dr. M.A. Borgerson - MD	(West Side)	1955			
FRONT STREET					
Julius T. Knudson - Lumber		late 1930s	1940s ?	ad in Sep 18, 1936 Cott. Current	
				Fred Aamodt bought from him	
				in area of 384 Front Street former	
				home of Ed&Dorothy Bjornebo	
				Info from Stan Aamodt	
WEST 1ST ST - EAST SIDE (NORTH - SOUTH)					
RESIDENCE	92 W 1st St N				
Delbert Hostetler - Ice Cream Shop					
Lloyd Kroger - Ice Cream Shop					
Delbert Hostetler, Ray Gigstad - Radio Repair					
Sisson - Newspaper Office - Print Shop			abt. 1951-1952		
Wesphal - Shoe Repair					
Tuthill Lumber Co. - Office					
Cottonwood Lumber Co. - Office					
IGLESIA APOSTOLICA CHURCH	78 W 1st St N	1999			
Rosaalyn Velde - Great Explorations Day Care		Jan. 3, 1994		Dec. 22, 1993 Tri Co News	Rosaalyn Velde
Connie Hanson Great Explorations Day care		Mar. 1993	Jan. 3, 1994	Mar. 3, 1993, Dec. 22, 1993 Tr Co	Craig & Connie Hanson
Jeff & Julie Meyer - Tri Co News		Jul. 1990	Feb. 1993	Jul. 25, 1990 & Mar. 3, 1993 TCN	
Bryon Higgin - Tri Co News		Jun. 8, 1988	Jul. 1990		
Bob Lancaster - I/C/E/ News		Apr. 1967	Jun. 1988		
Sisson - Cottonwood Current		1951/1952			
Don Juhl - Jewelry - Watch Repair		by 1952			

SITE		BEGINNING	ENDING	INFO FOUND	BLDG OWNER
George Gunderson - Watch Repair		by 1952			
Johnny Rewerts - Barbershop (1st location)		1950	1960	1963 business directory	
Henry Wesphal - Shoe Repair					
Les Arneson - Seed Corn					
Wally Olson - Hatchery					
Neil Kise - Hathery					
John Elmer - Wagon & General Repair					
IGLESIA APOSTOLICA CHURCH PLAY GROUND		1999			
Great Exploration Day Care Play Ground					
Cottonwood Farm Store - Shop				Mar. 31, 1993 Tri Co News	
" " "				torn down - Mar 1993	
Smith Farm Store - Tractor Repair Shop				Jan. 11, 1968 Cottonwood Paper	
" " "				gutted by fire - Jan. 1968	
Cliff Larson - Garage					
Calix Pilotte - Garage					
Gibb - Garage					
Leo Hostetler & Art Reber - Garage					
Custer - Blacksmith Shop					
SENIOR CITIZENS CENTER	**40 W 1st St N**				
Senior Citizens Center	(North Side)	Jul. 14, 1969		Pg 152 Centennial History	
City Clerk - Office	(South Side)	1974	Apr. 1, 1992	Chronology of City 1963-2013	
Lyon County Library	(In Basement)	early 1974	Apr. 16, 1992	Chronology of City 1963-2013	
North Star Mutual Insurance Co		1950	1968	Pg 121 Centennial History	
Creamery Mutual Insurance Co					
Charlie Madison - Plumbing					
Harry Stephens - Cream Station					
Klontes - Barbershop					
Krogstad - Barbershop					
Ray Grover - Barbershop					
M.B. Anderson - Barbershop					
Henry Stellmacher - Cream Station					
NORWEGIAN MUTUAL INSURANCE PARKING LOT		2012			
Jody Isaackson - Office			2012		
Bill Van der Hagen - Computer Sales & Service		Jul-07		Jul. 18, 2007 Tri Co News	
Dan Blower - Computer Sales & Service			Jul-07		
Dan Dahl & Jason Fischer - D & J Sports Cards		Jun-96		Ju.l 15, 1996 Marshall Ind.	
Kevin Anundson - State Farm Insurance					
Swan Lake Church - Office					

SITE		BEGINNING	ENDING	INFO FOUND	BLDG OWNER
City Jail (2nd jail)				demolished in 2012	
VACANT LOT					
Town Council Rooms					
Fire Station					
Public Rest Rooms					
Library					
Jail (1st jail)					
LE ROYS - FOOD & SPIRITS	89 W 1st St N	Jan. 2010		City News Letter	
Municipal Liquor Store		1969	2009	Chronology of City 1963-2013	
Cottonwood Co-op Oil Co		1921	abt 1969	City Chronology 1963-2013	
WEST 1ST ST - WEST SIDE (NORTH-SOUTH)					
VACANT LOT	63 W 1st St N				
Adrian Golberg - Storage Rental		1995	Jun. 12, 2003	1995-1996 City News Letter	Adrian Golberg
" "				destroyed by fire - 6-18-2003 TCN	
Glen Gniffke - Cottonwood Farm Store					
John Smith - Cottonwood Farm Store		1940	Mar. 1977	Mar, 17, 1977 Cottonwood Paper	
Douglas and John Smith (Douglas left '55, John then on own)		1940	1955	1963 businesss director	
G.A. Smith & Son Trucking		1940	1960	75th Cottonwood History	
				at farm on Nov 11, 1931	
Walter Roti - I.H. Dealer			1940		
J.E. & Merle Albertson - Garage					
Adolph Johnson - Livery Barn					
LAUNDROMAT					
Jim Munson - Laundromat		Jun. 2, 1997			Jim Munson
Eugene DeSmet - Laundromat		Jun. 1977	Jun. 2, 1997		Eugene DeSmet
Martin Bahn - Laundromat		1963	Jun-77	1963 business directory	Martin Bahn
Erv Schwartz - Insurance Service Agency (1st location)		1953	1963?	Info from Erv & June Schwartz	Erv Schwartz
Lester Christianson - Lawyer		by 1963			
Clarence Reishus -C.W. Reishus Insurance Agency			1953		Clarence Reishus
John Kolhei - Insurance					
Kolhei & Eickschem Insurance					

SITE	BEGINNING	ENDING	INFO FOUND	BLDG OWNER
U.S .BANK PARKING LOT				
Don Lenard - Body Shop			torn down - Jul. 1980	
Ron Deuel - Body Shop	Dec. 1974	Jan. 1980	12-26-74 & 1-24-80 Cott. Paper	Ron & Alan Deuel
Grover Gniffke - Garage	1962	by 1974	1963 business directory	
Grover, Ed & Henry Gniffke - Garage	1928	by Jul. 1962	July 1962 "Real McCoy" articvle	
Alphie Hanson - Garage				
Power plant				
U.S. BANK PARKING LOT				
Tony Nordli - Blacksmith			Apr. 2, 1970 Cottonwood Paper	
" "			demolished - Mar. 1970	
Carl Nordli & Son - Blacksmith	1904		75th Cottonwood History	Carl Nordli
Casper Johnson - Blacksmith				
Custer - Blacksmith				
JOHN MURPHY STORAGE 80 W 1st St S				
John Murphy Storage	2013			John Murphy
Bernie Heck - Shop	2009	2013		
Robert Haugen - Shop				
Dale Reishus - Carpenter				Dale Reishus
Dale Reishus - Carpenter	1949		Marlin Reishus	Orville Reishus
Loris Gniffke - Carpenter	1947	1949	Marlin Reishus	Orville Reishus
Orville Reishus - Carpenter	1938	1947	Marlin Reishus	Orville Reishus
Hans Applethun - Carpenter		1938	Marlin Reishus	Hans Applethun
Doug Smith - Seeds				
Beu - Photography				
BARSTAD RD (SOUTH - NORTH)				
NORTH STAR MUTUAL INSURANCE 269 Barstad Rd S	1968		North Star History	
COTTONWOOD CO-OP OIL 147 Barstad Rd S			Organized in June 1921	
Cottonwood Co-op Oil & Convenience Store	1994		Co-op 75th Ann. Booklet	
Cottonwood Co-op Oil - present location	1969		Co-op 75th Ann. Booklet	
COTTONWOOD FIRE STATION				

SITE		BEGINNING	ENDING	INFO FOUND	BLDG OWNER
TRI COUNTY NEWS	**1 Barstad Rd N**				
(listed with Main St. businesses)					
VACANT LOT	**Barstad Rd N**				
Remer Building				have photo	
Saloon					
Margaret Jurgenson - Bakery					
Tailor					
Agre Produce		1936			
Fossum					
APARTMENTS	**91 Barstad Rd N**				
Bob Haugen - Apartments					
LeRoy and Steve Alm Drainage					
Joe Derynck Drainage		1953		1963 History Book	
Joe Derynck & Carl Boedigheimer Drainage/Hi-Way Garage		1959		1963 business directory	
Cliff Larson - Garage					
Arcade Hotel					
Hopland - Photography					
PRIVATE PROPERTY	**115 Barstad Rd N**				
Greg & Pat Laleman - Pappy's General Store		Jul. 1, 1978	Apr. 30, 1993	Jun. 22, 1978 Cottonwood Current	
" " "				burned, Jul. 30, 2003 Tri Co News	
Dave Hoff - Convenience Store					
Dave Idso - Convenience Store					
Jim Martin - Oil Station		Jul. 1977		Jul. 8, 1992 Tri Co News	
Floyd Pfarr - Floyd's 66 Service		Jan. 1976		Jan. 27, 1977 Cottonwood Current	
Vernon Clair - Clair's Cities Service		1955		75th Cottonwood History	
Fred & Duncan McLennan - Oil Station		early 40s		Dec. 28, 1945 Cottonwood Curr.	
Manhattan Oil Station		1921		May 6, 1921 Cottonwood Curr.	
PRIVATE PROPERTY	**251 Barstad Rd. N**				
Roger Nelson - Nelson Repair		1955			
VACANT	**333 Barstad Rd N**				
Lakeview Ranch					Julie Jaeger
Pizza Ranch		Nov. 1989			Bob & Julie Jaeger
Wayne & Deb Erickson - Lakeside Ranch House					Wayne & Deb Erickson
Ron Gilb - Lakeside Drive Inn				Ron's Obit - Feb. 5, 2011 Mars. Ind	Ron Gilb
Glenda Vanlerberghe - Lakeside Drive Inn		Apr. 1978		Apr. 6, 1978 Cottonwood Current	Glenda Vanlerberghe
Ivan Hill - Drive Inn		by 1975			Ivan Hill

SITE		BEGINNING	ENDING	INFO FOUND	BLDG OWNER
Mr. & Mrs. Clifford Bauman - Shure Drive Inn		1963		75th Cottonwood History	Clifford Bauman's
				first Drive Inn	
SOUTH COTTONWOOD					
WEST PRAIRIE APARTMENTS	425 W Prairie St	Apr. 1974		Chronology of City 1963-2013	
" "				First residents moved in	
OLD CITY MAINTENANCE SHOP	W 1st St S	1975			
LINDSAY MOBILE HOME COURT	Lindsay Rd				
Rick Christians - Lindsay Mobile Home Court		Apr. 1, 2002		Apr. 3, 2002 Tri Co News	
Steve & Robin Alm - Lindsay Mobile Home Court		Feb. 1, 1995	2002	Jan. 25, 1995 Tri Co News	
Gilbert & Rosella Lindsay - Lindsay Mobile Home Court		May-71	Jan. 1995	Jan. 25, 1995 Tri Co News	
FIELDCREST ASSISTED LIVING	80 E Vermillion St	1998			
AGRONOMY CENTER / CO-OP OFFICE	999 W 1st St S				
Co-op Office		Dec. 2009			
Neil's Plumbing / Cottonwood Co-op		Jan. 1, 2007			
Agronomy Center		Oct. 1992			
LYON COUNTY EVERGREEN NURSERY		1904	after 1908	chronological list in 1938 History	
				& ads in 1906-1908 Cotton. Curr.,	
				10 acres on So edge of Cotton.	
EAST COTTONWOOD					
ELEVATORS					
Farmers Co-op Elevator					
Peavey Elevator					
Northwestern Elevator					
Interstate Elevator					
Monarch Elevator					

SITE		BEGINNING	ENDING	INFO FOUND	BLDG OWNER
Mr. & Mrs. Clifford Bauman - Shure Drive Inn		1963		75th Cottonwood History	Clifford Bauman's
				first Drive Inn	
SOUTH COTTONWOOD					
WEST PRAIRIE APARTMENTS	425 W Prairie St	Apr. 1974		Chronology of City 1963-2013	
" "				First residents moved in	
OLD CITY MAINTENANCE SHOP	W 1st St S	1975			
LINDSAY MOBILE HOME COURT	Lindsay Rd				
Rick Christians - Lindsay Mobile Home Court		Apr. 1, 2002		Apr. 3, 2002 Tri Co News	
Steve & Robin Alm - Lindsay Mobile Home Court		Feb. 1, 1995	2002	Jan. 25, 1995 Tri Co News	
Gilbert & Rosella Lindsay - Lindsay Mobile Home Court		May-71	Jan. 1995	Jan. 25, 1995 Tri Co News	
FIELDCREST ASSISTED LIVING	80 E Vermillion St	1998			
AGRONOMY CENTER / CO-OP OFFICE	999 W 1st St S				
Co-op Office		Dec. 2009			
Neil's Plumbing / Cottonwood Co-op		Jan. 1, 2007			
Agronomy Center		Oct. 1992			
LYON COUNTY EVERGREEN NURSERY		1904	after 1908	chronological list in 1938 History	
				& ads in 1906-1908 Cotton. Curr.,	
				10 acres on So edge of Cotton.	
EAST COTTONWOOD					
ELEVATORS					
Farmers Co-op Elevator					
Peavey Elevator					
Northwestern Elevator					
Interstate Elevator					
Monarch Elevator					

SITE	BEGINNING	ENDING	INFO FOUND	BLDG OWNER		
COTTONWOOD BLDG - STORAGE SHED 42 E. Main St						
Darren Beck - Cottonwood Lumber Storage Shed	1-May-99					
Ross Lumber - Storage Shed						
Vacant Area						
Tuthill Lumber Yard	1911	1940	Pg 29 Centennial Hist. & Picture			
" " "			May 30, 1940 Cott. Current			
Martin Norseth / W.H.Curran	1888/1889	1911	Pg 29 Centennial Hist. & Picture			
DEPOT		1981	Chronology of City 1963-2013			
"			moved to wastewater plant			
Agents:						
Ralph Van Kempen						
H.J.Dickey						
George Koelz						
H.G. Judd						
W.L. Barnett						
COTTONWOOD BUILDING CENTER 31 E. Main						
Darren & Heidi Beck - Cottonwood Building Center	1-May-99		May 5, 1999 Tri Co News	Darren Beck		
H. W. Ross Lumber - Norman Geihl, Manager	abt 1947	May. 1999	May 5, 1999 Tri Co News			
H. W. Ross Lumber - Tom Gunderson, Manager	early 1940s	by Apr 1961	May 3, 1940 Cottonwood Current			
" " "			see Apr. 1961 "Real McCoy"			
H.W. Ross Lumber - P.H. Bly, Manager	by Apr. 6, 1917		ad - see P 68 Centennial History			
H.W. Ross Lumber	1912					
ROBIN'S NEST 61 E Main				Steve & Robin Alm		
Steve & Robin Alm -Robin's Nest	Oct. 2010		info from Robin	Steve & Robin Alm		
Norseth / Larsen Historical Society (House)	1993	2010	Cott. Area Hist. Soc. Info.	City of Cottonwood		
Evelyn Swensen	1992	1993	Cott. Area Hist. Soc. Info.	Evelyn Swensen		
Margaret Larsen	early 1970s	1992	Cott. Area Hist. Soc. Info.	Margaret Larsen		
John & Emma Kruese	1947		Cott. Area Hist. Soc. Info.	John & Emma Kruese		
Hjalmer & Emma (Norseth) Larsen	abt. 1911	1947	Cott. Area Hist. Soc. Info.	Hjalmer & Emma Larsen		
Martin Norseth	Aug. 20, 1898		Cott. Area Hist. Soc. Info.	Martin Norseth		
NORCRAFT COMPANIES, INC 67 E 2nd St N	1990		Mar. 1998 Spotlight on Business			
Mid Continent Cabinetry, Inc	1-May-84		Mar. 1998 Spotlight on Business			
Mid Continent Millwork	1974		Mar. 1998 Spotlight on Business			
Marshall Millwork	1971		Chronology of City 1963-2013			
Cottonwood Co-op Creamery	1924					

SITE	BEGINNING	ENDING	INFO FOUND	BLDG OWNER	
LIVING QUARTERS (Log House) 275 E 4th St S					
Laurie Gregoire - Classic Images Portrait Studio	May-04		Log Cabin		
Living Quarters					
MINK FARM			Aug. 16, 1979 - bulldozed down		
INDUSTRIAL PARK					
COTTONWOOD BODY SHOP 410 E 4th St S					
Dave Wiesen - Cottonwood Body Shop	Apr. 1984		Apr. 7, 2004 TCN & Dave	Dave Wiesen	
Ron Deuel - Body Shop	1980	1982 or 1983	Dave Wiesen	Ron Deuel	
STERLING EQUIPMENT & REPAIR 235 E 4th St S					
Craig & Joy Kesteloot - Sterling Equipment & Repair	Jan. 1, 2010		Mar. 3, 2010 Tri Co Progress	Craig & Joy Kesteloot	
Matt Mohn - Prairie Wild					
K& S John Deere Implement Lot					
XCALIBER GUNSMITHING 235 E 4th St S				Craig & Joy Kesteloot	
Brent Kesteloot - Xcaliber Gunsmithing	Mar. 1, 2010		Mar. 3, 2010 Tri Co Progress		
HOT TUBS & MORE 190 E 4th St N					
Jason Fischer / Terry Lange - Hot Tubs & More	Jun. 2003				
Jason Fischer / Terry Lange - Precision Auto	Jun. 2003				
Jason Fischer / Terry Lange - CJT Claims	Jun. 2003				
PAUL GEIHL CONSTRUCTION 220 E 4th St N					
CITY MAINTAINCE SHOP 300 E 4th St N					
City & County Maintaince Shop	2012		Chronology of City 1963-2013	City of Cottonwood	
Brian & Theresa Kerkaert - Trucker's Pride Truck Wash	Jun. 11, 2007			Brian & Theresa Kerkaert	
Marty & Jeramiah Javens - Lone Wolf Logistic	Mar. 7, 2003		Mar. 12, 2003 Tri Co News		
" " "			Truck Wash & Welding Shop		
HYDRO SWING HYDRAULIC DOORS & WALLS 400 E 4th N					
Marshall Parker - Hydro Swing Hydraulic Door & Walls	Nov. 1, 2006	2011			

SITE		BEGINNING	ENDING	INFO FOUND	BLDG OWNER
Bob Eichenlaub - Cotton. Welding, Mfg./Hydro Swing		2-Jun-05		2006 Tri Co Progress	
Doug Kerkvliet - Cottonwood Welding Machine Shop		about 1997			
COTTONWOOD SELF STORAGE	470 E 4th St N	fall of 1995		City News Letter	Gaylen & Nancy Prairie
SPIN ZONE	480 E 4th St N				
Dave Hoff - Spin Zone		2003		Mar. 7, 2012 Tri Co News Progress	Dave Hoff
Bob Moore & Ron Anderson - Worm Farm		2002		Dave Wiesen	Bob Moore & Ron Anderson
Helena Chemical Warehouse		1999		Dave Wiesen	Dave Wiesen
Dave Wiesen - Master Blaster, Inc		Oct. 17,1994		Dave Wiesen	Dave Wiesen
EXTREME PANEL TECHNOLOGIES, INC	475 E 4th St N				
Terry & Linda Dieken - Extreme Panel Technologies, Inc		1994		1992 - 1994 at familyfarm	
Terry & Linda Dieken & Brad & Shirley Gniffke		1994		Jul. 27, 1994 Tri Co News	
" " "				As Prairie Wind Enterprises	
DAKOTAH GRAPHICS	475 E 4th St N				
Brad & Shirley Gniffke - Dakotah Graphics		1994		Jul. 27, 1994 Tri Co News	
" " "				As Prairie Wind Enterprises	
PALMER BUS GARAGE	305 E 4th St N				
G & B WOOD CHIPS	225 E 4th St N				
Doug & Laurie Gregoire - G & B Wood Chips		1999		Sep. 30, 2010 Gran. Falls Advocate	
" " "				Burned in Sep 2010/rebuilt	
Al & Kathy Martin			1999		
COTTONWOOD AREA HOME-BASED					
BUSINESSES AT SOME POINT					
IN THE LAST 25 YEARS					
Don Fischer-Wood Carving				Sep. 7, 2011 Tri Co News	
Jon Jeseritz - Electrician		1998			
Bill Weinhold - Electrician		1977			
Julius Coudron - Electrician		1971			
Dave Giehl - Carpenter					

SITE	BEGINNING	ENDING	INFO FOUND	BLDG OWNER
Jon Schmidt - Carpenter				
Gene VanDeViere - Carpenter				
Bernie Heck - Carpenter				
Steve Gregoire - Carpenter				
Damian Javens - Construction	2011		Lisa Varpness	
Loren Anderson - Dekalb Seed Dealer	1996		Oct. 2, 1996 Tri Co News	
Robert Matthys - Pioneer Seed Dealer	1993		Robert	
Dale Louwagie - Seed Dealer				
Scooter Javens - Scooter's Seeds			Channel seeds, info from Lisa V	
Bob Bossuyt - Garst Seed Dealer				
Norman Anderson - Dekalb Dealer	mid-1960s	early 2000s	Oct. 2, 1996 Tri Co News & Beulah	
Einar Oftedal - Garst Corn Dealer		2007		
Matt Mohn - Green Valley Seed & Supply	2009		Mar. 7 Tri Co Progress	
Dani Brower - Day Care				
Lona Neville - Day Care				
Jody Dubbeldee - Day Care				
Crystal Smith - Day Care				
Cindy Harris - Day Care				
Crista Post - Day Care				
Michelle Moseng - Day Care				
Barb Anderson - Day Care				
Melissa Selbo - Day Care				
Laura Kosen - Day Care				
Mary Lund - Day Care				
Kary Brower - Day Care				
Arvid Lund - Photography	early 1950s	late 1990s	info from Marlys Lund	
Laurie Gregoire - Classic Images Portrait Studio	2005		Laurie	other locations earlier
Laurie Gregoire -Arbonne Consultant	2006		Laurie	
Mary Lund - Photography	2007		Oct. 31, 2007 Tri Co News	
Rachel Boe - Photography	2006		Sep. 3, 2008 Tri Co News	
Mike Maxwell - Masonry				
John Murphy - Land Scaping				
Brian Gniffke - Brian's Tree Service	2003		Brian	
Bill Magnuson -Bill Magnuson Painting	1966	2011	Linda Magnuson	
Jeff Dahl - Painter	1982	1997	Jean Dahl	
Dave Idso - Painter	1963	mid-70s	Nellie Bjornebo	
Don Rosa - Don's Repair (farm machines)	1984	1989	Jul. 3, 1985 Cotton Paper & obit.	
Gary Gabrialson - Horse Trainer	1991		May 27, 1998 Marshall Ind.	
Jon Hoehne - Engine Repair	Oct. 1, 2001		Dec. 17, 2001 Marshall Ind.	
Mike Lee - Lee's Country Woods	2006		Mar. 11, 2009 Tri Co News	
Sandy Dovre - Defying Gravity Design	2010		Feb. 26 ,2011 Marshall Ind	
Al Martin - Martin Sanitary Service	1978	Sep-99	Sep. 15, 1999 Tri Co News	
			& Chronology of City	
Cindy Purvis - Mobile Veterinarian	Jun. 2009		Jun. 17, 2009 Tri Co News	
Alfred Fenger - TV Repair				

SITE	BEGINNING	ENDING	INFO FOUND	BLDG OWNER	
Rick Jeseritz - Jeseritz Construction Inc.	1983				
Lou Ba's Lunchwagon	1986				
Tom Schmidt - Trucker					
Keith Anderson - Trucker					
Rob Hoff - Trucker	Nov. 2005				
Jeff Wee - Trucker					
Tom Bahn - Trucker					
Marty Javens - Trucker					
Gregoire Trucking					
Don & Rose Bot - Cottonwood Farm Foods, Inc	1975	late 1990s	Don & Rose/wheat flour & honey		
Byron Kompelien - Road Maintenance	Fall 1981		Danielsons		
Lyle Danielson - Road Maintenance	1995		Danielsons		
June Kroger-Grandma's Café					
Sandy Dovre - Defying Gravity Design	abt. 2011				
Shane Lozenski - Nature's View Taxidermy	Dec. 1, 2010		Tri Co News		
Heather Gniffke - Oopsie Daisy Designs	Jan. 26, 2011		Tri Co News		
LeeAnn Boehne-LAMB Country Embroidery					
Wayne & Pat Peltier - P&K Fabricating					

Arbonne – Laurie Gregoire, Consultant

By Laurie Gregoire

I have been using Arbonne products since 2003 when my grandson had a horrible diaper rash. We tried every over-the-counter and homemade remedy possible. Then a friend gave me a tube of Arbonne diaper rash ointment. The diaper rash cleared up almost immediately. I began trying more and more of the products. In 2006 I signed on as a consultant and began going to meetings to learn more. There are some health facilities that recommend Arbonne products. The Rochester Mayo recommends their burn patients use the rejuvenating cream because it is free of fragrance, alcohol and has no harsh ingredients. It worked amazingly on my nephew, who suffered a burn to his arm, face and side of the body. To this day, we can hardly tell he was burned. Arbonne products are pure, safe and beneficial. The company has been around for 35 years offering over 350 products.

Arbonne uses premium botanical ingredients, innovative scientific discovery, and a commitment to pure, safe and beneficial products. Arbonne creates personal care and wellness products that preserve and enhance the skin, body and mind for an integrative approach to beauty. Working closely with scientists around the world and the Arbonne Research and Development laboratories (ARDL), to continually explore and develop scientifically advanced, botanically based proprietary formulas that meet our exacting standards for quality, safety and sustainability.

Arbonne's personal care products are formulated without animal products or animal by-products, no parabens, no formaldehyde-donating preservatives, no petroleum-based ingredients such as Benzene, Mineral Oil, Petrolatum, Phthalates, Toluene, PABA. In Arbonne nutrition and weight loss products there are no artificial colors, flavors, sweeteners, animal products, animal by-products or cholesterol, saturated fats and trans fats. Parabens are replaced by other safe and effective preservation systems. They've screened out gluten and ingredients that contain GMO. These are top-quality products that are carefully reviewed to meet the high standards of purity.

I like knowing that I am doing as much as I can to keep my skin safe from chemicals and harmful ingredients that don't belong on the skin or in the body. I like helping others with sensitive skin or skin disorders find a product that works for them. My health and well-being is important to me and I like feeling great. I am confident these products are as they say... Pure, Safe & Beneficial.

Art's Repair

Art Milner opened Art's Repair — an auto diagnostic and repair service business — in 2009.

The business is located where Robert Hoff's former auto mechanic garage the Performance Center was, at 190 West Main St.

Milner used to work at the Performance Center, so he moved into a familiar place when he opened Art's Repair. "I used to work in this building 15 years ago," he told the Marshall Independent for its June 29, 2009, issue.

As he opened, Milner already had 20 years of experience repairing cars and trucks. He worked in Cottonwood and later in Marshall, the Independent said.

"He said it was knowing that there wasn't service available in Cottonwood that helped him choose to go into business for himself," the newspaper said.

"'There were a lot of cars that were being taken to Marshall or Granite Falls," Milner said. Depending on where a customer lives and what kind of repairs they need done, a trip to either location could be inconvenient. "I thought it would be good to open a business in Cottonwood.

"I do a lot of diagnostic stuff, oil changes, brakes, pretty much all repairs," Milner added.

The Independent also wrote:

It's getting harder to find small-town businesses besides car dealerships that will do auto diagnostics, Milner said. Diagnostic tests on a car or truck can be time-consuming, and it often requires specialized knowledge and equipment.

"I think that's why a lot of places don't do it, because of the equipment," he said.

Brian's Tree Service LLC

From the March 25, 2013, Farm Focus special section of the Granite Falls-Clarkfield Advocate-Tribune and Tri-County News of Cottonwood

By Kim Louwagie
Editor, Tri-County News

Trimming trees, removing trees and tree stumps may seem like an easy job to some. One might think all you need are the right tools and a tree and you can begin to trim or remove. But it's not quite that simple. If you have ever watched people equipped with a ladder, a saw and tree on the TV show America's Home Videos try to remove or trim a tree, you can draw an obvious conclusion there is much more to trimming and removing trees than an average person might think.

Brian Gniffke not only has the proper equipment, he also has the expertise and a dedicated crew to remove and trim trees safely. Gniffke also has a commercial pesticide applicator license and is a Qualified Line Clearance Arbonist.

Gniffke began his business, Brian's Tree Service LLC, in July 2003. Growing up on a farm he always enjoyed tree trimming, and in 2003 decided it was a job that was compatible with his farming operation. Today the father/son business, along with a crew of two full-time and two part-time employees, specialize in tree removal, tree trimming, stump grinding and land clearing. They also remove and spray volunteer trees in road ditches for township and county projects. They specialize in the removal of trees on houses/machine sheds because of storm damage. They will also remove snow and ice off roofs of houses, cattle sheds, machine sheds, businesses or other structures needing snow and ice removed.

"Neat, clean and detailed" is how Gniffke describes the condition of the property when they leave a customer's yard. They are equipped with quality equipment, crew and expertise to accommodate the customer's needs, big or small, and will leave a customer's yard and property in next-to-perfect condition.

Along with the knowledge of trimming and removing trees, the proper equipment and a dedicated crew, Gniffke says safety has to come first. "It is an art and a science. There are absolutely no short cuts. One mistake can be very serious." There is a great deal of risk involved in his field of work and he prides himself on doing a job well in the safest possible way.

Having a love of trees himself, Gniffke can understand a special attachment a customer may have to a particular tree and takes this into consideration when removing trees.

Brian's Tree Service LLC is available for emergency service 24/7.

CENTROL Crop Consulting

By Leo Langer

CENTROL was founded in 1979 in a joint effort between CENEX and Control Data and, within a year or two, nearly 20 regional CENTROL offices were established. The joint effort between CENEX and Control Data did not survive long but the name stuck.

The CENTROL office moved into the old bank building at 90 W. Main Street in Cottonwood in February 1983, with one employee in Cottonwood and another working out of his home in Renville. The office had been established in Renville in 1980 as a co-op to serve farmers from Maple Lake to Cottonwood.

The CENTROL mission was to provide technical expertise to farmers in order to improve their crop yields and profits. The operation grew from the two original consultants to some 35 consultants spread through southwest and west central Minnesota and eastern South Dakota.

CENTROL continues with the same mission it had in 1983, when it moved to Cottonwood. CENTROL consultants continue to test soil, monitor fields, and make recommendations to farmers on crop inputs. The difference now from 30 years ago is that everything has become so much more complex. For example, taking one soil sample per acre grew into sophisticated grid sampling to bring global-positioning system (GPS) technology to each acre of the farm.

Bryan Smith of Balaton succeeded Leo Langer as general manager of CENTROL in 2003. CENTROL employees from the Cottonwood area include the coordinator of soil mapping, Rose Bot, bookkeeper Belynda Metz, and crop consultant Brian Velde.

The CENTROL office moved to Marshall in December 2010.

Classic Images Portrait Studio

By owner Laurie Gregoire

I opened my studio October 1992, while working at the school as a teacher's aide for kindergarten, renting space from the Village Court, in the room that is presently occupied by Inee's Alterations. I attended Southwest State University in 1990-1992 for black and white photography, taught by Professor Henry Kyllingstad, and continued the color segment at the Photography School of Winona. Over the next 10 years, I attended yearly classes at Mid-America Institute of Professional Photographers and completed the 25-merit requirement of Master's degree program.

In my work at Classic Images, I photographed aerials, school pictures, sport memory mates, high school seniors, families, children, weddings. In 1996, I outgrew my space and moved to the building on the end of Main Street, the corner building which is occupied by the newspaper office. The company expanded with more props, backgrounds, computers and the hiring of an office assistant. I outgrew the building in 2003 and moved once more to the log cabin location along Highway 23. My studio clientele continued to grow, drawing customers from an 80-mile radius.

In 2005, with the advent of new digital technology, the affordability of digital cameras, five commercial photographers in town, I chose to downsize and ride out the economic turmoil. I got a job in the corporate world and to-date, I continue to offer part-time environmental photography to a handful of high school seniors, a few family events, and an occasional wedding. I love photographing wildlife and look forward to what each new season brings.

Cottonwood Body Shop

By owner Dave Wiesen

In 1980, Ron Deuel built the body shop at its present address at 410 East 4th Street. he had sold his old shop to Empire State Bank, which is now the parking lot for the bank. The only thing on this side of town was the K&S John Deere dealer machinery lot (now Sterling Repair). I believe the shop sat empty for a year or two before I bought it.

In 1984, I bought the body shop.

I started with just myself working the shop. In about three to four years, I hired my first employee. Through the years I have had one to two employees all the time. The shop started doing just auto body repair, but started doing a lot of sand blasting also. At one time, we had two trucks set up with sandblasters and a semi tractor/trailer hauling sand out of Woodbury, Minn. The traveling sandblasting equipment was called "Master Blaster." In 1994, Master Blaster moved a building to the new industrial park out on East 4th Street, doing in-house sandblasting and paint instead of portable sandblasting.

In the late 1990s, the body shop started to repair boats and jet skis. The experience with working with fiber glass allowed us to expand into boat repair. We had to learn how to apply gel-coat finishes (gel-coat is the outside finish on a fiberglass boat). On the aluminum boats we had to learn how to rivet. The aluminum boats are held together by rivets. At this time, we are in the process of buying the equipment to do spray in bedliners in pickup boxes. The spray on bedlining can also be used on sandblasted equipment to prevent rock chipping to the painted surface.

In 2009, I renovated the outside of the building to its present look.

MASTER BLASTER

In 1994, I bought the old fertilizer plant shop and moved it out to the new industrial park. The building was used for the Master Blaster shop (sandblasting and painting business). In 1999, the building was rented to Helena Chemical Co. for a warehouse. In 2002, the building was sold to Bob Moore and Ron Anderson for a worm farm. In 2004, the building was sold to David Hoff for Spin Zone.

Cottonwood Building Center Inc.

By owner Darren Beck

The business at 31 East Main Street was originally the H.W. Ross Lumber Company. The original building was built in 1904.

After working for H.W. Ross for 52 years, Norman Geihl retired and it was then that Darren and Heidi Beck purchased the business. On May 1, 1999, it became the Cottonwood Building Center In. Norman still worked part-time for the Cottonwood Building Center until March of 2009.

Since its purchase by the Becks in 1999, some of the changes that have been made are:

1999: The office area was moved from the back of the store to the front.

2001: All of the buildings were repainted (with the exception of the pole shed across the street).

2006: New steel was put on the exterior of the main building, as well as new concrete out front, and new windows.

2013: The office area was remodeled with a new ceiling, flooring, and the retail space was reorganized.

Top: A current photo of Cottonwood Building Center. Below that, a photo of the lumber yard from 1941.

Cottonwood Co-op Oil Co.

In the last 25 years, the physical changes — new construction, renovations, relocation of facilities — undertaken by the Cottonwood Co-Op Oil Co. have been significant and impressive.

Yet, even with the growth, the additions of services, the remodeling, there's another aspect of the Co-op that ranks first on general manager Brad Rosa's list of the business' priorities and helps explain why the Co-op remains such an essential part of Cottonwood and the area.

"Community loyalty is key to our success.," Rosa said. "Repeat satisfied customers are very important. We have tried to keep the original idea of what a Co-op was designed to do: Providing service and products to the community.

"We strongly believe in community! I would like to think we compare well to other Co-ops in other communities. I think people of this area are proud to do business with the 'World's First' Oil Cooperative."

Along with that commitment to customer service , there has been a steady march of overall transformation at the Co-op. One place where change and improvements has been noticeable is at the convenience store located on Barstad Road.

"Expansion at our facilities is in response to the changes or potential changes demanded by our customers," Rosa said. "At the C-store, we try to provide items that the fast-paced consumer needs. Changing the 'face' to keep the store looking 'fresh' is an important factor in keeping customers coming back.

"In 1988 the current C-store location was a 'traditional' gas and service station," Rosa added. "Products sold included hardware-store-type products, lawn mowers and automobile supplies. Soda was sold outdoors from vending machines and we had a candy vending machine indoors."

That changed, though, when the convenience store took on a more modern form.

"In 1993, some people wondered if we had lost the farm focus," Rosa said. " Customers wondered if selling convenience items in Cottonwood was a necessary thing. They didn't believe it to be a successful endeavor. Even vendors didn't see the potential that the location offered. By the fall of 1993 the community, farm and city, had bought into the C-store concept.

The C-store sold many pizzas to sport fans on the way to games and to farmers waiting in line to dump grain at the elevator.

"In 2004 the interior of the C-store was remodeled. The kitchen was moved and larger freezer and coolers were installed, increasing the amount of products sold. The accounting offices were moved into a remodeled shop service bay. The till area was moved and enlarged to handle more customer traffic."

Murl Fischer was the Co-op's longtime general manager until he retired in 2002, and Rosa was promoted to the position. In 2007, the Co-op purchased the former Lakeview Schools athletic property — the old football and baseball fields — adjacent to the west edge of the Co-op's property.

"The property was needed to install a new diesel island," Rosa said. "With the increased traffic to the C-store, the old location of the diesel pumps became congested when cars and semi's tried to get at parking spots or the island. In 2008 new diesel pumps were installed southwest of the building, separating cars from the truck traffic. An E-85

Roger Dale drives his converted fire truck in area parades to promote the world's first co-op oil company.

and gasoline blender pump was also installed to offer various blends of ethanol.

"In 2010 we added a broasted chicken line, adding new equipment. This offered our customers another choice of items. This expansion went into the accounting office space, forcing [those offices] to move to the agronomy center. A seating area [in the convenience store] was also added for dine in customers."

The agronomy center is a large complex located at 999 West 1st Street S. on the south edge of town — a different location from where it could be found 25 years ago. From the current site, the agronomy center staff has kept pace with a rapidly changing agribusiness climate that has brought high-tech equipment and advanced science to the farm. The Co-op's service area is northeastern Lyon County and southeastern Yellow Medicine County.

"At the Ag Center, the volatile commodity prices make it necessary to have the storage needed to be competitive on pricing," Rosa said. "Also the precision agriculture trends are requiring new facilities and equipment to provide what the farm demands. Improvements keep us ahead of the competition with other dealers.

"In 1988 our entire Agronomy Center was located along the railroad by the lumberyard and Norcraft [near Main Street on the east side of Barstad Road]. We were planning at that time to relocate to our land purchased on the south side of Cottonwood. We built a chemical storage facility in late 1988 and early in the 1990 we built ag office facilities and a 3,500=ton dry fertilizer storage facility. Since then we have developed the Agronomy Center campus to include a repair shop and seed storage facilities, and built another dry fertilizer storage facility in 2009 allowing us to store around 13,000 tons of dry fertilizer at one time. In 2009 we remodeled the ag offices to bring in the accounting offices and accommodate more agronomy staff.

"The newest building was added in 2012. This is a larger liquid chemical and liquid fertilizer storage facility built on land acquired in 2011 from the small farm to north of our campus.

"The agronomy center has employees that take soil analysis of nutrient values in a farmer's field, give advice to the farmer on what recipe they would need to restore the soil back to a productive area to grow crops. We will apply the fertilizers and chemicals to the fields to help the farmer get the highest return per acre on his crop inputs. The sales people are trained agronomists and the applicators attend classes on procedure that they need to know to properly apply products to the soil."

Cottonwood Co-op Oil Company Agronomy Center

Written by Roger Breyfogle, Al VanOverbeke, John Regnier

Changes on the Farm

There have been several high impact changes in our industry. One has been the onslaught of new hardware and software technological advancements, almost all of which have their origins in the earth orbit of a basketball-size sphere called "Sputnik" 50 years ago. Satellites provide navigation and communication for much of this technology and computers control it. When considering the average age of people in our industry, this required a steep, rapid and continuing learning curve for most of the people in the Ag industry.

Another huge change came in the field of genetics with the ability to isolate and identify different traits within DNA and utilize them in plant breeding to provide the plant with natural resistance to diseases, insects, herbicides, drought, etc. or to enhance the content of specific nutrients to meet specific dietary needs. The DNA identification technology also speeds up the plant breeding process considerably, allowing for much faster development of plant improvements. This is all a giant step forward toward feeding and clothing a growing world population with limited land resources for production.

The communication advancements literally brought the world into the farmers' homes, vehicles, equipment cabs, and even their shirt pockets. They are now competing in a world market, versus the 1988 Upper Midwest Corn Belt market, and they have instant access to that market. This technology also allows growers to farm more acres and still micro-manage small individual zones within a particular field for maximum economic yield using the best agronomic and environmental practices.

Improved herbicide programs, especially glyphosate (Roundup), reduced the labor per acre required and allowed growers to farm more acres and to adopt more environmentally favorable minimum-tillage practices.

When first introduced, Auto-Steer (the ability of a machine to steer itself on a pre-determined course) seemed to be the most ridiculous of innovations to growers who took pride in their equipment operation skills. It has become one of the most popular and justifiable options and one most operators would not want to relinquish.

Basic agronomics have not changed much, i.e. quality seed, good fertility, timeliness, proper tillage, planting and harvesting etc. However, good business skills are becoming as important, if not more important, than production skills in the success or failure of today's farm operations. There has been a tremendous reduction in the physical labor required in a farm operation. This, along with more creature comforts in farm equipment and with instant communication anywhere in the world from where ever the grower is, makes conducting this business much easier and more efficient.

Agronomy Center Changes

1989 – Began the move from downtown to the present location

        Bulk Chemical Storage - 1989

        3,500-ton Fertilizer Plant - 1991

        Office/Chemical Warehouse - 1992

        Shop – 1994

1990 – Began Variable Rate Precision fertilizer application

1993 - Won the State Environmental Respect Award

1993 – Began conversion to larger, more powerful 4 wheel drive sprayers to accommodate increased demand for custom application.

1995 - Won the National Environmental Respect Award

1996 – Began using Global Positioning System (GPS) for custom application navigation

2006 - Added Seed Warehouse and Seed Treater

2007 – Acquired a local plumbing business to complement our heating and air conditioning sales and service

2009 - Added new 9,700-ton Fertilizer Plant

2010 - Office addition at the Agronomy Center to accommodate the entire office staff

    - Bulk Seed Tanks

2012- Added new bulk chemical and liquid fertilizer storage and load-out facility

Other changes:

Custom Application Fertilizer (conventional and precision)

Custom Application Spraying (with the ability to create as-applied maps)

Custom Application NH-3 (conventional and precision)

Custom soil Sampling (conventional, grid, zones)

Bulk Chemicals and Liquid Fertilizer

Develop Annual Customized Individual Farm Plans and Maps for each grower

Bagged and Bulk Seed and Seed Treatment

Grain Bin and Corn Dryer Sales and Service

Many basic services are very similar to 1988 operations but are done with much more precision and data verification that is based on sound agronomic, economic and environmental practices. As an industry leader in our area, we began offering precision sampling and application over twenty years ago. About 60-70% of our fertilizer is now applied by some form of a precision application system.

The industry has become much more highly regulated with involvement from; the Minnesota Department of Ag, OSHA, Minnesota and Federal DOT and the EPA. Farmers must now have a Private Pesticide Applicator's License to purchase Restricted Use Products. Compliance with these regulations consumes a greater share of our business time and expense but has improved workplace, highway and environmental safety, and that is a benefit to the entire community.

Like our customers, our learning curve has been steep and rapid also. There is a steady stream of new computer programs and monitor systems to implement and become proficient with. All of our office staff are now Certified Crop Advisors. They each had to pass State and National exams to become certified and have to complete 40 hours of continuing education credits every two years to maintain their certification. All of the custom applicators must be licensed annually by the State of Minnesota and must complete a one day training/update session every three years plus equipment manufacturers' training and update meetings. Most of the younger employees are immensely better back rounded to step into today's technological world than employees who were around in 1988.

Our trade area encompasses Northeast Lyon County and Southeast Yellow Medicine County and we service about 100,000 acres of cropland and 150 to 170 growers within that area.

We are in our 92nd year as a member of the Greater Cottonwood Community. We take pride in our relationship with the community and the ag industry and deeply appreciate the loyalty and support the community has shown to us. We have been very successful and have been pro-active in making available new technology, excellent equipment, facilities and employees. Our story is one the entire community can take pride in because we are owned by our patrons and none of this would be possible without their loyalty and support.

The Cottonwood Dental Clinic

The Cottonwood Clinic recently purchased a new Platinum Series Digital X-ray Sensor and Intra-Oral camera, which offers patients the latest technology in dental imaging, reported the city of Cottonwood newsletter in spring 2013.

The digital X-ray sensor is a small computer device that is placed inside a patient's mouth and takes an instant X-ray. The digital sensor allows staff to take X-rays with 75 percent less radiation than traditional film X-rays and makes

it possible to see the images instantly, so there is less waiting time for the patient. The clear, precise image quality allows patients to have a better understanding of the treatment advised, and the ability to magnify the image allows the patient to see exactly what the clinic staff sees.

The Intra-Oral Camera is a small digital camera that is placed inside the mouth to capture images of the teeth and oral structures. Once the image is taken, it can be immediately viewed on the computer screen, which allows staff to better educate patients on what treatment is needed. Both the digital X-rays and the Intra-Oral Camera are pain-free and allow for improved patient diagnosis and treatment planning.

As of 2013, Dr. S.A. Patel has been practicing general dentistry for the past 35 years in Cottonwood and Clarkfield.

Currently, the Cottonwood Dental Clinic employs eight staff members and offers a wide variety of dental services, including white tooth colored fillings, emergency dental care, orthodontic treatment, complete smile reconstruction, crowns, bridges, restoring implants, periodontal therapy including deep cleanings and periodontal maintenance care, bleaching, routine preventative care including exams, prophylaxis cleaning, sealants and fluoride varnish treatments.

The dental clinic now has its own web site at www.clarkfieldcottonwooddental.com

Cottonwood Farm Foods Inc.

Cottonwood Farm Foods was started in 1975 by Rose and Don Bot. The main purpose of the company was to market honey and whole-wheat flour. These two products were produced by the Bot family. Don and Rose, and children Chad and Jill produced these products on their own farm, which was two miles west of Cottonwood. They managed several hundred colonies of bees, which produced the honey. The honey was extracted, bottled and sold through grocery distributors.

The wheat for the whole-wheat flour was grown on their farm, milled into flour and also sold through grocery distributors.

By the late 1990s, both Chad and Jill had graduated from college, so without their help the business was discontinued.

Cottonwood Farm Service

Since about 2005, Doug Winn has owned and operated Cottonwood Farm Service at 15 West 2nd St. N, at the corner of Second Street North and Main Street.

In about 2009, he also bought the empty Casey's building across from him on the south side of Main Street (215 W. Main St.) and expanded his business into the lot there.

Prior to that, he operated the business from 1991 to 2005 in the rear of the Cottonwood Farm Service / later Hardware Hank store at 177 W. Main Street.

Cottonwood Grocery

Cottonwood Grocery Building Location History

Address: 104 W. Main Street

Compiled by owner Jim Munson

1905-1907	Arneson & Olson	General merchandise and machinery
1907-1910	G.A. Arneson	Mercantile
1910-1911	Eischen	Mercantile
1911-?	Eischen & Kolhei	Mercantile
?-1918	Kolhei	Mercantile
1918-?	J.T. Knudson	Grocery

Shortly after he purchased the store, Knudson changed it from mercantile to grocery

?-1938	Ristvedt & Johnson	Grocery
?-?	Alf Ristvedt	Grocery
?-Sept. 1962	Clarence Runholt	Grocery
Sept. 1962-April 1977	Martin Bahn	Grocery
August 1977-June 1997	Gene and Carol DeSmet	Grocery
June 1997-present	Jim/Sandy Munson family	Grocery

The current building has had groceries for sale for more than 100 years.

History of the lot where Cottonwood Grocery, the Post Office, laundry and upstairs apartments are located:

The lot changed hands many times before the building was constructed. The first dated exchange was in 1888 to Martin Ness, but there were five owners before him.

The lot changed hands 12 more times between 1888 and 1905.

Three different owners (Clarkfield Bank, Cottonwood State Bank, and H.C. Anderson) are listed as owning the property in 1905 when the building was built.

Eighteen other owners are listed between 1905 and 2002, when I bought the building in June of 2002 from Gene and Carol DeSmet.

By Pat Aamodt — addendum

The accounts on the Cottonwood Grocery building vary from the legal papers.

The Cottonwood Current newspaper dated March 25, 1893, makes this statement: "Immediately upon completion of the railroad (in 1888), the boom for Cottonwood took place. Martin Ness built the building now occupied by himself as a furniture store and Bomstad's station."

Page 4 of the 1938 Cottonwood History book says: "After there was regular train service begun on Sept. 11, 1888, preparations for the town were forging ahead rapidly. The second lot was purchased by Martin Ness whose choice of location was where now Ristvedt and Johnson (the site of Cottonwood Grocery in 2013) operate a general store. In September (1888) Martin Ness erected a double building, in a part of which he operated a hotel while the other part was rented to Oluf Pehrson of Marshall who opened a branch store under management of C.T. Hanson.

DID A DIFFERENT BUILDING USED TO STAND WHERE THE CURRENT ONE DOES? The double building would be the building where Jim Munson's Cottonwood Grocery and the Post Office are now located.

Crystal Smith Photography

158 W Main St.

From her website http://www.crystalsmithphotography.com/

I have been interested in photography since I was young, always anxious for the day that I could pick up my photos to see what I had captured. I love to photograph all kinds:

- Newborns, babies and children
- Maternity
- Family
- Seniors
- Engagement/couples
- Product photography
- Custom photo collages, invitations, birth announcements, holiday and birthday cards also available.

My style is by no means traditional, and I'm not out to create a "sit still, look at the camera and say cheese" style portrait. I think that some of the best photos come from children doing what they do best. My favorite photos are the unexpected ones. The wonderful moments that show a child's true spirit, and warm your soul. I love capturing natural expressions that celebrate the stages of life. Capturing moments in time so that we may hold onto them forever.

Jeff Dahl Painting

By Jean Dahl

1982-1997

Drywall, interior and exterior painting.

Jeff painted independently, but frequently worked with Bill Magnuson (Bill Magnuson Painting). They were a great pair, taking pride in the high quality work that they did.

I am not sure if this is a "serious" presentation or not, but if humor is allowed, then this tidbit might be interesting: Bill always loved to have Jeff working with him because of Jeff's height (6-foot-5). Bill would often say, "if Jeff is along, then I don't need a ladder!"

Extreme Panels Technologies Inc.

By Terry and Linda Dieken

Extreme Panels Technologies Inc. is owned by Terry and Linda Dieken. Both Terry and Linda were born and raised in the Cottonwood area. Terry graduated from Marshall Public School and Linda (Varpness) graduated from Cottonwood School.

After farming for 20 years, they were approached by Brian Gniffke, formerly from Cottonwood, to see if they would be interested in providing a lot on the north side of Cottonwood Lake and buy structural insulated panels (SIPs) from a Washington state panel company to erect a house and see how it performed.

After the house was completed, Terry and Linda couldn't see how SIP's wouldn't be accepted by the public. They were much more energy efficient and would save trees, which was a big thing at that time.

So, along with two employees, in 1992, they started manufacturing structural insulated panels in a 1,500-square-foot shop on their family farm to provide structural insulated panels mostly for the hog-confinement business. Because of continued demand for the product, using their panels, they built a 10,000-square-foot manufacturing plant and office in 1994 on land purchased from the Cottonwood EDA. They added a 25,000-square-foot addition in 1996, and completed a 30,000-square-foot addition in 2004 to accommodate an 8-by-24-foot press to start manufacturing jumbo panels in 2005.

Terry is CEO of the company and Linda is chief financial officer. Their daughter works in the office and is responsible for accounts payable and human resources. Their son is operations manager and purchasing agent and their son-in-law is the plant manager.

They currently have 24 employees. They credit their hard work, dedication and loyalty for their ability to grow their business to what it is today.

They have gone from a manual line of production to a fully automated laminated line, producing up to 8-by-24-foot panels, and installed a completely computerized cutting machine purchased from a German company in 2008. Panels are shipped mainly to the Upper Midwest states. Internationally, they have shipped to Japan, England, Africa and are currently expanding into Australia.

Farmers Cooperative Elevator

You don't have to go very far in any direction from Cottonwood to find grain elevators or other agri-business plants that are owned by some of the largest corporations in America.

But on Main Street in Cottonwood, just east of the intersection with Barstad Road, you'll find an elevator and feed mill that is still locally owned — and thanks to the foresight of patrons in an overwhelming vote in 1997 — probably going stronger than it ever has.

The Farmers Cooperative Elevator Company emerged after a vote on Nov. 25, 1997, by patrons of the Farmers Cooperative Elevator of Cottonwood and the Hanley Falls Farmers Elevator approved joining the two together. The new company started doing business under its new name a few weeks later, on Jan. 1, 1998.

Both elevators were already strong businesses. Fifteen years later, at its Cottonwood location and throughout the organization, FCE has continued to grow.

"The cooperative has been on a steady growth curve and vows to never forget its roots," said FCE General Manager Scott Dubbelde.

Since 1998, the company has repeatedly invested in expansion and improvements at its Cottonwood site. It has also grown as a cooperative, adding sites in several other local cities. FCE also owns the Hardware Hank store in Cottonwood.

The Cottonwood and Hanley Falls elevators joined together, in good part, out of a desire to keep themselves independent but competitive in a market dominated by big-name businesses like Cargill or Archer Daniels Midland. Another big-name business, the Burlington Northern railroad, played a role in the consolidation, too. Burlington Northern wanted the elevators in both Cottonwood and Hanley Falls to double the size of their rail loadout areas, from 55 rail cars to 110, said FCE Board of Directors President Mark Vandelanotte.

"I got on the board in March or April [of 1997] and we started talking with Hanley Falls not too long afterward," said Vandelanotte. Doubling the loadouts would allow the elevators to ship more grain and stay competitive in the market, but also would be costly to do.

Consolidating made it possible to handle the finances of expanding the rail loadouts, and also brought many more financial efficiencies for the new FCE, he said.

"I think it's worked well," Vandelanotte said of the FCE, adding that he is not surprised, given the Cottonwood area's long-standing spirit of economic independence ("it's always been head-strong that way. There is a good, loyal base of customers.") and deep tradition of supporting local cooperatives.

Dubbelde expanded on the decision to consolidate and form FCE:

"When the Cottonwood Elevator and the Hanley Falls Elevator both dissolved to form a new cooperative together, each was proud, financially strong, successful local cooperatives," he said. "But each respective board knew that the loading of unit trains of grain for export was moving from the 54-car units that each currently had the capabilities to load, to a doubled 110-car unit size. Without the ability to load 110s, the co-ops would not have access to a competitive marketplace.

"And they also knew that all projections pointed to the fact that it took a lot more grain volume to profitably operate a 110-car loader. After much study by both cooperatives, they both decided that to consolidate was the best option. The Consolidation Agreement stated that the Grain Department was to be headquartered in Hanley Falls and the Feed Department was to be headquartered in Cottonwood. "

Vandelanotte actually joined the board of the Cottonwood elevator a few months before the vote to consolidate with Hanley Falls. At that time, Cottonwood also already owned elevators in Echo and Ghent.

Dubbelde said: "Since January 1, 1998, the New FCE has added locations in Minneota, Taunton and Montevideo. The Cooperative has been on a steady growth curve and vows to never forget its roots. FCE is owned by the patrons that it serves."

The FCE pays annual dividends to patrons and has done so well that the retirement-age requirement for getting their equity payout has dropped from 75 to 69. That's a big positive for current patrons, Vandelanotte said. Years ago, a patron may not have even lived long enough to have enjoyed his retirement payout. Now, with the age at 69, "they're getting paid out while they're still young and have a lot of years to enjoy it."

Dubbelde said FCE exists for the benefit of its patrons/owners, and the improvements in Cottonwood bear that out.

"The Feed Department of FCE has an excellent production facility in Cottonwood that has had many expansions, upgrades and enhancements over the years. Increased customer service, increased efficiency, increased quality control, and a positive return on investment have driven the spending of capital on the Cottonwood Feed Mill," he said. "In 1999 the first semi delivery unit was purchased. Today the Feed Department uses eight semis and two tandem delivery units to deliver feed on a daily basis. FCE is mindful that the Cooperative exists for the benefit of its patron/owners. That is by definition the philosophy of a local cooperative and is included in the Mission Statement of FCE."

Vandelanotte and Dubbelde both say Cottonwood's tradition of being home to independent, locally-owned cooperatives is a major factor in FCE's success. The elevator is one of two successful co-ops in Cottonwood, with the other being the Cottonwood Co-op Oil Co. Vandelanotte said he's been aware since boyhood of the presence of both. He said he can remember old advertisements that promoted the Cottonwood Co-op Oil Co. "the world's first co-operative," and he still sees a sense of independence among local residents who take pride in local control, instead of watching important entities getting lost to national or corporate ownership. "We've been very fortunate to have two very good co-ops in Cottonwood."

Vandelanotte said it is a competitive market for FCE, nodding to corporately owned competitors just down the road, north, south and southeast of Cottonwood. But FCE succeeds because, like Dubbelde said, it treats its customers/patrons well. Neighbors and owners, not lines in a distant corporate database.

"We've got good management and employees at the elevator," Vandelanotte said. "You want to be able to provide good services at a fair price, and if you do that — if you become [relied on] for providing good services and a fair price — people are going to stay with you. People just keep coming back."

Dubbelde said the gratitude runs both ways:

"Cottonwood is a great community to operate a business in," he said.

"The City Council and residents are supportive of the business community and FCE views them as partners and co-inhabitants. The Cottonwood Fire Department, Cottonwood Ambulance and Rescue Squads, and Cottonwood city crews are valuable assets to the business community and rural area."

(Dana Yost contributed reporting to this story)

Farmers Cooperative Elevator's Vision, Mission and Values statements:

Vision

The Farmers Cooperative Elevator Company will be a member-owned and controlled, diversified agricultural service company that anticipates changes in agriculture and the resulting needs of its members. It will be recognized by its members, competitors, employees, and vendors, and by the communities in which it is located as an innovative leader.

Mission

To provide a variety of products and services to its members that will improve their profitability and result in the Farmers Cooperative Elevator Company being a profitable, financially sound company.

Values

Endorse and promote the basic coop principles.

Be an effective listener and communicator with our member-owners.

Acknowledge the contributions made by older patrons by retiring equities and support the efforts of current members with cash patronage refunds, as the financial condition of the company will allow.

Accept change as a normal business environment.

Operate competitively and with the utmost form of integrity.

Be responsive to the needs of our members.

Be a good company to work for.

Pursue new business ventures that have a high probability of success and will enhance the profits of our members.

Encourage training for members, the Board of Directors, and employees.

Respect and protect the environment.

Support communities within our market area.

Farmers Cooperative Elevator Timeline

Compiled by Scott Dubbelde and Mark Vandelanotte / 1988 to Present

1991: Completed a remodel of the Feed Mill. Cost $203,750. Done by Hogenson Construction of Fargo, ND

1992: Updated the Hardware Store that was being rented to Gislason's

1992: Installed a bulk weigher on the Corn House so we could get origin official railcar weights. Cost $127,785. Done by Hogenson Construction of Fargo, ND

1993: Purchased the Hardware Store for $105,000. Carol Kompelien was hired as the Hardware Store Manager. Coast to Coast was the previous Hardware Supplier. The new supplier will be Hardware Hank.

5-10-93: The Board passed unanimously to bring a vote to the Patrons a merger plan with the Farmers Warehouse Association of Echo.

6-15-93: The Farmers Co-operative Elevator Company of Cottonwood (FCEC) Patrons voted to merge with the Farmers Warehouse Association of Echo (FWA). FCEC tallies were 119 votes for and 11 votes against. The FWA of Echo also passed the merger vote. FWA tallies were 139 votes for and 11 votes against. Over 2/3 majority voted for the merger from both cooperatives so it passed. The merger will be effective 1-1-1993.

1993: Feed Mill pelleting expansion. Cost $550,000. Ted Miller of Cenex/Land O Lakes is the General Contractor.

1994: Bought Loris Gniffke property next to the Corn House for $15,000.

1995: Built 44x30 building for hardware storage. Cost $16,156. Done by Geihl Construction.

1995: Purchased B&H Feed Supply in Ghent from Joyce & Will Blowers. Cost $300,000.

6-30-97: Jim Duncan retired after 24 years of service as Manager.

7-1-97: Leonard Doom was hired as the new manager.

9-3-97: The Board passed unanimously to bring a vote to the Patrons a consolidation with the Hanley Falls Farmers Elevator (HFFE).

11-25-97: The FCEC Patrons voted to dissolve and form a new Cooperative with the HFFE. The vote was 226 Yes and 14 No. The HFFE Patrons voted to dissolve and form a new Cooperative with the FCEC of Cottonwood. The vote was 267 Yes and 23 No. Over 2/3 (two-thirds) majority voted for the unification by both cooperatives so it passed.

The new Entity will be the Farmers Cooperative Elevator Company with the corporate address to be Hanley Falls. A 108-car load out will be built in Hanley Falls and the Feed Division will be located in Cottonwood. Facilities are located in Cottonwood, Hanley

Falls, Echo, Ghent, Granite Falls, and Minnesota Falls. The General Manager will be Scott Dubbelde. The new cooperative will commence doing business on 1-1-98.

6-8-99: The FCE Board voted unanimously to bring a merger by acquisition plan to a vote to the Taunton Patrons, to merge the Taunton Cooperative Elevator Company, with a branch in Minneota, into the Farmers Co-operative Elevator Company.

6-15-99: The Taunton Cooperative Elevator Company Board voted unanimously to bring a vote to their Patrons a plan to merge into FCE.

7-14-99: The merger by acquisition vote was passed by the Taunton Patrons. The vote passed with 98 Yes and 3 No. Merger effective 9-1-99.

2000: The Cottonwood Feed Warehouse added a 25' x 40' addition. Cost $20,000.

8-2-01: There was a fire at the Cottonwood Elevator. A leg belt started on fire due to a hot bearing. The Cottonwood Fire Department with the help of mutual aid used foam to put out the contained blaze. There was no explosion and no injuries.

2002: Feed Mill was expanded with new feed load outs and feed ingredient storage on the east side. Cost $315,000. CEEC, Inc. from Wabasso was the contractor.

2003: New conveyor was added so the Elevator could convey corn to the Feed Mill directly. Cost $33,895. CEEC, Inc. of Wabasso was the contractor.

2003: Hardware Store remodel approved. Cost $25,000.

2004: Additional storage for bulk ingredients added at the Feed Mill. Cost $300,000. CEEC, Inc. of Wabasso was the contractor.

9-23-04: The Montevideo location was purchased from Montevideo Grain, LLC which was a joint venture between CHS, Inc. and the Farmers Union Oil Company of Montevideo.

2006: Installed a computerized feed grinding and mixing feed system in the Feed Mill. Cost $370,114. Contractors were CEEC, Inc. of Wabasso, WEM Automation Company of New Berlin, WI, Abel Manufacturing of Appleton, WI, and Potter Electric of Montevideo.

2007: Replaced the Feed Mill's roller mill with a larger one and added more load out bins on the east side. Cost $561,412. CEEC, Inc. of Wabasso was the contractor.

2008: Added a new conference room and office addition at the Feed Mill office. Cost $17,000. Contractors were Elmo Volstad, Geihl Construction, and Jeseritz Electric.

1-1-12: Carol Kompelien retired as the Hardware Store Manager after 19 years as the Manager. Jessica Laleman was hired as the new Manager.

7-28-12: The 100th Anniversary Celebration for FCE was held at the Minnesota Machinery Museum grounds in Hanley Falls. Famous Dave's catered the meal. Surf City All Stars from Southern California provided the entertainment. Board President Mark Vandelanotte, General

Manager Scott Dubbelde, and Assistant General Manager Bill Doyscher emceed the event. All former Managers and Directors were recognized.

2013: Bought the City Maintenance shed and property across the street from the Feed Mill. Cost $70,000.

Hardware Hank / owned by Farmers Cooperative Elevator

(Carol Kompelien contributed information and reporting to this story)

When Glenn Gniffke retired in 1991, the Cottonwood Farm Store was purchased by Virgil Gislason, who had an Ace Hardware Store in Minneota. It became the Cottonwood Home and Farm. It was managed by Don and Barb Rye (Barb is Virgil's daughter). In 1992, they became a Coast to Coast.

On April 1, 1993, the Farmers Co-op Elevator purchased the store from Gislason and hired Carol Kompelien to manage it. At this time, it became a Hardware Hank Hardware Store. When the Cottonwood and Hanley Falls elevators merged, the Cottonwood Farmers Elevator office employees, who occupied half the hardware store building, eventually moved to the feed mill and Hanley Falls main office.

At that time, the hardware store underwent a major remodel and almost doubled in size in 2001. The hardware store has carried many farm-related products along with hardware supplies, household, paint, electrical, lawn and garden, and pet supplies. They have offered many services such as making and repairing hydraulic hose. Over the years it became very successful in the paint department, earning many awards.

On Dec. 31, 2011, Carol retired and the new manager, Jessica Laleman, took over the position.

Carol Kompelien started working for John Smith at Smith's Farm Store in 1965. In 2013, she recounted her career to Scott Dubbelde, the general manager of Farmers Cooperative Elevator, which owns the hardware store:

"As Carol says in her own words, 'I was sold along with the inventory every time!'" Dubbelde said. "Carol worked all of the various duties at the Smith Farm Store, Cottonwood Farm Store, Gislason's Hardware, and FCE Hardware Hank and eventually assumed the role of Store Manager in 1993 when FCEC purchased the store.

"Carol retired after 47 years of service to several owners but virtually the same customers. Carol also wanted to remind us that she starting working in 1965, 'at a very young age.' Carol was described as a hard worker, a person who cared for the customers and liked to serve them, dedicated, and having very good business sense."

In March 2013, the Granite Falls-Clarkfield Advocate-Tribune and Tri-County News of Cottonwood reported that Cottonwood's Hardware Hank store earned the "Most Improved" award from United Hardware, with the award citing a 72 percent increase in paint sales after a new paint room was installed. United Hardware is the parent company of Hardware Hank, a wholesale distributor serving 11,100 retailers throughout the Upper Midwest.

Laleman focused on increasing advertising for the store, including a Youtube video made by her daughter Lexy and a friend, boosting its Facebook presence and planning a float for the 125th anniversary parade.

Bill Doyscher, assistant manager of Farmers Cooperative Elevator, praised Laleman's creativity and results in her first year in the position. Asked about the future, Doyscher told the Advocate-Tribune and Tri-County News: "The big thing is to continue the trend of increased sales and make the store more profitable. We want to offer things the community wants and needs without duplicating what other stores in the community are already offering."

Laleman manages eight employees in the store and said working for a cooperative is "completely different" than anything she's done before. But, the newspapers said, store employees with as much as 20 years of experience have helped her.

"Everyone here just keeps coming in with new ideas," she told the newspapers. "Everybody has ideas and we can try out most of them. Several people are working on new projects. We just keeping going forward and trying things. I think when you're doing that it makes a place fun to work at and fun for people to come to."

Along with Jessica Laleman, current store employees are Cheryl Laleman, Ardyce Louwagie, Ruth Louwagie, Stacy Plotz, Sandy Doyscher, Abby Lee and Cody St. Aubin.

Fieldcrest

Fieldcrest Assisted Living is an assisted living facility at 80 East Vermillion Street that offers independent living options and daily support.

Fieldcrest offers a warm, safe home with 24-hour nursing care, emergency call system, medication management, laundry services, housekeeping and three home-cooked meals daily, all provided by the caring staff.

G & B Woodchips, Inc.

By Doug and Laurie Gregoire

Doug and Laurie Gregoire purchased Gold Dust Woodchips from Al and Kathy Martin of Cottonwood in 1999, and changed the name to G & B Woodchips, Inc. To-date, the business

operates as a resource recovery unit offering recycled wood waste that is processed into livestock bedding. The business delivers bulk loads of bedding to dairy and turkey farms within a 200-mile radius in Minnesota and South Dakota. G & B Woodchips on average processes and delivers 150 to 200 tons of bedding per week, or the equivalence of 16 million pounds of bedding a year. This is a product that is recycle and not put into a landfill or burned.

In September of 2010, a fire destroyed our warehouse, shop and office buildings and the majority of all our equipment. We rebuilt in the same location and were able to continue to serve our customers throughout the rebuilding process. We were fortunate enough not to lose any customers.

G & B Woodchips is a family-owned and operated business, employing five family members and four other full-time employees. In 2010, we incorporated Gregoire Trucking, LLC providing hopper bottom and van trailers hauling throughout the Upper Midwest.

We take pride in offering quality livestock bedding with great customer service.

Handeland Chiropractic

Handeland Chiropractic opened its Cottonwood office at 231 W. Main St. on April 25, 2013. Cottonwood office hours will be Tuesdays 9 a.m.-noon, and Thursdays 2 p.m.-4:30 p.m.

"Handeland Chiropractic is very excited to be opening a chiropractic clinic in Cottonwood," said an early 2013 issue of the city's newsletter.

Dr. Brad Handeland, a 2007 graduate of Northwestern Health Sciences University, already had a chiropractic office in Clarkfield and expanded into Cottonwood.

"At Handeland Chiropractic, our primary goals are to provide exceptional, gentle and effective chiropractic care to our patients across the age continuum from birth through the elder years and to educate our patients about chiropractic and other natural solutions to common health problems," Handeland said in the city newsletter.

Handeland Chiropractic is equipped to diagnose and treat many areas of discomfort, including neck, back, shoulders and overall body pain. Services provided include adjustments/manipulations, ultrasound, electrical muscle stimulation, DOT/sports physicals and nutritional counseling. Handeland is also a certified kinesio taping practitioner.

Teresa J. Hoff CPA

Information from Teresa Hoff

190 W. Main St.

She started doing tax work for a few clients from home in 1980.

She purchased the tax preparation business from Erwin Schwartz and started working in the Insurance Service Agency building in January 1982.

She purchased the building at 190 W. Main Street in October 1986, and moved the accounting business from the Insurance Service Agency building to the 190 West Main Street building Jan. 1, 1988.

Services provided include:

Tax planning and preparation

 individual

 partnership

 estate and trust

 corporate

Monthly accounting services

 business

 farm

Payroll services

Hot Looks

By Lisa Fratzke

Current owners of Hot Looks are Megan Jeseritz and Lisa Fratzke.

Deb Ness and Lisa Fratzke opened Hot Looks in November of 1986. It opened up as a two-chair salon. In the summer of 1987 tanning was added.

June 1989 Deb Ness sold her portion of the business to Carla (Timm) Schlenner.

Two more stations were added in the 1990s. Carla Schlenner and Lisa Fratzke owned and operated the business until March 2005. At that time Megan Jeseritz bought Carla Schlenner's portion of the business and Megan Jeseritz and Lisa Fratzke continue to own and operate Hot Looks together.

Currently Erin (Kroger) Geistfeld rents a station at Hot Looks. We all enjoy working side by side in our hometown.

There has been a number of stylists that have worked at Hot Looks. Bea Hartke, Laura Oftedahl, Tara (VanMaldeghem) Balding, Sharon Johnson, Natalie (Ozmun) Pederson, Desire (Tolk) Timmerman, and Kelsey Labat.

Inee's Alterations

By Dana Yost

In her clothing alteration business on Cottonwood's Main Street, Inee Loke tackles jobs that can be as small as fixing a single jacket's broken zipper to making certain pretty much every girl in the area's prom dress fits exactly right.

Big or small jobs, she said May 12, 2013, in an interview for this history book. "Like this: I just finished 43 prom dresses. I keep busy, believe me."

She has for many years, as one of southwest Minnesota's most-trusted tailors. She has owned and operated Inee's Alteration in Cottonwood since 1992. She opened the business when the Village Court opened that year, and later moved to the back of the building and out of Village Court itself, renting space privately from building owner John Murphy. The Village Court has closed, but Inee's is one of three businesses still operating in the building.

A Cottonwood native, she went to technical college in Pipestone, earning a diploma in tailoring in 1971. She started her profession in Mankato in 1971, before moving back to the area after she married. She was a tailor for 24 years at Olson & Lowe clothing store in Marshall. While she was working at Olson & Lowe, she opened Inee's Alterations in Cottonwood, and for a time the two jobs overlapped.

"I repair and do alterations on clothing, is mainly what I do," Inee said.

She has a heavy-duty sewing machine at her business, which lets her replace such difficult items as leather zippers, hems on jeans and stretch stitching. She doesn't have a serger-sewing machine, and does not do embroidery. She stays current on trends in her profession, but also trusts her experience and own knowledge as she works with clients to meet their needs.

Her customer base reaches through much of southwest Minnesota.

"I am doing a wedding party for people in Worthington right now," she said. "Montevideo, Ruthton ... from all over I have quite a clientele."

She keeps a sizeable stock of supplies on site, including zippers, so repair work can be done quickly.

She joked that she is a "one-man show," but says she enjoys being the owner/operator of her business. She's stayed at it because she loves it, she said.

"I do," she said. "I like people, and here I am in contact with a lot of people. And I like keeping up with trends and styles."

Insurance Service Agency

From the Tri-County News

Insurance Service Agency of Cottonwood has been in business since 1932, during the Depression, when John Kolhei moved the business out of the Cottonwood State Bank.

Clarence (C.W.) Reishus operated the agency until Erv Schwartz took over in 1952. Schwartz moved the agency from its former office (where the laundromat is now located) to its present location at 68 W. Main Street.

In 1972, Dennis Vien took over the agency from Schwartz and operated it until 1990.

Kirk Lovsness began working for Vien in 1984 and took over the agency in 1990 after Vien retired.

On Jan. 1, 2013, Derek Dahl of Cottonwood joined the agency as a full-time agent.

Insurance Service Agency strives to bring the best insurance companies in Minnesota to Cottonwood. They have direct contracts with several highly regarded companies to give their clients many options.

The agency is locally owned and operated. Their clients get to deal with the same licensed agents when they have a claim as when they put their insurance plan together. They are local, invested in the community and available for service.

Jess Citrowski — Hair Stylin'

Jess Citrowski started her career at Hot Looks in November 2005-December 2006. She then relocated to the Neil's Plumbing building from January 2007-2009. In January 2010, she moved to her present salon which is in the rear of the former Village Court building on Main Street.

Jeseritz Construction

By owner Rick Jeseritz

Jeseritz Construction started business in 1983.

My first pieces of equipment were an old International 190 tandem gravel truck and a tracked loader purchased from Steve and Leroy Alm. Digging basements, burying rock piles, and hauling gravel were some of the jobs of the time.

As time went on, and still working alone, I purchased a used tractor/loader/backhoe and started installing farm septic systems, which we still do to this date. Years passed and workload increased, so finally I had to hire employees. With employees, I could take on more and bigger jobs, but, then again, I had to buy more equipment.

The last 30 years have been very successful because of the many loyal customers in our community and I hope there will be many more. Our equipment has grown throughout the years, along with the number of employees. My son Wade and grandson Jordan, along with two other part-time employees, are part of the work force that keeps us going.

Thank you Cottonwood for helping us get to where we are today, and congrats on your 125th!

Jeseritz Electric

From owner Jon Jeseritz

Jeseritz Electric, located at 3832 320th Avenue in rural Cottonwood, is owned by Jon Jeseritz.

The company started in 1998. "I started on my own with one truck and a credit of $1,500, worked out of my home. Things went good the first year," Jon Jeseritz said.

In his second year, he hired a part-time employee and then hired a full-time employee and put another truck on the road in the first five years of the company's existence.

Through its first 10 years, Jeseritz Electric "kept really busy and redid a machine shed — completely cemented out and heated it — added two scissor lifts, one electric that fits through a door with non-marking tires and goes 26 feet high, and the other a four-wheel drive, fueled by gas or LP. We also added a skid loader and trencher," Jon said.

Now, after 15 years of being in business, "we have four full-time employees, three trucks on the road, a remodeled shop (put on an office and parts room) and an upgraded skid loader and trencher," Jon said.

"What we wire: houses, farms, commercial, bins, dryers, trenching, install TV cable, telephone cable, speaker cable.

"We would like to thank everyone for all the business and we hope to continue serving you. Thank you. Jon, Tyler, Jeremy, Carl, Eloy."

Joyce Warnke Doll Clothes

By Joyce Warnke

I started making doll clothes for my two granddaughters when they received "American Girl" dolls. I happened to show them to my boss, Glenda VanLerberghe, at TNT, and she asked me to make some doll clothes for her granddaughters, too. So I did.

After she saw them, Glenda said she wanted them in her store. That was in the beginning of the fall of 2010. Later, Glenda closed her store and I moved to Village Court on Aug. 1, 2011.

The doll clothes sold more than I dreamed possible. Then on March 31, 2013, Village Court closed. Where to go now? With thanks to John Murphy, owner of the building, and Irene Loke, who offered to receive the money for my clothes, I was able to stay in the former Village Court building.

Thank you to all who helped make this possible, and to all of you who bought my doll clothes.

Kompelien-Danielson Maintenance

Kompelien-Danielson Maintenance is a business that maintains township roads.

In the fall of 1981, Byron Kompelien bought two road graders and the maintenance business from Arvid Anderson.

Then in 1995, Lyle Danielson became a partner in the business.

Over the years, we have increased the number of townships that we provide service for and upgraded equipment to the present number of four road graders and two snow-plow trucks.

LeRoy's

The owner of a Marshall restaurant bought the city of Cottonwood's former municipal liquor store on Nov. 3, 2009, for $75,000.

The building still stands, but it has a new look, a new name and now sells more than liquor.

Tom Handeland, who owns the Hitching Post restaurant in Marshall, became the new owner of the liquor store after the Cottonwood City Council approved its sale, ending several months of debate over its future.

Handeland extensively remodeled the interior of the store, converted it to a bar-and-grill and renamed it LeRoy's. It opened in 2010.

It is often a busy eating establishment, with a vaulted ceiling, and Handeland brought in a restored antique wooden bar, with backdrop, that anchors the bar area.

The council voted unanimously for the sale, contingent on Handeland meeting requirements for a liquor license.

Handeland and Carey Field of Montevideo submitted the only two bids for the liquor store. Field bid $25,000.

Along with food, LeRoy's sells both on- and off-sale liquor.

Cottonwood had a municipal liquor store since 1937, the Marshall Independent reported. However, in recent years the business struggled with declining sales and operating losses.

The city council had been discussing whether to sell the liquor store since 2007. The possibility of private ownership for the store was brought up at a November council meeting.

Bids were opened by Isaackson and members of the city council's liquor store committee the afternoon of Nov. 3.

"We did have an extensive discussion" after the bid opening, Isaackson told the city council, and he recommended that the council act on a sale. Handeland's bid offered to contract with the city for the full $75,000 price at a 5.5 percent interest rate. Payments to the city would work out to be about $813 a month, Isaackson said.

"If the business works out for the owner, it would be good for the city."

Additionally, Handeland offered to pay to refurbish the interior of the liquor store himself.

The city began advertising for bids on the liquor store in September. Isaackson said the city had gotten seven requests for bid applications, but only Field's and Handeland's had been returned.

"We'd be looking at about $9,700 a year coming in for deed payments," he said.

The building originally had been the first Cottonwood Co-op Oil Station.

LouBa's Lunchwagon

By owner Laurie "LouBa" Kuyper

For the past 27 years, I've run LouBa's Lunchwagon and have enjoyed it tremendously. The people I've met and the places I've been have been quite an adventure.

I started out with step vans, but then went to a pull-type trailer, which is a lot easier. We do catering and serve at auctions, birthdays, picnics, town events, horse shows, snowmobile races, fairs, fishing events, parades, dances and have even been to Sturgis, S.D., to serve for the motorcycle rally a few times.

In the summertime, I go to the Cottonwood Lake beach on Tuesday and Thursday for noon and supper meals.

My family and the people of Cottonwood have been very supportive of me, and I greatly appreciate it.

I couldn't have made it 27 years without them, and I hope the next 27 years are just as much fun.

MaCKs Salon

By Shari Wee

MaCKs Salon opened their doors on January 1, 2010, at 158 West Main Street in Cottonwood. Owner Shari Wee named the business after her three daughter's initials, Morgan, Corbyn and Kennar (MCK). She used the beginning letter of their middle names (a) and added the "s" for herself.

To date, she has 26 years in the hair industry. In November 2011, she added an employee, Mallory Gregoire, to the salon. Salon services include haircuts, colors, multi-dimensional colors, hi-lites, perms, reconditioners, waxes, rust removals and a thorough consultation to kick-start your visit. Different retail products to help in your home hair care are also offered. Although the location had been a salon for a few years before, furniture was added and the space was updated and has a welcoming, up-to-date relaxing spa-like atmosphere.

Matthys Pioneer Seeds

By Robert Matthys

Matthys Pioneer Seeds is celebrating its 20th year in business during 2013. Owner Robert Matthys started selling Pioneer seed in 1993 with about 15 farmers in the Cottonwood area. Today, the business has grown to roughly 80 farmers in the local area, extending from Cottonwood down toward Marshall and Milroy.

Pioneer Seeds offers a complete line of corn, soybean and alfalfa seed, along with silage inoculants for area farmers. Pioneer offers farmers the latest products that offer patented herbicide and insect resistance in the seed to help farmers manage risk while increasing yields on every acre in their farming operation.

Matthys Pioneer Seeds is a full-service business that works with farmers on their planting plans, hybrid selection, seed financing, soybean seed treating, on farm-product delivery, in-season crop scouting, and harvest yield data collection and analysis.

Mid Continent Cabinetry

From Mid Continent's corporate web site and the city of Cottonwood

Mid Continent Cabinetry, as part of the Norcraft Companies brand, is one of the longest-running cabinet producers in the industry. In 1966, Mid Continent started in Marshall, began manufacturing operations in Cottonwood in 1971 in the old creamery building. The company's headquarters are now in Eagan, a Twin Cities suburb.

Starting as a small regional manufacturer, Mid Continent Cabinetry has grown through the last five decades to become the United State's fifth-largest cabinetry producer. Our work culture extends out to this tradition in stability. To have two generations of a family working within our company is not uncommon, and some of our employees have been with us since our opening in 1966.

Today, Mid Continent Cabinetry is a leader in the cabinet market, creating glazed cabinets, kitchen cabinets, bath vanities, entertainment centers, wine racks and cabinets, and more. Our design philosophy extends past the cabinets themselves, as we continue to find more uses and solutions for our cabinets and vanities. As we move forward, we will continue to innovate and deliver top-quality cabinets and vanities to our distributors and our customers.

There has been steady expansion at the Cottonwood site.

In 1978, the city of Cottonwood donated land to Mid Continent and made infrastructure improvements for an expansion project.

In 1982, street, bridge and water and sanitary sewer improvements were made to the Industrial Area around the Mid Continent Cabinetry building with funding from a Community Development Block Grant.

In 1989, a new 150,000-gallon water tower was constructed in the city's Industrial Area to accommodate an expansion by Mid Continent, funded with federal EDA and Small Cities Development Program grant funds, and Tax-Increment Financing.

In 2005, funded with city and state grants, the city undertook sanitary sewer rerouting and lift station construction around the east side of the industrial plat to accommodate Mid Continent's expansion project on East Second Street.

At Mid Continent Cabinetry, we hold our products to precise quality standards. Throughout our decades of experience, we have built solid relationships with the industry's best suppliers. We combine our culture of innovation and continuous improvement with the time-honored joinery techniques to make solid, modern cabinetry solutions for your home.

How our cabinets are built

Our doors are built to ensure quality, while still meeting the demands of a short production cycle.

The wood used in creating our frames and doors are native species grown in the United States. We have specifically machined frames designed to meet our exact standards.

The cabinet case is made from sheets of plywood or furniture board produced in the United States.

The functional hardware, including the drawer glides and hinges, are built for Mid Continent Cabinetry by some of the best manufacturers in the industry.

The finishing techniques used on the cabinets are some of the best in the industry. The stains and paints are applied by hand, and the finish coat is oven cured. This gives Mid Continent Cabinets their strength, durability, and the outstanding grain clarity.

Our product care extends out to our shipping as well. The cabinets are packaged individually using the proper corner protectors. We utilize dedicated trucks to ship our product to the local dealer, as well as utilizing carries that are experienced in handling cabinetry.

Mid Continent has earned several awards for its products and how they are built.

Mid Continent Cabinetry is an active member of the National Kitchen and Bath Association (NKBA) helping to support, educate and lead the kitchen and bath industry.http://www.kcma.org/ Mid Continent Cabinetry retains the KCMA seal of certification on its Signature Series, Pro Series and Norcraft Cabinetry Series door styles. http://www.greencabinetsource.org/

Mid Continent Cabinetry was awarded the Environmental Stewardship Program Certification in January 2007. Developed through the KCMA, the annual certification enables cabinet manufacturers to demonstrate their ongoing commitment to sound and sustainable environmental practices in the production of their products in areas that impact the environment and their community. Certification include rigorous review and compliance in five categories: Air Quality, Product Resource Management, Process Resource Management, Environmental Stewardship, Community Relations.

Mid Continent is committed to protecting the environment. Our goal is to provide consumers with high-quality, durable cabinetry using sustainable manufacturing methods.

To meet this goal, we strive to manufacture products that are both good for the environment and healthy and safe for our customers and their homes. Also, we are reducing waste consumption. We believe a sustainable future can be achieved by following the three basic "R's" – reuse, reduce, recycle.

Our facilities have recycling bins setup to collect a variety of items including paper, plastic, glass, stain canisters, cardboard, scrap wood and metal.

We use green-certified printers that use e-certified renewable energy to produce paper. We also use corn-based inks and print on recycled paper. Additionally, all discounted and/or outdated literature is recycled.

Our plant facility employees work four, 10-hour work days, helping to reduce the amount of harmful greenhouse gases emitted from vehicles and decreasing the amount of daily energy used.

Mirror Solutions

A business that offers a non-surgical method for people to lose body size opened in May 2011 on Cottonwood's Main Street.

Mirror Solutions is owned by Kim Sander. The business is located next to Hot Looks, in the former CENTROL offices.

It uses a non-surgical liposuction treatment that was first developed in France in the 1990s, and has been in use in the United States since 2002, said a May 11, 2011, issue of the Tri-County News.

Sander said she knows the method works, because she has used it herself. She first heard about non-surgical liposuction at a women's expo, and was convinced by a friend to try the procedure. She and her friend made appointments at a spa.

"I lost six and a half inches at the first treatment," she said. "I was totally sold. I could immediately tell the difference."

After four treatments, Sander said in the Tri-County News, she had lost a total of 20 inches.

"I haven't gained an inch back, and I'm not a workout person," she said.

Sander decided to invest in the equipment and supplies, which come from France, and went into business for herself. She went through a certification process, before opening the location in Cottonwood.

"It's a good location, with the salon next door," she said.

She said the process is similar to getting a massage.

"There are two phases of detoxification on the entire body," she said. "It involves deep breathing and gentle massage to open the lymphatic system. With the remodeling phase, we call it, we deliver the microcurrents that breaks up and actually melts the fat and moves it toward the lymphatic drain points to get rid of it permanently."

All of the materials used in the process are natural products designed specifically for the treatment, the newspaper reported.

"The average inch loss is four to six inches with one treatment," Sander said. "The treatment increases metabolism for 21 days, so a lot of people will do a series of three treatments, 21 days apart. That trains the metabolism to stay at an increased rate."

The treatments can take about an hour and a half, she said.

Murph's

When Andy's Place closed in 2001, about 20 men ended up buying it so they had a place to play cards.

Then, in December 2007, John Murphy made the Main Street building that formerly housed the Tri-County News into what was unofficially called "the new pool hall."

Then, in December 2008, because of Snooks Café having been closed in March 2008, Murphy's building also became the place for Cottonwood's coffee drinkers to come. It is now known as Murph's.

Murphy began converting the building into a pool hall in late 2007, the Tri-County News reported in its Dec. 5, 2007, issue. "The local card sharks are only too happy to put up with the construction and the place has a number of card players on nearly a daily schedule, which includes Sunday afternoon poker games," wrote Ida Kesteloot in the newspaper. Card players range in age from 21 to 70.

Murphy planned to move the "Andy's Place" sign to the new location from the building where Andy's had been owned and operated for more than 40 years by Andy Viaene.

"Beverages and candy bars are available to ward off any hunger pangs that might threaten to break up the game. Most of the regulars are appreciative of the smoke-free atmosphere," Kesteloot's story in the Tri-County News said.

When the new site formally opened in early December 2008, there was debate about what it should be named.

"I like the sound of Murph's, that has a friendly sound to it," Kathy Dahl said in the Dec. 3, 2008, issue of the Tri-County News.

"Murphy's or Murphy's Place sounds good, too," added Erma Huso.

There aren't set prices for cups of coffee or snacks. People are trusted to pay a proper price for what they drink and eat, or, in other words, to follow the honor system. The Dec. 2, 2008, story, also written by Ida Kesteloot, continued:

"The honor system is something that one wouldn't find in a large coffee shop but it seems to work for a small town with a big conscience. Everyone pays for their coffee and whatever they decide to indulge in. Rolls are purchased from Carl's Bakery in Granite Falls or the fixings for toast are available. Or you might get lucky and hit a morning when someone brings in homemade treats in the honor of a birthday or just for the fun of sharing.

"The one hazard of joining the coffee crowd at the new location is the ever-ready danger of being asked to purchase the latest raffle tickets that are circulating.

"The current raffle tickets making the rounds are for the Lady Auxiliary Quilt raffle. Tickets are available for a mere dollar at the United Southwest Bank in Cottonwood or through Erma Huso.

"It appears that the new permanent coffee drinking place has definitely filled the bill for the Cottonwood community."

Neil's Plumbing

From the March 14, 2007, issue of the Tri-County News of Cottonwood

The transfer of ownership of Neil's Plumbing in Cottonwood took place Jan. 1, 2007, when Neil Kroger's business was purchased by the Cottonwood Co-op Oil Co.

"The Board of Directors had discussed enhancing its department that already provides cooling and heating," Co-op general manager Brad Rosa said. "They were looking for ways to increase this division and decided to approach Neil Kroger about the possibility of selling his business.

"Kroger will stay on board with the business and services won't change that much. One thing that will change is the opportunity to reach someone in an emergency. The phone line will still be answered at Neil's but there will be back-up numbers and someone at the Agronomy Center. "There are technicians at the Agronomy Center, so if Neil is out on another job or unavailable there will still be a service person ready to cover calls. It is just another way that the Cottonwood Co-Op has found to enhance its services."

North Star Mutual Insurance Company

Company history and data provided by Joe Hoff

The North Star Mutual Insurance Company was founded in 1920 by farmers to provide insurance protection for themselves and their neighbors. The company's office, originally

located in Redwood Falls, was moved to Cottonwood in 1926. In its 93 years of existence, North Star has grown to be one of the larger regional property and casualty insurance companies in the Midwest.

And it continues to call Cottonwood home.

"From our perspective, Cottonwood *is* home," President Jeff Mauland said. "Our employee base is here. We have loyalty here. We've got our facilities and extra land here. We've got some considerable investments here. The quality of the workforce – the people – make that work."

North Star moved to its current location at the south edge of Cottonwood in 1968 after outgrowing its previous locations on Main Street. At the time of the move, the company had 27 employees with annual premium writings of about $2,500,000 and assets of just over $4,000,000. In 1979, an addition was completed, more than doubling the size of the 10-year-old building and providing adequate space for the staff that had grown to 70 full-time employees.

The past 25 years have seen dramatic changes in the company. North Star is still a local company with its only office in Cottonwood. Farm, homeowners, auto and commercial insurance is now written in six states with annual premium writings of about $300,000,000 and assets of over $460,000,000. The staff at North Star has grown rapidly also in the last few years, now numbering just over 200.

Because of the strong growth, a second building addition was required in 1994. This addition added more than 20,000 square feet, almost doubling the size of the building again. In 2001, Cliff Hanson retired from the company after 47 years of service, 28 of them as President. Jeff Mauland replaced Cliff as President upon his retirement, and still serves in that capacity today.

Many of North Star's employees are graduates of the Cottonwood/Lakeview school system, although Mauland said employees at the home office may come from a 50-mile range of Cottonwood. That helps build stability, longevity and familiarity with the company and community, he said.

"Sometimes it can be hard to attract (employees from outside the area), so we end up growing our own. We feel we provide an excellent opportunity for our own people. We promote from with in. I guess I am a good example of that. The quality of life here, and the work ethic here, that has all worked well for us."

In 2009, the company purchased a large portion of the adjacent athletic complex to allow for future expansion needs. In 2010, a shelter house along with playground equipment was constructed on the property, which was made available to the city as a park until such time the company may have need of it.

"We certainly want to be good corporate citizens, too," Mauland said. "For the local area, we try to help the schools out where we can, and the town itself, as well."

Mauland said the company invests in factors that are important amenities for both the community and North Star's employees: golf course, lake, schools, Lions Club projects, the park on its own property. It also has been a prominent sponsor of Coming Home Days. Plus, employees of the company themselves get very involved personally in many local organizations and events.

"It's important to keep the community moving forward," he said. "The things that improve the quality of life, if we are able to support those types of things, we will."

Norwegian Mutual Insurance Company

Norwegian Mutual Insurance Company started in 1879. We are a property and casualty insurance carrier. Over the last 25 years, there have been several changes, with most occurring in the last five years.

Pete Hellie, the previous manager, took a position with North Star Mutual and was replaced by Mark Nelson. The  company also changed its logo. The logo used to be a green Viking shield and now it has a more modern look.

Our company name has also changed. We have removed the word "Fire" from our company name.

In 2012, the company moved out of the North Star building to our new office building at 95 W. Main Street in Cottonwood. Our company employs four full-time employees and one part-time employee.

Snooks Cafe

More than three years after it closed its doors as a cafe, demolition equipment tore down the former Snooks Café on Main Street in Cottonwood in early December 2011.

The café building, and a building next to it, were demolished by Jeseritz Construction to make way for new development.

The new development is a new office building for Norwegian Insurance Company, which was constructed in 2012 at the site at 95 West Main Street.

Snooks, owned by Joel and Brenda Krumrey for about seven years, closed its doors March 14, 2008. It had been a café for several years before that, as well, and was known as Jim's Café while owned by Jim Schrupp. The building was not always a café. It also served as the A.G. Nelson and Art Olson Produce Store at one time.

The decision to close was difficult but necessary, Brenda Krumrey told the Marshall Independent.

Business hadn't been good enough to pay the bills, Krumrey said, and the café already had been listed for sale before the closing.

"We just can't afford it," she said. "We're going to try and sell it, hopefully."

The former Snooks Café building is shown being demolished in this photo from the Dec. 22, 2011, issue of the Granite Falls Advocate-Tribune. A new office for Norwegian Mutual was built in its place.

For the last year before it closed, Brenda Krumrey worked full-time on her own at the café. At first, the restaurant did good business selling breakfast and lunch.

"It wasn't really until the last two years that it started getting hard," Krumrey said. Now, Snooks is "more of a coffee place. We have an early-morning crew."

Krumrey said she wasn't sure what caused the slowdown in business, but she thought the economic downturn that began in 2008 might have led people to cut back on spending, including eating out at restaurants.

"I don't know. I think a lot of it is the economy. People are a lot more cautious about how they spend their money. I am," Krumrey said. "There are some people who will disagree with me, but I think the no-smoking law affected my business. Not a lot — the majority of my customers are nonsmokers — but the ones who smoked, stayed and ate."

With Snooks closed, its regulars looked for new places to gather for coffee. Village Court planned to offer coffee and rolls for a while, City Clerk-Administrator Greg Isaackson told the Independent.

Krumrey said she thought people in the community have been pretty understanding about the decision to close the cafe. With Snooks closed, there are still other places for people to gather. Overall, she said, the experience of running the cafe had been positive.

Sterling Equipment & Repair Inc.

By Craig and Joy Kesteloot

Sterling Equipment & Repair Inc. opened in January 2010. Craig and Joy Kesteloot purchased the property and buildings in August 2009 and did extensive remodeling to the building that houses the business now. It began as an agricultural equipment repair business but quickly added truck repair, as well, because of demand.

When Sterling opened, they had one part-time and four full-time employees. Sterling has continually grown since opening their doors. Three more employees were added in 2011 because of growth and, in the spring of 2012, Sterling became a dealer for Ag Leader Technology, the leading innovator in precision farming technology. In June 2012, Sterling became a Gehl Skidloader and Manitou Telehandler dealer.  They also offer consignment sales. Because of their great location along Highway 23 on the edge of Cottonwood, sales has been a nice addition to Sterling.

2012 proved to be a year full of growth for Sterling Equipment & Repair Inc, which included adding a larger parts department and a parts manager; also increasing the shop work space along with a larger service office. The Sterling Family has grown to ten employees at the current time. They feel very blessed to have the support of the Cottonwood community and surrounding areas and look forward to what the future holds.

Tri-County News

There has been a newspaper in Cottonwood for nearly as long as the city has been incorporated. The first issue of the Cottonwood Current was printed Feb. 6, 1892, according to a story a century later in the Jan. 29, 1992, issue of the Current.

The first issue was literally a limited edition: "According to local historian Torgny Anderson, there was only one copy of the first issue printed because a fire destroyed that issue of the paper before any other copies could be printed," the Jan. 29, 1992, Current reported in a story marking the centennial of the paper.

"W.H. Mulhane was the first publisher of the Current and he founded the newspaper after would-be publisher G.E. Graber left town in August of 1891. Graber left behind a newspaper plant and Mulhane took over.

"According to an article written by Mulhane in the Feb. 6, 1892 issue, G.E. Graber came to Cottonwood with the promise of starting a newspaper [called the Leader]. He collected payment for subscriptions in advance, and obtained the materials necessary for publishing a newspaper. After two months of drunken loafing, Graber left town, Mulhane wrote.

"Mulhane said in his story. 'This paper is not G.E. Graber's Leader. It is THE CURRENT and does not feel that it is fair that the ghost of a defunct paper should haunt it.' Mulhane stated the purpose of The Current was 'to publish local news and place the advantages of Cottonwood before the outside world … and as to the way The Current succeeds is left for the people of this vicinity to judge.'"

Mulhane was succeeded by E.I. Raymond, who, like Graber, disappeared from Cottonwood with unpaid bills. Residents took over the paper and published it themselves until J.F. Paige became publisher in 1893. The office of the newspaper was destroyed by fire in April 1893, and the Current went through several owners until 1905, when W.A. Sisson and a partner bought the paper.

The Sisson family was associated with the Current for more than 50 years. W.A. Sisson bought out his partner in 1929, and, in 1938, his son Keith Sisson bought a half interest. Through the 1940s, Mrs. W.A. Sisson, Keith and Mabelle Sisson and Keith's brother, R. Ward Sisson, operated the paper.

Tom Idso started working for the Sissons while he was in junior high. He said in 1992 that the Sissons were determined to continue to print the paper even as their health began to fail. "You have to hand it to them," Idso recalled. "They could have sat home and felt sorry for themselves, but they didn't." Ward Sisson wrote editorials for the Current. "He was witty. He'd always write a good editorial to get people stormed up, " Idso said.

In 1954, Keith Sisson bought his brother's inherited interest and was the sole operator of the Current until he sold it to Robert and Lorraine Lancaster. Under the Lancasters, the paper combined the Current with the Belview Independent and the Echo Enterprise and renamed the paper the Current/Enterprise/Independent News. The Lancasters sold the paper in 1988 to Byron Higgin, who renamed it the Tri-County News.

Higgin combined the News and the Clarkfield Advocate and renamed the paper the Tri-County Advocate.

In 1990, Higgin's stepson, Jeff Meyer, and his wife Julie, bought the paper and renamed it the Tri-County News. They did not purchase the Clarkfield portion of the paper. Higgin kept the Clarkfield portion and merged that with the Granite Falls Tribune to form the Granite Falls-Clarkfield Advocate-Tribune.

"We know this is a wonderful area and the residents are very interested in keeping a newspaper active in each community — and so are we," the Meyers said when they took over the paper.

In 1999, the Meyers sold the paper to the Liberty newspaper chain. The paper is currently owned by Gatehouse Media, a corporate chain based in Fairport, N.Y. It has a local office in downtown Cottonwood at 1 Barstad Road N., on the north side of Main Street where it intersects with Barstad Road. Kim Louwagie is the present editor. Published every week on Wednesdays, its circulation in 2013 was 963, according to the Minnesota Newspaper Association.

The Tri-County news is one of 10 newspapers and five shoppers Gatehouse owns in Minnesota. The company owns newspapers and other publishing properties in 20 states throughout the U.S.

United Southwest Bank

A Chronological Look at United Southwest Bank / update provided by Greg Golberg

August 1, 1916 — Articles of incorporation were drawn and charter issued to Farmers State Bank of Hanley Falls.

September 30, 1922 — Merger with First State Bank of Hanley Falls. Farmers State Bank is the surviving corporation.

1929 — The two Cottonwood banks merge, with the Cottonwood State Bank surviving.

September 1931 — Banks in Cottonwood, Echo and Clarkfield failed to open doors for business.

September 23, 1931 — The Board of Directors of the Farmers State Bank of Hanley Falls resolved "that the Board of Directors hereby order the bank closed to protect the interests of its depositors and conserve its assets." A run on the bank because of the closing of other banks in the area was a definite possibility.

July 22, 1932 — Farmers State Bank of Hanley Falls re-organizes and thereby avoids liquidation process.

December 21, 1932 — Stockholders approve moving the Farmers State Bank from Hanley Falls and further acted to change the name of the corporation to the Empire State Bank of Cottonwood.

February 6, 1933 — The Empire State Bank opened its doors for business in Cottonwood, occupying the former Cottonwood State Bank building.

January 1, 1934 — Empire State Bank approved for FDIC insurance.

January 11, 1936 — First dividend of 5% paid on the results of 1935 business.

May 9, 1940 — Air conditioning equipment installed in bank building at cost of $692.

April 24, 1965 — Grand opening held to celebrate expansion and renovation. The expanded facility is nearly twice the former bank size.

1973 — Empire State Bank parking lot is acquired on southwest corner of First and West Main streets in Cottonwood.

1975 — Dell Theatre Building acquired as a possible "new" bank building site in Cottonwood.

October 13, 1977 — Request approved for the operation of a detached banking facility in Hanley Falls.

January 2, 1978 — Opened doors for business at the detached banking facility in Hanley Falls.

December 1980 — Construction commences on new bank building in Cottonwood.

February 24, 1981 — Final authorization received from the State Banking Commission and FDIC to relocate Empire State Bank.

November 10, 1981 — Construction completed and the Empire State Bank opened for business in its new banking house at 111 W. Main St. in Cottonwood.

December 28, 1990 — Adrian C. Golberg purchases interest in Vesta State Bank.

June 26, 1992 — Adrian C. Golberg purchases controlling interest in Vesta State Bank.

August 16, 1993 — Vesta State Bank changes name to United Southwest Bank.

November 22, 1993 — United Southwest Bank opens branch in Marshall.

January 1, 1997 — Empire State Bank merges with United Southwest Bank located in Cottonwood.

May 16, 2000 — Hanley Falls branch moves into new building at 101 1st Street North.

OFFICERS

1916 — John Lee, president; J.W. Tanquist, cashier

1928 — E.H. Anderson, president; A.O. Thostensen, cashier

1932 — Reed N. Johnson, president; R.A. Gluth, cashier

1934 — T.F. Spreiter, president; R.A. Gluth, cashier

1939 — Guy S. Bacon, president; H.P. Peterson, cashier

1961 — Paul O. Pearson, president; Emil V. Stavick, cashier

1973 — Adrian C. Golberg, president; Douglas Anderson, cashier

1981 — Adrian C. Golberg, president; Douglas Anderson, vice president; Mark Bjornebo, assistant vice president; Mark Elston, assistant vice president; Ruth Post, cashier

1983 — Adrian C. Golberg, president; Douglas Anderson, vice president; Mark Bjornebo, assistant vice president; Mark Elston, assistant vice president; Loretta Dieken, cashier

1988 — Adrian C. Golberg, president; Douglas Anderson, vice president; Gary Gabrielson, senior loan officer; Ron Bortnem, loan officer; Loretta Dieken, cashier; Mark Elston, insurance manager; Ardith Grothen, Hanley Branch manager

1997 — Adrian C. Golberg, president; Douglas Anderson, vice president; Gary Gabrielson, senior loan officer; Ron Bortnem, loan officer; Loretta Dieken, cashier; Glenda Vizecky, auditor; Ardith Grothen, Hanley Branch manager; Richard Eilders, Vesta loan officer; Karen Lemcke, compliance and training officer; Connie House, assistant cashier; Dan Raduns, Marshall loan officer

2000 — Adrian C. Golberg, chairman; Greg Golberg, president; Douglas Anderson, vice president; Gary Gabrielson, senior loan officer; Ron Bortnem, loan officer; Loretta Dieken, cashier; Glenda Vizecky, auditor; Ardith Grothen, Hanley Branch manager; Richard Eilders, Vesta loan officer; Karen Lemcke, compliance and training officer; Ellen Golberg, insurance/marketing officer; Bruce Rupp, Marshall loan officer

2008 — Adrian C. Golberg, chairman; Greg Golberg, president; Douglas Anderson, vice president; Ron Bortnem, vice president; Glenda Vizecky, cashier; Nancy Dahl, Hanley Branch manager; Micheal Core, Marshall loan officer; Karen Lemcke, compliance and training officer; Ellen Golberg, insurance/marketing officer; John Classen, junior loan officer; Judy Ozmun, loan administrator; Brenda Lynner, auditor

2013 — Adrian C. Golberg, chairman; Greg Golberg, president; Douglas Anderson, vice president; Ron Bortnem, vice president; John Classen, loan officer; Nancy Dahl, Hanley Branch manager; Ellen Golberg, insurance/marketing officer; Deb Zimmer, compliance and training officer

BOARD OF DIRECTORS

1916 — John E. Lee, A.O. Simundson, B.C. Green, W.W. Olson, J.W. Tanquist

1922 — E.H. Anderson, C.S. Orwoll, G.M. Gustafson, T.A. Veldey, Oscar Johnson, J.M. Gustafson, J.K. Holum, C.H. Hellie, A.O. Simundson

1932 — R.A. Gluth, A.O. Simundson, H.O. Riisnoes, E.H. Anderson, Reed N. Johnson

1933 — T.F. Spreiter, Reed N. Johnson, Ludwig Dahl, R.A. Gluth, Christ Sather

1934 — T.F. Spreiter, R.A. Gluth, Ludwig Dahl, Chris Sather, Julius Sween

1937 — T. F. Spreiter, C.O. Sather, Julius Sween, Ludwig Dahl, H.P. Peterson

1941 — G.S. Bacon, C.O. Sather, Julius Sween, Ludwig Dahl, H.P. Peterson

1946 — G.S. Bacon, C.O. Sather, Julius Sween, Ludwig Dahl, Paul O. Pearson

1951 — G.S. Bacon, C.O. Sather, Julius Sween, Paul O. Pearson, Emil V. Slavick

1954 — G.S. Bacon, C.O. Sather, Paul O. Pearson, Emil V. Slavick, Rachel Bacon

1955 — G.S. Bacon, Paul O. Pearson, Emil V. Slavick, Rachel Bacon, Russell Bacon

1961 — G.S. Bacon, Paul O. Pearson, Emil V. Slavick, Helen Pearson, Ida Slavick

1969 — Paul O. Pearson, Emil V. Slavick, Helen Pearson, Ida Slavick, Adrian C. Golberg

1973 — Paul O. Pearson, Emil V. Slavick, Adrian C. Golberg, Douglas Anderson, Judith Golberg

1980 — Emil V. Slavick, Adrian C. Golberg, Douglas Anderson, Judith Golberg, John Loe

1984 — Adrian C. Golberg, Douglas Anderson, Judith Golberg, John Loe

1997 — Adrian C. Golberg, Douglas Anderson, Judith Golberg, John Loe, Lee Holmberg, Dan Raduns

1999 — Adrian C. Golberg, Douglas Anderson, Judith Golberg, John Loe, Lee Holmberg, Greg Golberg

HOLDERS OF CONTROLLING INTEREST

1916 — no single party control

1932 — Hacking Brothers, Minneapolis

1936 — T.F. Spreiter

1939 — Guy S. Bacon

1961 — Paul O. Pearson/Emil V. Slavick

1972 — Adrian C. Golberg

Xcaliber Gunsmithing

Xcaliber Gunsmithing has moved to a new building at 235 E 4th St. South. Xcaliber relocated to Cottonwood in the spring of 2010 and until spring of 2013 had been sharing a building with Sterling Equipment.

Owner Brent Kesteloot was busy moving into new space at the same address in the spring of 2013, which would allow Xcaliber to increase its inventory and provide additional services, including the hosting of concealed-carry classes starting March 9, 2013, a city of Cottonwood newsletter said.

Xcaliber Gunsmithing specializes in firearms repair and customization, as well as retail sales of guns and gun products. Its website is www.excalibergunsmithing.us

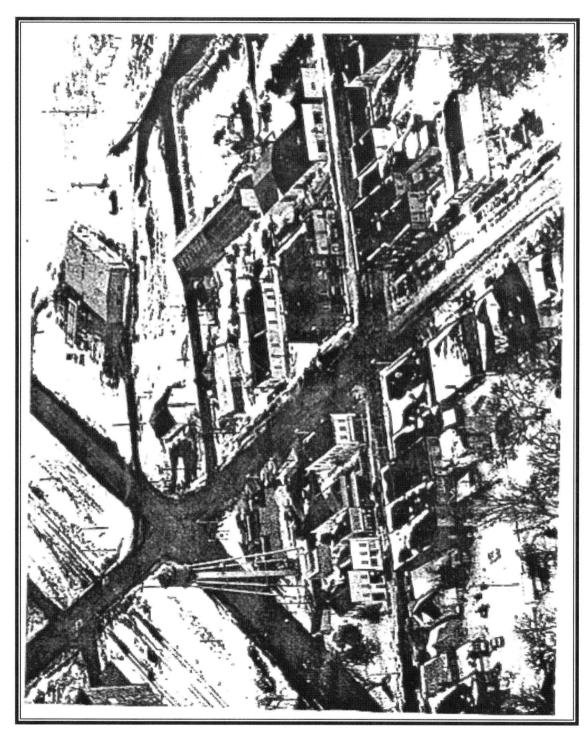

An overhead view of central Cottonwood taken between the years 1940 and 1946. (Courtesy of Audrey Hostetler)

Former Cottonwood Area Business Owners Who Have

Died in the Last 25 Years

Compiled by Pat Aamodt

Name	Death	Business
Alm, LeRoy	Dec. 15, 2005	Tiling
Bahn, Martin	Feb. 18, 2007	Star Market Grocery
Baumann, Ruby	Feb. 12, 2010	Owner of Drive-In
Carlson, Marge	Oct. 26, 1994	Marge's Beauty Shop
Colburn, Gordon	Dec. 13, 2012	Meat market
Coudron, Julius	March 22, 2000	Electrician
Dahl, Jeff	Sept. 30, 2009	Painter
Deuel, Ronald	May 5, 2011	Body shop
Ericksen, Edna	June 5, 2012	Ericksen Furniture
Ericksen, Loren	July 21, 1990	Furniture and hardware
Erickson, Wayne	Jan. 22, 2009	Drive-Inn
Fenger, Alfred	Jan. 25, 2007	TV sales and repair
Fruin, Duane	Oct. 24, 2001	Trucking
Gilb, Ronald	Jan. 24, 2011	Drive-Inn
Gniffke, Edward	Nov. 22, 1990	Garage
Gniffke, Glen	May 1, 2008	Farm Store
Gniffke, Grover	May 10, 1996	Garage
Gniffke, Loris	Dec. 22, 2005	Carpentry
Hill, Ivan	Nov. 24, 2006	Drive-Inn
Hostetler, Delbert "Bud"	July 13, 2006	Ice cream shop
Huso, Kermit	Oct. 19, 1991	Huso's Grocery/dry goods
Jaeger, Robert	Jan. 3, 1997	Pizza Ranch
King, Charles "Bud"	Dec. 7, 2002	Shoe Shop and The Family Store
King, Eleanor "Dot"	Dec. 15, 2000	The Family Store
Knudson, Gordon	Oct. 16, 2003	K&S Implement
Knutson, Wendell	June 6, 1991	Fleet of buses

Kroger, June	April 17, 2013	Grandma's Kitchen Café
Krumrey, Leland	May 18, 1998	Carpenter
Lancaster, David	April 15, 1998	Tri-County News
Lancaster, Lorraine	June 30, 2004	Cottonwood Current/Tri-County News
Lange, Merle	Jan. 4, 2006	Lange's Family Restaurant
Lewis, George	Dec. 16, 2007	George's Café
Lindsay, Rosella	May 5, 2008	Lindsay Trailer Court
Lund, Arvid	March 4, 1996	Lund Studio
Mauland, Bernhard	March 21, 1990	Carpentry
Morken, Olaf	June 30, 1994	Soft water hauling
Nelson, Kenneth	Nov. 17, 1997	Nelson Hardware
Nelson, Roger	Sept. 3, 1998	Bus repair
Nordli, Thorfinn "Tony"	Aug. 3, 1994	Blacksmith
Oftedahl, Clarence	March 11, 2002	Oftedahl Insurance
Oftedal, Einar	March 19, 2007	Seed sales
Olson, Art	Dec. 2, 1995	Olson Produce
Peterson, Wayne	Dec. 27, 2000	Movie theater
Reishus, Dale	Dec. 30, 2002	Carpentry
Reishus, Theron	Jan. 27, 1994	Trucking
Retrum, James	Feb. 1991	Retrum's Grocery
Retrum, Paul H.	Feb. 1991	Retrum's Grocery
Rewerts, John	June 23, 2003	Johnny's Barber Shop
Ricke, Ben	March 24, 1990	Plumbing
Rosa, Don	July 27, 2005	Farm machine repair
Seitz, Wilson	Sept. 14, 1988	Druggist
Slette, Ben	Sept. 6, 1989	Slette's Café
Slette, Stella	Nov. 15, 2003	Slette's Café
Smith, John	Feb. 2, 1997	Smith's Farm Store and Trucking
Snyder, Bruce	Oct. 11, 2006	K&S Implement
Thompson, Ervin	March 9, 1997	K.A. Thomson & Sons Road Const.
Van DeViere, Gene	Sept. 20, 2011	Carpentry
Viaene, Andy	Nov 4, 2007	Andy's Pool Hall
Vien, Dennis	May 14, 2010	Insurance Service Agency

THROUGH THE YEARS

A Chronology of Headlines: 1988-2013

Researched and compiled by Steve Lee and Pat Aamodt from issues of the Tri-County News

Year / Month / Week   Incident / Occurrence / Item of interest

BEGIN 1988

Date: **Subject/Information**

Year	Month	Week		Subject/Information
1988	Jan.	13	➡	Work on the dam at Cottonwood Lake — Geihl
1988		20	➡	Cash rents number $55 an acre
1988	Feb.	10	➡	Dam discussions
1988		17	➡	Philip Dacey - a Fulbright Scholarship
1988		24	➡	Aeration in Lady Slipper Lake
1988	Mar.	2	➡	Cliff Hanson elected vice-chairman of the Minnesota Association of Farmers Mutual Insurance Companies
1988		23	➡	Jerome Hatlestad passed away
1988		30	➡	Car sank on the lake on March 25
1988	May	4	➡	Need for a new water tower discussed
1988		18	➡	High winds up to 70 mph
			➡	new siding on DeSmet's store
1988	June	1	➡	Change in newspaper ownership - Lancaster
1989		8	➡	New water tower information
1988	July	6	➡	About the Centennial
1988		27	➡	Lake facelift
				Florence Dacey, Loft-McKnight Grant
1988	Aug.	24	➡	English Lutheran Centennial
				Birdwatching on Page 3
1988		31	➡	Drought of 1988
1988	Sept.	7	➡	Early harvest.

1988		14	➡	In-depth article on the new dam - $55,088.
			➡	New roof on the City Hall / Senior Citizen Center.
1988		21	➡	Cora Sather dies @ 91.
1988	Oct.	5	➡	Clean up day at the lake.
			➡	Olaf Sather dies @ 89 years - the last of the Sather family.
1988		12	➡	New dam installed on the lake.
1988		19	➡	Harvest finished.
1988		26	➡	Work day.
1988	Nov.	23	➡	New construction at Mid-Continent
1988	Dec.	7	➡	Moose pictures.
1988		21	➡	Henry Broughton plays the saw.

END 1988

BEGIN 1989

1989	Jan.	18	➡	New Cottonwood aerations.
1989	Feb.	1	➡	Brynelsons attend inauguration.
1989		8	➡	Fishless Derby.
			➡	Article about Torgny Anderson.
1989	Mar.	29	➡	Schools: Echo-Wood Lake and Cottonwood discuss pairing.
1989	April	19	➡	Article about Harold Fratzke ramp.
1989	May	3	➡	Cottonwood-Wood Lake school discussions.
1989		24	➡	Jim Cole retires
			➡	Dennis Vien gets a new kidney.
1989	June	7	➡	Girls win the state Golf Tournament.
1989		14	➡	Harold Fratzke wins award.
1989	July	5	➡	Howard Mohr - New book
				A Minnesota Book of Days (and a Few Nights.)
			➡	Grasshopper infestation.

1989		12	➡	Senior Citizen Center celebrates 20 years.
1989		26	➡	Discussions about the lake.
1989	Aug.	9	➡	Fire at Mid–Continent.
1989		16	➡	New water tower for Mid–Continent.
1989	Sept.	13	➡	Ben Slette dies.
1989		20	➡	Tae Kwon Do comes to Cottonwood.
1989	Nov.	15	➡	City buys the old depot and considers it for a museum.
1989		29	➡	Liquor Store shows loss.
1989	Dec.	6	➡	About saving the school — Brynelson.
1989		13	➡	Talk about school pairing.
1989		27	➡	Year in Review Issue with items of interest.

END 1989

BEGIN 1990

1990	Jan.	3	➡	Marvin Belling story.
1990		31	➡	Water tower still going up.
1990	Feb.	7	➡	Mary Javens dies @ 89.
			➡	Mrs. Endre Rebecca Anderson died Dec. 2/lost son in WWII.
1990		14	➡	Mid–Continent Cabinets adds 27 new jobs.
1990		28	➡	About the new water tower.
1990	Mar	14	➡	Margaret Rewerts - "Postmaster of the Year" in the 562 area.
1990		21	➡	Kermit Carlson — WWII stories.
1990		28	➡	Gordy Knutson retires from the fire department.
			➡	Bernie Mauland dies @ 90.
1990	April	4	➡	Cottonwood-Wood Lake talk about pairing.
1990		11	➡	Cottonwood, Echo, Vesta elevators consider merging.
1990		18	➡	Article about the Dick Gullickson sailing ship.
1990		25	➡	Dennis Allex- Naval Reserve- hunting submarines.

			➡	Cottonwood-Wood Lake school pairing discussed.
			➡	Oscar Volden dies.
1990	May	9	➡	Cottonwood-Wood Lake schools to pair.
1990	June	6	➡	Stories about the Bjornebo brothers in WWII.
1990		13	➡	Cottonwood-Wood Lake schools to pair.
1990		20	➡	Heavy rains inundate fields.
1990	July	4	➡	Swan Lake Church celebrates its 100th anniversary.
1990		11	➡	Carl Carlson-WWII.
1990		25	➡	Loren Ericksen dies.
1990	Aug.	1	➡	New water tower construction.
1990		15	➡	Formation of the Cottonwood Historical Society.
1990		22	➡	Avis Kroger retires from being Christ Lutheran custodian.
1990	Nov.	14	➡	Ida Desilet dies.
1990		21	➡	Article on school pairing.
1990	Dec.	26	➡	Brynelson steps down after 38 years.

END 1990

BEGIN 1991

1991	Jan.	9	➡	Mike O'Reilly retires after 25 years.
1991		23	➡	Gary Anderson in Operation Desert Storm.
1991	Feb.	6	➡	Last Man Club ends-Tom Gunderson dies in California in December 1990. Last meeting in 1980.
1991		13	➡	Fishless Derby held.
		20	➡	Article about Greg Isaackson
1991		27	➡	Javens and Gregoire killed in auto accident.
			➡	From Norm's Plumbing (21 years) to Neil's Plumbing.
1991	Mar.	6	➡	Farm Store Closing.
			➡	18 people move to Cottonwood.

			➡	Historical Society formed.
1991		13	➡	New high school sports name "Lakers."
1991	April	3	➡	Possible new Farm Store-Yes: Gislasons.
1991		24	➡	Two Retrum brothers die in California 12 hours apart.
1991	May	15	➡	Elizabeth Huso dies @ 91 on May 14.
1991		29	➡	Gislasons open Farm Store.
1991	June	12	➡	Torgny Anderson Tribute to Wendell Knudson/Died June 06.
			➡	Article about Thelma Egeland.
1991		19	➡	About the popcorn stand-built in 1948.
			➡	Heavy rain.
1991		26	➡	High water.
			➡	Margaret Rewerts retires as postmaster after 23 years.
1991	July	3	➡	Wet fields.
			➡	Harold Gredvig dies @ 86.
1991	Sept.	4	➡	Classes start at the newly formed school.
1991	Oct.	9	➡	Linda Magnuson-new postmaster.
1991		16	➡	Construction of new Norcraft Warehouse.
1991		23	➡	About the good harvest.
			➡	Filming about Howard Mohr's book.
			➡	Kermit Huso dies @ 75.
1991	Nov.	6	➡	Early snowstorm.
1991	Dec.	11	➡	Myrtle Olson dies @ 91.
End 1991			➡	Year in Review Issue

Early snowstorm

Sept.1st school year starts @ Lakeview.

Snowstorms @ Halloween & Thanksgiving.

END 1991

BEGIN 1992

1992	Jan.	29	➡	Cottonwood population @ 1,005.
1992	Feb.	5	➡	About the upcoming Fishless Derby.
1992		19	➡	Kathy Dahl hired as city secretary.
1992	April	8	➡	Eliots close the TV store.
1992		15	➡	Cherry Olson dies @ 87.
1992	June	3	➡	Bob Jaeger retires.
		10	➡	Earl Post dies.
1992		24	➡	Ardell Lerstad (Mrs. Nalum) dies @ 86.
1992	July	1	➡	Cottonwood receives grant.
1992		15	➡	North Star claims estimates @ $12 million.
1992		29	➡	Margaret Larsen dies @ 80 on July 26.
1992	Sept.	9	➡	Casey's considers store.
1992		16	➡	Housing shortage in Cottonwood.
1992	Oct.	7	➡	Work on the Co-op Agronomy Center.
1992		14	➡	URSA plans Cottonwood plant.
1992		21	➡	Village Court opens.
End 1992			➡	Year in Review Issue

END 1992

BEGIN 1993

1993	Jan.	6	➡	Police chief Lowell Fenger dies.
1993		13	➡	A shoreline ordinance.
1993		20	➡	Floyd and Eleanor Hovdesven killed on Jan 13.
1993		10	➡	Rough fish removed from Lake
				Fishless Derby-Sunday, Feb. 14.

1993		17	➡	Derailment of 24 rail cars.
1993	Mar	24	➡	Elevator-about Echo merger.
				About Farm Supply store.
1993	April	7	➡	Elevator buys Farm Store.
1993	May	5	➡	Bill Bly dies on April 30.
1993–		12	➡	Tornado in the area.
1993	June	16	➡	Bill Holmberg dies on June 13.
1993		23	➡	6 inches of rain on June 16-17.
1993		30	➡	Cottonwood Fire Department to celebrate 100ᵗʰ anniversary.
1993	July	7	➡	Cottonwood Fire Department celebrates 100ᵗʰ anniversary.
1993	Aug.	11	➡	Selmer O. Rosvold dies on Aug. 9 @ age 90.
1993	Sept.	15	➡	Norcraft discusses expansion.
1993	Oct.	6	➡	Voters approve school cooperation and consolidation
				of Cottonwood and Wood Lake, paired since 1991.
1993		20	➡	Lake draw down. Fish kill planned.
1993		27	➡	Low yields.
1993	Nov.	3	➡	Fish kill in Cottonwood Lake.
1993		10	➡	North Star expansion.
				Idso Addition.
				Council denies zoning request.
1993		17	➡	Fishless Derby to summer.
End 1993			➡	Year in Review Issue

END 1993

BEGIN 1994

1994	Jan.	5	➡	Sherry Kosen (Nagel) works on Rose Parade Float
			➡	Kacy Idso business/sporting goods and small engine repair.
			➡	Jane Lange dies on January 3.
1994		12	➡	Snow and high wind.

1994		19	➡	Bitter cold: down to -30°.
1994	Feb.	2	➡	Break-in at the Pizza Ranch.
			➡	Theron "Sandy" Reishus dies on January 27.
1994		16	➡	Co-op burglarized.
1994		23	➡	Swan Lake commits to a new building-about 90 attendees.
1994	Mar.	23	➡	Car on the ice.
1994	April	27	➡	Additional construction @ North Star.
			➡	Talk about improvements at the Liquor Store.
1994	May	4	➡	Up to 8" of snow at the end of April.
1994		18	➡	Cottonwood plans for a summer celebration to replace the Fishless Derby.
1994		25	➡	A big article about fish stocking.
1994	June	1	➡	City audit report-good.
1994		8	➡	Norcraft request for the north end of 1st Street to be vacated.
			➡	George Davis and wife retiring after 30 years at Cottonwood-Wood Lake.
			➡	North Star expansion.
1994		22	➡	Restart the 10:00 p.m. curfew for minors.
			➡	Garbage at the compost site.
1994		29	➡	Article about Loris Gniffke flew on Marauders on D-Day with the 9th Air Force.
1994	July	6	➡	Discussions on housing.
			➡	Article about Erv Schwartz.
			➡	Olaf Morken dies June 30 @ 75.
			➡	Lee Swennes dies July 1 @ 90.
1994		20	➡	2" of rain in a short time: flooded streets.
1994		27	➡	Extreme Panel start-up.
			➡	DNR installs new aerator.
1994	Aug.	3	➡	Norcraft expanding, to add 20 jobs in 2 years.
			➡	Thorfinn Nordli (a 7th generation blacksmith by trade) dies @ 78 in Long Beach. Had moved away in 1968.
1994		10	➡	Article about Cottonwood's infrastructure.
1994		17	➡	Article about City employees.

1994	Sept.	14	➡	Incidents of vandalism.
1994		21	➡	Mabel Aamodt dies on the 13th @ 100 years.
1994		28	➡	Fall harvest starts.
			➡	Plans to expand the Liquor Store.
1994–	Oct.	19	➡	Ida Loe dies @ 93.
1994		26	➡	Article: "Harvest means waiting in Line."
1994	Nov.	9	➡	Cottonwood studies Liquor Store, possibly will sell.
			➡	Working on the infrastructure.
			➡	Dedication of the new Swan Lake Church.
1994		16	➡	Stella Olson dies @ 88 on November 7.
1994	Dec.	14	➡	Thinking about selling the Liquor Store.
1994		28	➡	Year in Review:

> #1   Record harvest.
>
> #2   Record construction permits.
>
> #3   Record snow and cold.

END 1994

BEGIN 1995

1995	Jan.	4	➡	Loading grain.
1995		11	➡	Discussions about Liquor Store.
			➡	discussions about infrastructure.
1995		25	➡	The Alms buy Lindsay Mobile Court.
1995	Feb.	1	➡	Liquor Store talks.
1995		8	➡	Article about Einar Oftedahl.
1995		15	➡	City looks to sell the Liquor Store.
1995	Mar.	1	➡	"Council to address streets, sewers."
			➡	"Incubator short on objectives."
			➡	Thilda Nelson dies @ 87 on February 24.

1995		15	➡	"Coming Home Days" theme for the summer celebration.
			➡	Cora Geihl dies @ 99 on March 9.
1995	April	12	➡	Continued vandalism at parks.
1995		26	➡	Bob Molstad retires after almost 35 years at the Co-op.
1995	May	3	➡	Roland Boehne dies April 27 @ 75.
			➡	Ollie Rewerts dies April 25 @ 79.
1995		10	➡	Warnke marks 20 years with NorCraft.
			➡	Article-WWII-Leif Bjornebo.
1995		17	➡	Work on Highway 23.
1995		24	➡	"Development … generates shoreline discussion."
1995		31	➡	Rain delay to planting.
1995	June	14	➡	NorCraft marks 20 years.
			➡	City to keep Liquor Store.
			➡	Theft @ Hardware Hank.
1995	July	5	➡	Improvements @ the Bel-Mar addition and the Northwood Addition.
1995		12	➡	Highway 23Cottonwood to Green Valley nearing completion.
			➡	Coming Home Days-started from the Fire Department centennial in 1993.
1995		19	➡	Photos from Coming Home Days.
1995		26	➡	City dissatisfied with the telephone service.
			➡	About shoreline changes and runoff.
			➡	Ella Rowberg dies @ 97 on July 22.
1995	Aug.	2	➡	Policy about kids in the Liquor Store.
			➡	Algae season on the lake.
1995		9	➡	Robert Hoff closes The Performance Center.
			➡	Agronomy Center work under way.
1995		16	➡	Arden Kremin dies.
1995		23	➡	Extreme Panel proposes expansion.
1995		30	➡	Familiar tree cut down.
			➡	Susan Roe Weber (Anderson) dies @ 53 on August 20.
1995	Sept.	6	➡	Assistant manager for the Liquor Store.

1995		13	➡	City approves budget.
			➡	Bart Fauteck: 31 years without taking a sick day (5,000) days.
			➡	Kermit Rolan Johnson dies @ 77 years on September 5.
1995		20	➡	Extreme Panel builds a lodge in Alaska.
1995	Oct.	11	➡	Lakeview levy increase of 13.8%.
1995	Nov.	1	➡	Construction ongoing in the North woods addition.
1995		8	➡	Crop prices hit highs;
				Corn @ $2.89 to $2.95 per bushel.
				Soybeans around $6.35 per bushel.
1995		22	➡	City to increase tax levy by 9.5%.
1995	Dec.	6	➡	Arthur Olson dies @ 87 on December 2.
				He was over 40 years in produce business.
1995		13	➡	Blizzard strands travelers in area towns.
1995		20	➡	Year in Review Issue.

2   Agronomy Center

3   Liquor Store

910   Record harvest and prices.

➡ Article about the Norwegian Mutual Insurance Company

END 1995

BEGIN 1996

1996	Jan	3	➡	3% full-time employee raise.
1996		10	➡	
1996		17	➡	Gertrude Roland dies @ 90.
1996		24	➡	Blizzard strands travelers
				Drifts on 1st Street.
1996		31	➡	Winter kill of birds.
				Deer herd up by Hanley Falls.

1996	Feb.	7	➡	GTE upgrading.
1996		21	➡	"Extreme needs a day to build a house."
				"Water damage @ Lakeview School."
				Hazel Loe dies @ 85 on February 17.
1996		28	➡	Coop Convenience Store expanding.
1996	Mar	06	➡	Arvid Lund dies @ 70 on March 14.
1996		20	➡	"City wants signal …"GTE.
				"Oil Company … $8 million in sales."
				Elevator has a record year.
1996	Apr.	10	➡	Andrew Anderson dies @ 89 on April 4.
1996		17	➡	Another heavy snowfall.
1996	May	8	➡	Dead fish in Lake, DNR contacted.
				Helen (Lohman) Yahnka dies @ 71 on May 2.
1996		15	➡	Grover Gniffke dies @ 87 on May 10.
1996		22	➡	A hard wind damages buildings.
				Repair work on the Norseth-Larsen House.
1996		29	➡	Norseth-Larsen Carriage House burns.
1996	June	5	➡	2 to 4 juveniles suspected as having been involved.
1996		12	➡	Work on Barstad Road.
1996		26	➡	Co–op 75th.
				Planning for Coming Home Days.
1996	July	3	➡	Co–op 75th.
				Corn borers return to area fields.
1996		10	➡	Storm damage spotty.
			➡	Coming Home Days preparations.
				Afghan with Cottonwood sites featured.
1996		17	➡	Coming Home Days.
1996		24	➡	City stops shoreline improvements.
				Award to Tim Fruin, the mayor
				Gordy Colburn attempts to water ski @ 80.
		31	➡	Alan Swennes hosts Norwegian relatives.
				Expansion @ the mobile home court.
1996	Aug.	7	➡	Shoreline letters generate responses.

				Tanks removed from Pappy's
1996		14	➡	Shoreline conditions require a drawing and written document.
				Lightning strike at the Byron and Janeen Kompelien
				home in rural Cottonwood.
1996		21	➡	Bituminous surfacing on Barstad Road.
1996	Sept.	4	➡	Liquor Store expansion-Estimated @ $50,000,
				low bids came in at $62,000 to $65,000.
1996		11	➡	North Star celebrates expansion and 75th anniversary.
1996	Oct.	9	➡	Robert Hoff-The Performance Center back in business.
				Ellen Holmberg (Mrs. Glenn) dies @ 85 on October 1.
1996		16	➡	Water tower needs repair$13,750 is the estimate.
1996		23	➡	Brad Rosa retires after 15 years as a football official
				Everett Willhite passes @ 85 on October 20.
1996		30	➡	Article about the elevator working long hours.
1996	Nov.	6	➡	City expresses concern about on street parking
				with apartments on Main Street.
1996		13	➡	Article about the St. Lucas stained glass windows.
				3 Bald Eagles on Cottonwood Lake.
				City to repair water tower for $50,000 estimate.
1996		20	➡	Ice storm power outage.
1996		27	➡	About Edna Ericksen and her use of the
				Farmer's Almanac to predict the weather.
1996	Dec.	11	➡	New bids solicited for the liquor store expansion.
				Bids solicited for the water tower repair.
				Laura Anderson (Mrs. Endre) dies @ 94 on December 6.
1996		18	➡	Snow closes school.

END 1996

BEGIN 1997

1997 -	Jan.	1	➡	The 1996 year in review issue.
				1. Grain prices up: corn @ $5, beans from $6 to $7 / bushel.
				2. Record snow falls.
1997		8	➡	Bob Jaeger dies on Jan 3 @ 68. 35 years a school coach.
				Snowstorm strands people in Cottonwood.
1997		15	➡	"Snow removal taking its toll on area budgets."
				Joe Hoff dies @ 74 on January 9.
1997		22	➡	"Area declared a snow disaster."
1997		29	➡	
1997	Feb.	5	➡	John Smith dies @ 84 on February 2.
1997		26	➡	Article about the theater.
				Ruth Applethun dies @ 98 years on February 20.
1997	Mar.	5	➡	School closes again.
1997		12	➡	City approves liquor store expansion @ $53,240.00.
			➡	Work on the "old" water tower.
1997		19	➡	Co-op sales increase
			➡	Remodeling of the Community center
			➡	Ervin Thompson dies @ 68 on March 9.
1997	Apr.	2	➡	"Flood waters rise in the region."
1997		9	➡	Flooding on the Minnesota River.
1997		16	➡	Joe Loe Sr. passes @ 94 on April 13.
1997	May	14	➡	Three options for the school
				1. Fix the building
				2. Abandon the district
				3. Plan for a new building.
			➡	"Liquor store finances improve." - Figures given.
1997		21	➡	Break-in @ Norcraft.
1997	June	4	➡	Jim Munson buys the grocery store from DeSmet.
			➡	Nadyne Balding buys the restaurant.
			➡	Jerry Sanders leaves the classroom, started in 1964.

1997		25	➡	Linda Magnuson elected president of State Chapter of the National Association of Post Masters in the United States.
1997	July	2	➡	Article about the popcorn stand.
1997		9	➡	Jim Duncan retires after 30 years with the elevator.
			➡	"Norcraft plans expansion."
			➡	About fireworks for Coming Home Days.
1997		16	➡	Article about Thelma Egeland and her peonies.
			➡	Coming Home Days main festivities on Saturday, July 12th.
1997		30	➡	High winds hit the area.
1997	Sept.	24	➡	"Patrons to vote on elevator consolidation." -- Cottonwood and Hanley Falls
1997	Oct.	8	➡	Sanford Gullickson dies @ 82 on October 2.
1997		15	➡	Elmer Bergdies @ 85 on October 9.
1997	Nov.	5	➡	"Developer proposes assisted living facility in Cottonwood."
			➡	Franklin Okrina dies @ 85 on November 1.
1997		19	➡	Kenneth Nelson dies @ 87 on November 7.
1997	Dec.	3	➡	"Voters pass consolidation." - elevators to merge.
1997		10	➡	Olive Fronsdahl dies @ 68 on December 7.
1997		17	➡	"Extreme Panel will expand its plant."
1997		24	➡	Helen Fenger (Mrs. Alfred) dies @ 70 on December 21.
1997		31	➡	Proposed pairing.
			➡	Nancy Duncan retires after 31 years as a bus driver.
			➡	Mabel Olena Enga dies @ 94 on December 22.

END 1997

BEGIN 1998

| 1998 | Jan. | 7 | ➡ | The 1997 year in review issue. |

#1. #5 The weather. Snow then flooding.

				# 8. Lakeview School district studies.
			➡	In 1997 Empire State Bank and United Southwest bank of Vesta merge
			➡	Gladys Swennes dies @ 91 on December 30, 1997.
1998		14	➡	Liquor Store hours extended.
			➡	Lorayne Rekedal dies @ 78.
			➡	Assisted living facility going up.
1998		28	➡	Ethel Dirnbergerr dies @ 79 on January 24.
1998	Feb.	4	➡	Marvel Naab dies @ 89 on January 31.
1998	Mar.	4	➡	"Dairy discussion" Lone Tree
			➡	"Assisted living on schedule"
1998		18	➡	Arlene Addison dies @ 82 on March 14.
1998		25	➡	George Van de Voorde dies @ 86 on March 22.
1998	April	22	➡	Dave Lancaster killed.
1998	May	6	➡	Services for Mrs. John Lines April 17. She was born in 1917.
1998		27	➡	Kenneth Oftedahl dies @ 73 on May 21.
1998	June	17	➡	"Barstad Overpass set for construction."
			➡	Incidents of break-in.
1998		24	➡	"Investor group buys Norcraft."
			➡	WCCO "Good Morning" - July 10: To be in Cottonwood.
1998	July	1	➡	WCCO Radio Farm Director Roger Strom in town Friday to gather material for July 10 "Good Morning" show
		1	➡	Belgian relatives visit Jasper Vandelanotte
		1	➡	Norwegian orchestra to perform in Cottonwood tonight at the Community Center.
		1	➡	Becky Bitker, representing Unit 503 American Legion Auxiliary of Cottonwood, spent the week at Minnesota Girls State.
		1	➡	Four members of Fire Department retire.
		1	➡	Emma Jane Carlson dies @ 96 on June 22..
		1	➡	Luverne "Louie" Severson dies @ 77 on June 28.
		8	➡	Fieldcrest assisted living facility is open.
		8	➡	Coming Home Days this weekend.

1998		15	➡	"Good Morning" show broadcasts live from Lakeview school auditorium.
1998		15	➡	First Little Miss Coming Home Days Pageant.
1998		15	➡	Dennis Ozmun runs for sheriff.
1998		22	➡	Gary Gabrielson holds horse clinic at his farm.
1998		22	➡	Victor Christian David Rebers dies @ 82 Jon uly 18.
1998		22	➡	Ardyce E. (Johnson) Solseth dies @ 64 on July 17.
1998		22	➡	Idella Henrietta Hanson Nikolaisen dies @ 75 on July 18.
1998		29	➡	Rev. Paul Hadusek new parish priest at St. Mary's.
1998		29	➡	Helen Hermina Boerboom dies @ 69 on July 24.
1998		29	➡	Arnold H. Schrupp dies @ 89 on July 22.
1998	Aug.	5	➡	Pearl Eaton dies @ 83 on August 2.
1998		19	➡	Cottonwood Area Historical Society celebrates 100th anniversary of Norseth/Larsen House.
1998		19	➡	Marilyn Rosa and son Braden meet and shake hands with President Clinton.
1998		26	➡	Jim Cole retires from teaching firearms safety.
1998	Sept.	2	➡	Dixon Anderson, former pilot, talks about Northwest Airlines strike.
1998			➡	Lakeview School will change to nine-week grading period this fall.
1998			➡	Thelmar Orin Volden dies @ 66 on August 23.
1998			➡	Roger Duane Nelson dies @ 71 on September 3.
1998		16	➡	Old #261 railroad steam engine goes through Cottonwood.
1998			➡	Harold Schlemmer dies @ 72 on September 14.
1998		30	➡	Article on Edna Ericksen and Helen Pearson, longtime teachers at Cottonwood.
1998			➡	Orvid Jerome Johnson dies @ 87 on September 23.
1998			➡	Richard Andre "Dick" Lynne dies @ 71 on September 26

1998			➡	Farm Focus issue
				Doug Olson: The Co-op tire man
				Loris Gniffke restores damaged barns
				German exchange student to live at
				Joe and Marcella Matthys'
1998	Oct.	7	➡	Jeff and Roberta Gniffke were on old #261
				steam engine passing through Cottonwood.
1998			➡	Halldor Cecil Hofteig passes away.
1998			➡	Robert Arnold Sandberg dies @ 62 on September 18.
1998		14	➡	Tour of Homes sponsored by Cottonwood Area Historical
				Society last Sunday.
1998			➡	Chicken dinner catered by Hy-Vee on first Wednesday
				of each month has been going on for more than 10 years.
1998		21	➡	Elevators find temporary storage for big yields.
			➡	Clara Alvina Thompson dies @ 92 on October 17.
1998	Nov.	4	➡	Sally Lynn Allison dies @ 37 on October 29.
1998			➡	Merle V. Bruns dies @ 90 on October 27.
1998		11	➡	Storm-related power outages.
1998			➡	Village Pub should break record sales.
1998		18	➡	Aubner (Bob) Gniffke dies @ 79 on October 7.
1998			➡	Thora Irene Myhre dies @ 72 on November 9.
1998		25	➡	Hector Matthys wins national FFA award.
1998	Dec.	2	➡	William "Bill" Kurtenbach dies @ 71 on November 25.
1998			➡	Photo of Bud Hostetler mowing his lawn on December 1.
1998		9	➡	Norman R. Pentila dies @ 66.
1998			➡	Pehrson family members enjoy sharing music together.
1998		16	➡	Toll-free calls from Cottonwood to Marshall start today.
1998			➡	Arden Kermit Lien dies @ 88.
1998			➡	Robert Albert Gerlach dies @ 90 on December 8.
1998			➡	Charlie Olson barn saved in fire.
1998		23	➡	Ordell Jerome "Esky" Lovsness passes away
				@ 87 on December 16.
1998		30	➡	The 1951 "Womenless Wedding" remembered

by former cast members.

| 1998 | ➡ | Maurice Remi Adam dies @ 74 on December 28. |
| 1998 | ➡ | Robert Theodore Carlson dies @ 90 on December 18. |

END 1998

BEGINNING 1999

1999-	Jan.	6	➡	Top 10 List From 1998 Year in Review
				# 1 "bumper crops, poor prices."
				# 2 The mild weather.
				# 5 "Norcraft changes and accomplishments."
				# 8 Fieldcrest.
				# 9 Schools plan.
			➡	"Cottonwood Muni. Liquor Store close to record net profit."
			➡	Alice Norland dies @ 83 on January 3
1999-	Feb.	3	➡	Article about coyotes.
1999		10	➡	About possible school consolidations.
			➡	Don Gniffke dies @ 70 on February 4.
1999		17	➡	"City seeks shelter funds.
				Improvements planned for Lakeside beach park."
1999		24	➡	Article about continued city support for the Village Court opened in 1995.
1999-	Mar.	3	➡	Herb Nelson dies @ 96 on February 28.
1999		10	➡	Ardis Michaelson dies @ 79 on March 3.
1999		17	➡	Bart F., Mike and Carol O'Reillly to retire at end of the school yeartaught for 35 years in Cottonwood.
1999		24	➡	"Co-operative posts more than $9 million in sales."
1999		31	➡	Article about the elevator: moving offices from Cottonwood.

			➡	Minnie Vien dies @ 94 on March 26.
1999-	Apr.	7	➡	Edwin Bjornebo dies @ 87 on March 23.
			➡	Raymond Gigstad dies @ 79 on March 31.
1999-	May	5	➡	Darren and Heidi Beck buy the lumber yard.
1999		26	➡	Work on the overhead ongoing.
1999-	Jun.	2	➡	Greg Isaacksonmarks 25 years as city clerk-administrator.
1999		9	➡	About Cottonwood businesses - Kroger Article!!
1999		16	➡	About Harold Fratzke.
1999		23	➡	Article about the Lone Tree Dairy.
1999	July	7	➡	Sophie Dickey on a motorcycle @ 95.
			➡	Erma Huso in the D. A. R.
1999		14	➡	"Grain prices hit 20 year lows."
				$3.66 / beans.
			➡	"Hot dish bakeoff."
1999	Aug.	4	➡	"City considers Northwoods addition."
			➡	Hazel (Runholt) Lund dies @ 99 on August 1.
1999		11	➡	Some rain but more is needed.
1999	Sept.	1	➡	Article about "The Overhead."
1999		8	➡	Article about rural lakes.
			➡	Glenn Holmberg dies @ 92 on August 31.
1999		15	➡	About street work in the North Wood Addition.
			➡	Article about St. Lucas Church.
1999	Oct.	13	➡	"Harvest Reports indicate good yields."
1999	Nov.	10	➡	"Extreme expands market base."
1999		17	➡	Willis Wells dies @ 56 on November 3.
			➡	Harold Gee dies @ 80 on November 10.
1999		24	➡	John Reishus dies @ 61 on November 22.
1999	Dec.	1	➡	"Norcraft expands to Arizona."
1999		15	➡	"Liberty Group purchases TriCounty News."
1999		22	➡	"Bomb threat. Lakeview Middle School receives threat Monday."
1999		29	➡	Roger Carlson retires from North Star after 35 years.
			➡	The 1999 year in review issue (Jan. 5.)

❶   Grain prices @ a 20 year low prices.

Corn @ $1.00 (+) / bushel.

Soybeans @ $4.00 (-) / bushel.

❻   Weather Extremes.

❿   Development in Cottonwood.

END 1999

BEGIN 2000

2000	Jan.	5	➡	Y2K Fireworks
			➡	John Hirmer dies @ 82 on December 31, 1999.
			➡	James Cravens dies @ 91 on January 2.
2000		12	➡	"Cottonwood greets Ventura." (Gov. Jesse Ventura)
			➡	"Liquor sales at an all time high in 1999."
2000		26	➡	Millennium Edition !!
2000	Feb.	2	➡	"Article about Lake quality."
			➡	"Moisture levels still low in area soils."
2000		16	➡	Orin Ericson dies @ 83 on January 10.
2000	Mar	1	➡	Possible end to Coming Home Days.
2000		8	➡	Bald Eagles in Normania.
2000		22	➡	"Cottonwood Chamber dissolves."
			➡	A solution to continuing with Coming Home Days.
			➡	"Cottonwood property values increase by 15 percent."
			➡	"Cottonwood Co–op has another good year."
			➡	A UFO sighted.
2000		29	➡	"Farmers Elevator has good year in 1999."
			➡	Julius Coudron dies @ 97 on March 22.
			➡	Eddie Van Eidie dies @ 51 on March 22.
			➡	Ardell Engum dies @ 83 on March 22.

2000	April	5	➡	"Lakeview student numbers to decline."
			➡	Rae Yost leaves as newspaper editor.
2000		12	➡	"Lake walk?"
			➡	Article about the old softball field.
2000		26	➡	"Lakeview plans for cuts."
			➡	Hugh Jones – new editor at Tri-County News.
2000	May	3	➡	"Dry weather allows farmers in field."
2000			➡	"Basic skills. Area schools compare well to state average."
2000		10	➡	Coming home Days will continue.
2000	June	21	➡	An old train comes through town.
2000		28	➡	Gordon Colburn – skydiving @ 81.
2000	July	5	➡	Planning for Coming Home Days.
2000		12	➡	About Coming Home Days.
2000			➡	Steeple on the old Presbyterian Church comes down
			➡	Erected in 1898.
			➡	Last service in 1990.
			➡	Closed in 1992.
2000			➡	Hot for Coming Home Days.
2000		19	➡	Curt Dahl dies @ 78 on July 13.
2000			➡	Dagny Rialson (nee Runholt) dies @ 85 on July 18.
2000		26	➡	Wallace Post dies @ 91 on July 21.
2000			➡	Harland Volden dies @ 71 on July 25.
2000			➡	Irene Kolhei dies @ 87 on July 31.
2000	Aug.	2	➡	Granite Falls tornado.
2000		9	➡	Hydroswing door start-up.
2000		16	➡	Article about Bud Hostetler's 1929 Model A Roadster.
2000		30	➡	Jim Schrupp back as owner of the Cottonwood Café.
			➡	Henry Versaevel dies @ 87 on August 25.
2000	Sept.	6	➡	Article about the problem with parking at the school.
2000		13	➡	"City proposes 10.6 % levy hike."
2000		20	➡	Early harvest since dry.
2000	Oct.	4	➡	Arleen Hawkinson dies @ 82 on September 26.
2000		18	➡	"Lakeview will see $12 million bond issue."

			➡	Martin Reishus dies @ 93 on October 9.
2000	Nov.	29	➡	"Thieves break into Lakeview High School for computers electronics."
			➡	"Lakeview sportsmen working on plan to aerate area lakes."
2000	Dec.	6	➡	Two men charged in burglary at Lakeview."
			➡	Proponents of referendum hold public meeting Monday."
2000	Dec.	13	➡	Dorothy Severson dies @ 76 on December 11.
2000		20	➡	Bond issue approved.
2000			➡	Eleanor "Dot" King dies @ 82 on December 15.
2000		27	➡	Mildred Huso dies @ 90 on December 22·

END 2000

BEGIN 2001

2001	Jan.	3	➡	Year in Review issue for 2000.
2001			➡	Wayne Pederson dies @ 89 on December 27, 2000.
2001		10	➡	"Andy's Place closes after nearly 43 years."
2001			➡	Jim's Café to be sold.
2001		24	➡	"Testing lake clarity."
2001	Feb.	14	➡	Article about Selma Rosvold.
2001		28	➡	Page 3A – Photograph of the old Empire State Bank building with the Ionic columns, the brick façade and the name centered in the window with a clock above it.
2001			➡	Page 4A – article about the Legion.
2001			➡	Page 6A – article about Hydroswing doors.
2001			➡	Note: The above is from the "Progress" Issue.
2001	Mar	7	➡	Elsie Isaackson dies @ 80 on March 9.
2001		14	➡	Elmer "Slim" Jarcho dies @ 87 on March 11.
2001		21	➡	Article about the Cottonwood Lake Association
			➡	79 members.

			➡	1 year old.
2001	Apr.	11	➡	Article about a pile of dead animals that was found
2001		18	➡	Article about the Historical Society
2001			➡	Sophie Dickey dies @ 97 on April 13.
2001			➡	Article about the change in ownership of "Jim's Café."
2001		25	➡	Article about the dead animals.
2001			➡	Article about the Lake Association.
2001	May	2	➡	Burton Mauland dies @ 75 on April 25.
2001		16	➡	"Cottonwood Girl's Club still going strong after 50 years."
2001		30	➡	Article about Mohn and "Wild" seeds.
2001			➡	Cliff Hanson retires after 47 years @ North Star.
2001	June	20	➡	"Budget cuts eliminate Lakeview teachers."
2001			➡	Donna Pringle dies @ 79 on June 12.
2001	July	4	➡	Magnuson elected vice president of NAPUS."
2001			➡	"Historical Quilts lists names of area residents." "Lakeview School board meets with architects."
2001		18	➡	Article about Coming Home Days.
2001			➡	"Lakeview School board to close on land, open bids."
2001		25	➡	"Debt Equalization secured for Lakeview."
2001			➡	"Crops finally get needed rain, wind causes damage."
2001			➡	Article about Harold Fratzke.
2001	Aug.	1	➡	"Cottonwood Lake Association awaiting test results for quality."
2001		8	➡	"Elevator damaged by four – alarm fire, business evacuated."
2001			➡	Bertha Anderson dies @ 86 on July 30.
2001		15	➡	Article about a lot of butterflies.
2001			➡	"Krumreys settling into café business."
2001		22	➡	Article about the bank lawsuit. "Lakeview selects Hasslen as contractor for new school."
2001	Sept.	19	➡	Pentagon attack – a missing sister.
2001		26	➡	About the school architect.
2001			➡	About pub remodeling.

2001	Oct.	17	➡	Funeral for Rhonda Boe's sister who died in 9/11.
			➡	Article about Curt Warnke, longtime Wood Lake publisher.
2001		31	➡	Duane Fruin dies @ 75 on October 24.
2001			➡	3 articles about area industries.
			➡	Extreme Panel.
			➡	Norcraft.
			➡	Hydroswing.
2001	Nov.	7	➡	"Area crops better than expected."
2001		28	➡	"18.5 " rain reported."
2001	Dec.	12	➡	Article about the new school going up.
2001			➡	About a bar fight.
2001		19	➡	Article about Torgny Anderson

END 2001

BEGIN 2002

2002	Jan.	2	➡	Adeline Bly dies @ 88 on December 24, 2001.
2002	Feb.	27	➡	"Dayton meets with 50 local farmers at Bossuyt's Farm."
2002			➡	Gertrude (Mossige) Chambers dies @ 82 on February 19.
2002			➡	Article about the railroad and shipping.
2002	Mar.	6	➡	Myron Hoiland dies @ 94 on February 25.
2002			➡	Marvin Belling dies @ 84 on February 20.
2002		20	➡	Foot of snow on the 14th.
2002			➡	Clarence Oftedahl dies @ 87 on March 11.
2002			➡	Ludwig Belling dies @ 83 on March 17.
2002			➡	"A review of farm income for 2001."
2002		27	➡	Picture of helicopters lifting heating and cooling units to the top of the new school
2002			➡	"Dahl will file for Lyon County Sheriff."

2002			➡	Article about the Yellow Medicine River watershed.
2002	April	3	➡	Work progressing on the new school
2002		10	➡	3 new sirens (+ 2 old ones.)
2002		17	➡	Torgny Anderson dies @ 97 on April 7.
2002		24	➡	"The History of Cottonwood Lake" – Part 1
2002	June	5	➡	"Wellstone and the green bus stop in Cottonwood."
2002			➡	Article about men arrested for killing owls & hawks.
2002			➡	Article about the Norseth Larsen house
2002		26	➡	Clinton Berg dies @ 85 on June 23.
2002			➡	Llewllyn Bahn dies @ 68 on June 21.
2002			➡	Kristian Idso dies @ 39 on June 20.
2002	July	10	➡	Article about Extreme Panel.
2002		17	➡	Article about Coming Home Days.
2002		24	➡	Article about Coming Home Days.
2002	Aug.	14	➡	Article about the Cottonwood Current.
2002	Sept.	4	➡	Article about the Wood Lake Battle.
2002	Oct.	2	➡	"Sirens to be installed in Cottonwood after months of waiting."
2002		16	➡	Interesting column on "old" Cottonwood.
2002			➡	"The history of the Cottonwood Fire department."
2002		23	➡	School has started but the building not yet finished.
2002	Nov.	7	➡	"Sheriff–elect Dahl wins big."
2002		13	➡	Marie Fruin dies @ 78 on November 6.
2002		27	➡	"Village Court celebrates 10 years."
2002			➡	"Old school building to find possible uses."
2002	Dec.	4	➡	Camille Hoflock dies @ 84 on December 1.
2002			➡	Charles "Bud" King dies @ 88 on December 7.
2002		18	➡	Orville Michaelson dies @ 84 on December 13.
2002		24	➡	"Doug Warnke retires after 33 years." @ Mid – Continent Cabinets.
2002			➡	"[Murl] Fischer retires after 30 years with Co-op."

END 2002

BEGIN 2003

2003	Jan.	8	➡	"Rosa new Co – op manager."
2003			➡	W. Dale Reishus dies @ 78 on December 30, 2002.
2003			➡	The Year in Review issue.
2003		15	➡	Selma Rosvold to turn 100.
2003			➡	Helen Pearson dies @ 88 on January 8.
2003	Feb.	12	➡	Harry Bouressa dies @ 88 on February 6.
2003	Mar.	5	➡	Selma Rosvold turns 100.
2003		12	➡	"New truck wash opens in Cottonwood."
2003		19	➡	Discussing options for the old school building.
2003	May	14	➡	"Pub sales remain down."
2003		21	➡	"Orville Kompelien remains active at 95 years young."
2003			➡	"Mossiges celebrate 57 years of 'wedded bliss.'"
2003		28	➡	"New railroad crossing in Cottonwood."
2003	June	4	➡	Article about the Norseth / Larsen Home.
2003		11	➡	"BNSF makes repairs to tracks in Cottonwood."
2003			➡	"Fratzke to show inventions at M. I. C."
2003		18	➡	"Old Smith Farm Store burns in Cottonwood."
2003			➡	"Where are the 'bubblegum' scholarships for Lakeview students?"
2003		25	➡	John Rewerts dies @ 77 on June 23.
2003	July	9	➡	"Preparations for Coming Home Days are under way in Cottonwood."
2003		16	➡	"Coming Home Days in Cottonwood."
2003		30	➡	"Cottonwood Landmark Gone." Pappy's – Vern Clair's station.
2003			➡	"Hydroswing Doors new addition …"
2003	Aug.	06	➡	"Old Cottonwood shop building goes down."
2003				Next to Andy's Place.
2003		13	➡	Article about Emily Weidauer.
2003	Sept.	24	➡	"Lakeview hires two contractors for demolition of sites."

2003	Oct.	15	➡	"Cottonwood Post Office predecessors mark 100th anniversary October 15."
2003		22	➡	"Norcraft bought by new investment asset management firms."
2003			➡	Gordon Knutson dies @ 73 on October 16.
2003	Nov.	19	➡	Amanda Slette dies @ 93 on November 15.
2003		26	➡	City approves beginning of construction for Extreme Panel.
2003	Dec.	3	➡	"End of an era: Cottonwood School Building goes down."
2003		10	➡	"Hardware Hank holds open house [to show remodeling]"
2003		17	➡	"Lakeview School Board hears offer for old school sites."
2003		31	➡	Pete Dandurand dies @ 90 – no date given.

END 2003

BEGIN 2004

2004	Jan.	14	➡	Reverend Burton H. Schwerin dies @ 79.
2004		21	➡	Loretta Dieken retires after 27 years @ United Southwest Bank.
			➡	Hannah Rosvold dies @ 91 on January 10.
2004	Feb.	4	➡	Virgil Lee dies @ 91 on January 29.
2004			➡	"The History of Cottonwood Lake, Part II."
2004		11	➡	"The History of Cottonwood Lake, Part III."
2004		25	➡	Article about Selma Rosvold turning 101.
2004	Mar.	3	➡	Avis Isaackson dies @ 79 on February 26.
2004			➡	Mayme Reishus dies @ 101 on March 1.
2004		17	➡	Glenn Isaackson dies @ 86 on March 10.
2004		24	➡	Jerrold Sanders retires after 40 years with the Lakeview schools, both as teaching and as finance officer.
2004	April	7	➡	"Wiesen operates Cottonwood Body Shop for 20 years."

2004			➡	Bernard Belling dies @ 55 on April 4.
2004		14	➡	Article about Emily Weidauer.
2004		21	➡	Article about the Cottonwood Grocery – Jim Munson.
2004		28	➡	Robert Isaackson dies @ 80 on April 21.
2004	June	2	➡	Sue Seldon retires from the school after 35 years.
2004			➡	Donna Fauteck retires from the school after 23 years.
2004			➡	Reverend David Halbakken dies @ 87 on May 28.
2004		30	➡	"Weidauer starts new band."
2004			➡	"City of Cottonwood asks for more law enforcement.'
2004			➡	Article about Coming Home Days.
2004	July	7	➡	Lorraine Lancaster dies @ 60 on June 30.
2004		14	➡	"Cottonwood was the weekend's Happenin' Place."
2004		21	➡	"Habitat for Humanity breaks new ground in Cottonwood."
2004		28	➡	Gloria Vien dies @ 77 – no date given.
2004	Nov.	10	➡	Article about "Bud" Hostetler.
				A Diary of the 307ᵗʰ Bombardment Group (H),
				By Sam S. Britt Jr.
2004			➡	Ruth Midboe dies.
2004		17	➡	Alvin Knutson dies @ 89 on November 14.
2004			➡	Randall Rickard dies @ 61 on November 13.
2004	Dec.	1	➡	Ione Knudson dies @ 79 on November 26.
2004		8	➡	Erling Mossige dies @ 86 on November 16.

END 2004

BEGIN 2005

2005	Jan.	5	➡	Deborah Van Uden dies @ 95 on December 29, 2004.
2005		19	➡	James Isaackson dies @ 84 on January 15.
2005		26	➡	Year in Review edition for 2004.

2005	Feb.	2	➡	Year in Review edition for 2004.
2005		9	➡	Article about the Fishless Derby.
2005			➡	Year in Review edition for 2004.
2005		23	➡	Jason Timmerman killed in Iraq on February 21.
2005			➡	Article about a Hellie, a pilot – a full commander.
2005	Mar.	2	➡	Progress Edition. Articles about
2005				➡ Extreme Panel.
2005				➡ Jeseritz Electric.
2005				➡ North Star.
2005				➡ Jeseritz Construction.
2005				➡ Cottonwood Co-op.
2005				➡ Insurance Service Agency.
2005				➡ City of Cottonwood.
2005				➡ Hydroswing Doors.
2005		9	➡	Linda Magnuson retires as postmaster
2005				➡ 1979 – started with the post office.
2005				➡ 1991 – became the Cottonwood Post Master.
2005			➡	Article about blizzards.
2005		16	➡	"Lovsness named Sportsman of the Year."
2005			➡	Josephine Prairie dies @ 88 – Exact date not given.
2005			➡	"Hoff house of great interest to Mid–Continent."
2005		23	➡	"Former Cottonwood resident turns 100 years young." — Myrtle Buysse
2005	April	6	➡	"Lakeview lawsuit goes to court." – about sexual discrimination.
2005		13	➡	Vandalism @ the closed Casey's store.
2005		20	➡	Marvin Rewerts recounts the attack on Pearl Harbor and his WWII Service.
2005	May	4	➡	Sylvia Mossige dies @ 86 on April 17.
2005		11	➡	"Lakeview School District saves over $700,000 by refinancing debt."
2005		18	➡	Myrtle Lovsness dies @ 91 on May 10.
2005	June	8	➡	"Historical Society seeks support."

2005			➡	SPC Terry Kesteloot – about his service in Iraq.
2005		15	➡	"Christ Lutheran Church congregation to celebrate 125 years of grace."
2005	July	6	➡	"Everything coming up roses – Cottonwood's first garden tour."
2005		20	➡	Marsha Gabrielson retires after 22 years teaching – 20 @ Lakeview.
2005		27	➡	"Wiesen builds wings."
2005			➡	"Garden Tour well attended."
2005	Aug.	3	➡	Don Rosa dies @ 70 on July 27.
2005		10	➡	"Fengers' fabulous fare." — About Cathie & Randy Fenger's garden
2005			➡	"Hokanson sings his heart out with All State choir."
2005		24	➡	"Old School Addition taking place."
2005			➡	"Cottonwood team takes five trophies in tractor pull." — About Ernie and Kevin Viaene.
2005			➡	Article about the Historical Society.
2005		31	➡	Herbert Mauland dies @ 82 on August 16.
2005	Sept.	7	➡	Appreciation expressed for Volunteers Genevieve Morken and Audrey Hostetler
2005		14	➡	Margaret Halbakken dies @ 88 on September 6.
2005			➡	Article about Viola Gigstad.
2005		21	➡	Article about Teresa and Robert Hoff's 30th wedding anniversary and their hike up Long's Peak in Colorado.
2005			➡	Article about Doris Lee.
2005	Oct.	5	➡	Catherine Krumrey dies @ 84 on September 30.
2005			➡	Article about Helen Dahl.
2005	Nov.	2	➡	Article about the Cottonwood Lions Club – a picture with 14 members.
2005			➡	Two new business in town. — A hair stylist — A massage therapist.

2005		9	➡	"Lakeview board talks athletic field move."
2005			➡	Elsie Oftedahl dies @ 83 on November 6.
2005		30	➡	Cottonwood meal site in operation for 22 years.
2005	Dec.	21	➡	Leroy Alm dies @ 84 on December 15.
2005		28	➡	Loris Gniffke dies @ 87 on December 22.

END 2005

BEGIN 2006

2006	Jan.	4	➡	Heavy snowfall at the end of December.
2006		18	➡	Article about Lillian Olsen turning 96.
2006			➡	Adam Rigge deploys to Iraq.
2006		25	➡	"North Star Insurance donates $5,000 to Lakeview Schools."
2006			➡	Article about Cub Scouts.
2006	Feb.	6	➡	Article about the Boy Scouts
2006		8	➡	Luke Anderson – Serving in Iraq.
2006			➡	Article about the St. Lucas Scouts.
2006		22	➡	Article about Cub Scouts.
2006			➡	Information about Hydroswing.
2006	Mar.	1	➡	"Cottonwood pursues trail development grant."
2006			➡	The progress edition. Articles about the following
2006			➡	Lakeview School.
2006			➡	Hydro Swing Doors.
2006			➡	Extreme Panel.
2006			➡	Jeseritz Electric.
2006			➡	TNT.
2006			➡	North Star.
2006			➡	Lions Club.
2006			➡	Insurance Service Agency.
2006			➡	Hardware Hank.

2006			➡	The Agronomy Center.
2006		8	➡	"Lucas Township loses landmark Barn." – The Elmer barn – 1st article.
2006			➡	John C. Peterson dies @ 78 on February 24.
2006		15	➡	"Lucas township loses landmark Barn." – The Elmer barn – 2nd article.
2006		22	➡	"Lucas township loses landmark Barn." – The Elmer barn – 3rd article.
2006		29	➡	Doris Alm dies @ 78 on March 27.
2006			➡	Dortha Hirmer dies @ 89 on March 15.
2006	April	5	➡	"Seniors share quilts skills and stories."
2006		26	➡	"Owls rescued in Cottonwood."
2006	May	3	➡	Green Valley elevator burns.
2006		10	➡	"Project nears commencement, construction on a new trail facility at Lakeview begins May 22.
2006		31	➡	Henry Broughton dies @ 93 on May 26.
2006			➡	"After 30 years it's still fun." Article about the Minnesota River canoe trip that Gary Hostetler, Paul Lines, Murray Smith and others have been taking for the past 30 years.
2006	June	7	➡	Article about Oceanna Knutson.
2006			➡	Article about Coming Home Days.
2006			➡	"Fire threatens feed supply." @ the Lone Tree Dairy.
2006		21	➡	Phyllis Bot dies @ 81 on June 14.
2006	July	5	➡	Cottonwood Historical Society – 2nd Garden Tour.
2006			➡	Article about Bud Hostetler – photos of old Cottonwood.
2006		12	➡	Article about Coming Home Days.
2006		19	➡	"Bud " Hostetler dies @ 82 on July 13.
2006	Aug.	2	➡	"Area in grip of a heat wave."
2006		9	➡	"Helen Langer, Lakeview teacher retires." – started in 1985.
2006			➡	Rain helps crop and aphid problem.
2006			➡	"The Pub needs a facelift."
2006		16	➡	Cathy Kosen retires from Lakeview – 25 years all total.

2006		23	➡ Lakeview Schools – wins harassment suit.
			➡ Judy Hisken retires – 22 years @ Lakeview.
2006		30	➡ School starts – 580 students @ Lakeview.
2006	Sept.	6	➡ "Road const. in Cottonwood delayed."
2006		13	➡ "Dental lab moving to Cottonwood."
2006			➡ Myrtle Buysse dies @ 101 on September 6.
2006			➡ Selma Rosvold dies @ 103 on September 7.
2006		20	➡ "Dirckx's invest time and energy in vines. Grape growing comes to Cottonwood."
2006		27	➡ "Hoffs go to the top this time." – about Robert and Teresa's hike to the top of Longs Peak in Colorado.
2006	Oct.	4	➡ Marie Johnson dies @ 74 on September 25.
2006		11	➡ Jessica Louwagie buys pony riding business.
2006			➡ Council addresses problems at the liquor store.
2006		18	➡ Article about Norman Geihl and his pigeons.
2006			➡ Bruce Snyder dies @ 73 on October 11.
2006			➡ Robert Lines dies @ 86 on October 5.
2006	Nov.	1	➡ Article about Alice Nelson quilts.
2006		8	➡ Article about the quilt show at the Norseth–Larsen House.
2006			➡ Article about Norman Geihl and his pigeons.
2006		15	➡ Further problems at the liquor store – smoke extractors.
2006		22	➡ Charlie Seipel – New city Community Development Coordinator.
2006		29	➡ Article about the building of the "Laker Lounge" @ Snooks Café.
2006	Dec.	6	➡ Article about Cottonwood native Terry Gniffke and his military support group.
2006			➡ Ralph Brynelson dies @ 85 on November 30.
2006		20	➡ Article about Paul and Karen Geihl's Christmas decorations.
2006		27	➡ Mildred Erickson dies @ 88 on December 20.

END 2006

BEGIN 2007

2007	Jan.	3	➡	The Year in Review Issue for 2006.
2007			➡	Viola Gigstad dies @ 90 on December 27.
2007		17	➡	Historical Society article.
2007			➡	Bernice Neuman dies @ 85 on January 14.
2007		24	➡	Neil's Plumbing purchased by Cottonwood Co-op.
2007		31	➡	Alfred Fenger dies @ 84 on January 25.
2007	Feb.	7	➡	A follow-up article about the old hotels in Cottonwood.
2007		14	➡	City and school at odds over the old athletic field.
2007			➡	Article about depot agent Fred Brookman working 37 years for the Great Northern – 1946 – 1983.
2007		21	➡	Historical article about the old hobo jungle.
2007	Mar.	7	➡	March snowstorm.
2007			➡	"Kroger named Sportsman of the Year."
2007		14	➡	Thelma Egeland to turn 100.
2007			➡	Article about the Norseth–Larsen house.
2007			➡	The Progress Edition. Articles about the following.
2007			➡	City of Cottonwood
2007			➡	Tri – County News.
2007			➡	Cottonwood Elevator.
2007			➡	Insurance Service Agency.
2007			➡	Gniffke Tree Trimming Service.
2007			➡	Jeseritz Electric.
2007			➡	Cottonwood School.
2007		21	➡	Shirley Fauteck dies @ 87 on March 12.
2007			➡	Article about Bob Molstad's service in Korea.
2007		28	➡	Einar Oftedahl dies @ 88 on March 19.
2007	Apr.	4	➡	Historical Society article about the old ice house.
2007		11	➡	Discussion on what to do with the old athletic field.
2007			➡	Arlo Hawkinson dies @ 88 on April 4.
2007		25	➡	Photograph on beginning

development at the old school location.

2007	May	16	➡	Janiel Lee dies @ 60 on May 3.
2007			➡	Alicia Reynolds with the 82nd Airborne in Iraq.
2007		23	➡	City meeting about strengths and weaknesses of the town.
2007		30	➡	Arthur Clementson dies @ 79 on May 19.
				A Cottonwood teacher from 1966 – 1991.
2007	June	13	➡	Trucker's Pride truck wash opened June 11.
2007			➡	Article about Harold Fratzke's "Step-up" invention.
2007			➡	LouBa's Lunchwagon in business 22 years.
2007		20	➡	Albert Viaene dies @ 85 on June 14.
2007		27	➡	Shore clean up on Cottonwood Lake
				by the Sportsmen's Club.
2007	July	4	➡	Anne Isaackson retires after 35 years teaching.
2007			➡	Cottonwood Co-op purchases land by the old athletic field.
2007		11	➡	North Star donates $5,000 to walkway project.
2007			➡	Article about Ray and Marlene Glenn –
				he's the new pastor at Swan Lake Church.
2007		18	➡	Article about Coming Home Days.
2007			➡	New business in Cottonwood – Computer Sales & Service –
				Bill Van der Hagen
2007			➡	School to return land to the city.
2007		25	➡	Article about pet ducks by the lake.
2007			➡	Penalties at the Lone Tree Dairy.
2007		15	➡	Article about Maxwell Construction
				constructing a "Cottonwood " Sign.
2007			➡	Article about the plantings at the Mid-Continent site
				separating parking from street and houses across the way.
2007		22	➡	Rod Kolhei home from Iraq – 22 months.
2007			➡	Lakeview enrollment up to 593
				(was 573 for the 2006–2007 school year.)
2007	Sept.	5	➡	School opens.
2007		12	➡	Fire at Prairie Wild hay bales that lasted 12 hours
				– east side of Cottonwood – John Mohn.

			➡	Lillian Olson dies @ 97 on October 3.
2007	Nov.	7	➡	"Fondly remembering the days of sarsaparilla at Andy's place." Closed January 2001 after 43 years.
2007			➡	Andy Viaene dies @ 81 on November 4.
2007			➡	Douglas Engereson dies.
2007		21	➡	Article about the Lions Club – @ one time had 120 members, now down to 40 people.
2007			➡	Helen Mary Dandurand dies @ 90 on November 13 – was from Cottonwood.
2007		28	➡	Article about Leona Pederson and Vi Nelson: "Two Cottonwood natives reflect on life, love, and loyalty. Sisters total nearly 200 years between the two of them."
2007	Dec.	5	➡	"The card sharks of Cottonwood playing everything but bridge." Article about John Murphy's building up town.
2007			➡	Marlene Gniffke dies @ 73 on December 3.
2007			➡	Article about the weekend snowstorm.
2007		12	➡	Article about Marlys Lund "Serving on the postal scene for 16 years."
2007		26	➡	Article about Mike Lee's woodworking business.

END 2007

BEGIN 2008

2008	Jan.	2	➡	Shirley Nelson dies @ 65 on December 24, 2007.
2008			➡	Year in Review Issue – 2007.
2008		9	➡	Doris Volden dies @ 77 on December 28, 2007.
2008			➡	Donna (Molstad) Sjolseth dies @ 82 on December 22, 2007.

2008		16	➡	Article about the closing of Israel Lutheran Church.
2008		23	➡	Muriel Maxwell dies @ 79 on January 19.
2008	Feb.	13	➡	Article about possibility of no parade for *Coming Home Days*.
2008		27	➡	Articles about the Bus tragedy:

      ➡ Emilee Olson   ➡   Jesse Javens

      ➡ Reed Stevens   ➡   Hunter Javens.

2008			➡	Boy Scouts go on a dog sledding trip in Wisconsin.
2008	Mar.	5	➡	Funeral for Reed Stevens.
2008			➡	Dorothy Bjornebo dies @ 87 on February 27.
2008			➡	The Progress Edition.

      ➡   The Village Pub.

      ➡   The Village court.

      ➡   Trucker's Pride.

      ➡   Extreme Panel.

      ➡   Cottonwood Co – op.

      ➡   A school photograph.

2008		12	➡	"City will re-zone for building of diesel island."
2008		19	➡	"Snook's Café of Cottonwood closes. Coffee drinkers have relocated.
2008			➡	Community receives grant for Walking / Bike path.
2008	April	2	➡	Article about 75 geese behind Ed & Leona's.
2008		9	➡	"Cottonwood selects Lovsness as first Business Person of the Year."
2008			➡	Thelma Egeland dies @ 100 on April 4.
2008		16	➡	
2008		23	➡	Prom Night – "A Night in the Spotlight."
			➡	Reduced bail denied for Olga Marina Franco.
			➡	[Old time Church Services @ Rock Valley & Hawk Creek Lutheran Churches.
2008		30	➡	Article about John and Taunya Geihl's house.
2008			➡	Jerrule O. Kise dies @ 91 on April 24.
2008			➡	"Cottonwood area Historical Society holds annual meeting."
2008	May	7	➡	"Lakeview feels trauma as student is

airlifted from playground."

2008			➡	"Cottonwood loses strong supporter.
			➡	"Gniffke's absence will be evident."
				Glenn Gniffke dies @ 77 on May 1.
			➡	Wade Geihl back from Iraq.
			➡	Hazel Anundson dies @ 87 on April 30.
2008		14	➡	"Orville Kompelien celebrates 100 years of good living."
2008			➡	Rosella Lindsay dies @ 84 on date not given.
2008		21	➡	Work starts on the new diesel island.
2008			➡	Beverly Lange dies @ 66 on May 18.
			➡	Laverne Lines dies @ 90 on May 12.
2008		28	➡	Esther Holmberg dies @ 84 on May 20.
2008	June	4	➡	Lakeview graduation – 40 graduates.
2008		11	➡	"No easy answers for a café in Cottonwood."
2008			➡	"Lions Club gives much to many."
				Donations to various causes.
2008			➡	Katie Geihl dies @ 69 on June 7.
2008		18	➡	Article about the kids recovering from the bus accident.
2008	July	2	➡	Diesel Island @ Cenex opens.
2008			➡	Janice Oftedahl dies @ 60 on June 24.
			➡	"Still no answers for café in Cottonwood."
2008		9	➡	Thomas Gunderson dies @ 84 on June 22.
				He was originally from Cottonwood.
2008		16	➡	"A big blast and a big splash @ *Coming Home Days*.
				Some old favorites and some new features offered."
2008		23	➡	"2008 Lyon County Farmer Family of the Year"
				– the Jonathan Olson Family.
2008		30	➡	Ernest Brusven dies @ 78 on July 25, 2008.
2008	Aug.	6	➡	"Repairs needed for Norseth–Larsen House."
2008			➡	"Something is cooking for a café in Cottonwood."
2008			➡	"The prosecution rests and defense begins calling witness in Franco trial."
2008		13	➡	"Brief deliberation brings guilty verdict to Franco."

2008		20	➡	"Family and friends gather to celebrate life sending message of love on high."
2008	Sept.	3	➡	Rain on the 1st day of school.
2008		10	➡	New playground equipment in City Park.
2008		17	➡	Article about Vi and Gordon Geistfeld house.
2008	Oct.	1	➡	Joel Dahl selected as Elected Official of the Year.
2008			➡	"Harvest of bean crop well under way." "… yields affected by lack of rain …"
2008		8	➡	Article about the tour of homes.
			➡	Paul and Karen Geihl
			➡	Laura and Perry Penske
			➡	Lael and LuAnn Bahn
			➡	Gordon and Vi Geistfeld.
2008		15	➡	"Franco is sentenced will serve at least 8 ½ years."
2008		22	➡	"Second fire call to dairy in Cottonwood."
2008			➡	"No easy Cottonwood Café solutions."
2008		29	➡	"Herrigan will clean up with new business."
			➡	Leaf vacuuming.
2008	Nov.	5	➡	"Cottonwood family enjoys its 28th annual hay ride." – Jim and Darlene Cole.
2008		12	➡	"A winter wonderland springs up over night."
			➡	"Lenz to serve another term in Cottonwood."
		19	➡	"One metal cross on the right side of the highway."
2008			➡	"Snook's Café goes on auction block but sale not completed."
2008		26	➡	Cottonwood Lake — photos.
2008			➡	"Cottonwood business confirms an upside for the economy. Hydro Swing looks at growth and expansion in 2009."
2008			➡	Trudy Anderson dies @ 92 on November 22.
2008			➡	"Cottonwood Senior Dining celebrates 25th anniversary."
2008	Dec.	3	➡	"A new gathering place on Main in Cottonwood."
2008			➡	"Memories of days gone by" – interesting article.
2008		10	➡	"Memories of days gone by in Cottonwood."
			➡	By Dorothy Fratzke Brown.

2008		➡	Carl Anundson dies @ 95 on December 5.
2008	24	➡	LGA to be cut – city waits on payment reduction.
2008	31	➡	Jessica Stölen joins the news staff.

END 2008

BEGIN 2009

* With limited time, just year-end review stories were searched and highlighted from 2009-2012. The obituary listings are complete for those years.

2009	Jan.	28	➡	Mineva Edith (Mickey) Fritze dies @ 86 on January 11.
			➡	Wayne Douglas Erickson dies @ 62.
			➡	Larry Krause dies @ 70 on January 15.
2009	Feb.	4	➡	Norman F. Varpness dies @ 88 on January 23.
	Feb.	11	➡	Ed Chambers dies @ 90 on January 26.
2009	March	4	➡	Donald J. Roby dies @ 74 on February 27.
		11	➡	Suzanne Cole dies @ 37 on February 26.
		18	➡	Margaret Wirtz dies @ 85 on March 11.
		25	➡	John Dieken dies @ 87 on March 18.
2009	April	15	➡	Arvid Bjornebo dies @ 95 on April 11.
			➡	Norma Reishus dies @ 67 on April 9.
2009		22	➡	Bob Crouse dies @ 67 on April 18.
2009	June	3	➡	Johnny Oftedahl dies @ 89 on March 10.
2009	June	17	➡	Arthur Paulson dies @ 84 on June 9.
		24	➡	Bertha C. Hanson dies @ 89 on June 17.
2009	July	1	➡	Leif Bjornebo dies @ 87 on June 28.
2009	Oct.	7	➡	Jeffrey Dahl dies @ 56 on September 30.
		14	➡	Christine Okrina dies @ 97 on September 26.
		21	➡	Darlene Clementson dies @ 76 on October 11.
2009	Nov.	4	➡	Gloria Rebers dies @ 79 on October 29.
		11	➡	Sylvia Dahl dies @ 76 on November 7.

2009	Dec.	23	➡	Rev. Lynn R. Broughton dies @ 70 on December 13.
		30	➡	Regina Kellen dies @ 97 on December 21.
2009	**Dec.**	**30**	➡	**Year in Review Issue for 2009**
2009	Feb.		➡	Daniel Lancaster published a book:
				John Beargrease – Legend of the Minnesota North Shore.
2009			➡	City council reduces expenditures due to LGA cuts.
2009			➡	Darlene Cole receives a plaque for 40 years
				service with Lakeview Schools.
2009			➡	Parents of the victims reflect on the bus crash.
2009	Mar.		➡	Mid – Continent lays off 80 – 85 people.
2009	April		➡	Landscape design underway for Memorial Garden
				for victims of the bus crash.
2009			➡	Cottonwood Historical Society requests community input on
				maintaining the Norseth – Larsen house.
2009	May		➡	New "Welcome to Cottonwood" sign being finished.
2009			➡	New business in town – "Art's Repair."
2009			➡	Greg Isaackson honored for 35 years
				of service to Cottonwood.
2009	June		➡	Jean Dahl retires after 19 years with Lakeview schools.
2009			➡	Rick Jeseritz named Cottonwood Business Person of Year.
2009			➡	Cottonwood native Susan Runholt publishes a book:
				The Mystery of the Third Lucretia.
2009			➡	Work begins on the Celebration Garden for the bus victims.
2009	July		➡	Concrete paving on Highway 23 to be ongoing during the
				summer. Highway 23 will be closed.
2009	Aug.		➡	Fireman's Open held at the Cottonwood Country Club.
2009	Sept.		➡	Cottonwood advertises sale of *The Village Pub.*
2009	Nov.		➡	New business: "The Escape" – therapeutic massage – in the
				Dental Center Building – Ashley Potter.
2009			➡	**End Year in Review Issue for 2009**

BEGIN 2010

2010	Jan.	6	➡	James A. Cole dies @ 82 on December 31, 2009.
			➡	Andrew Boerboom dies @ 90 on January 3.
		27	➡	Virgil Hoff dies @ 95 on January 20.
2010	Feb.	3	➡	Idalene A. Boehne dies @ 86 on January 26.
		17	➡	Ruby S. Sandland dies @ 94 on February 12.
		24	➡	Norman Knudson dies @ 76 on February 19.
2010	Mar.	3	➡	Iona May Budolfson dies February 15.
		24	➡	Phyllis E. Ricke dies @ 80 on March 15.
2010	April	28	➡	Ordell I. Mortensbak dies @ 83 on April 21.
2010	May	12	➡	Roger Keepers dies.
2010		19	➡	Dennis Vien dies @ 77 on May 14.
2010	June	16	➡	Morris Behrman dies @ 83 on June 8.
2010	July	14	➡	Esther Titrud dies @ 86 on July 10.
2010	Aug.	4	➡	Carl Stanley Christensen dies @ 88.
		11	➡	Edward Wallace Olson dies @ 73 on July 31.
		18	➡	Bernice Peppersack dies @ 86 on August 14.
2010	Oct.	13	➡	Lillian Falkum dies @ 88 on October 3.
2010		20	➡	Raymond Janachovsky dies @ 77 on October 12.
2010	Nov.	3	➡	Bertha Louwagie dies @ 89 on October 27.
			➡	Myrna Broughton dies @ 98 on October 27.
2010	Dec.	15	➡	Dale Bahn dies on November 27.
2010		29	➡	Shirley Kennedy dies @ 88 on December 8
2010		29	➡	Gordon Yahnka dies @ 53 on December 18
			➡	**Year in Review Issue for 2010 (published Jan. 5, 2011)**
2010		Jan.	➡	L. E. D. Stop signs placed at 2 Cottonwood intersections.
2010		Feb.	➡	Feb. 19th, 2nd anniversary of the bus crash in which 4 children died and 16 of the 28 on the bus were injured.
2010		Mar.	➡	Marvin Boerboom lives through an earthquake in Chile.
2010		April	➡	Cottonwood Historical Society turns care taking of Norseth–Larsen house over to the city of Cottonwood.
2010		May	➡	City of Cottonwood discusses a new city facilities building.
2010		June	➡	Norseth – Larsen house to be sold.

2010	Aug.	➡	Proposed levy referendum of $800 per pupil for the November election.	
2010		➡	Public hearing on a proposed ordinance for ATV and Snowmobile use on city streets.	
2010	Sept.	➡	Norseth – Larsen house sold to Steve Alm.	
2010	Oct.	➡	BNSF crews at work repairing tracks in the area.	
2010		➡	Ellen Lenz elected mayor.	
2010		➡	**End Year in Review Issue for 2010**	

END 2010

BEGIN 2011

2011	Feb.	16	➡	Doris Post dies @ 95 on February 9.
		16	➡	Evangeline Kraft dies @ 83 on February 7.
2011	May	18	➡	Walter Boerboom dies @ 86 on May 13.
			➡	Wesley Reishus dies (born April 17, 1941).
		25	➡	Lorene Elsie Smith dies @ 90 on May 12.
2011	June	1	➡	Edward Heidemann dies @ 82 on May 22.
		8	➡	Candace "Candy" Demke dies @ 55 on June 4.
2011		15	➡	Harold Yahnka dies @ 86 on June 10.
			➡	William "Bill" Snyder dies @ 83 on June 12.
		29	➡	James Schwerin dies @ 59 on June 20.
2011	July	20	➡	June Krause dies @ 73 on July 13.
		20	➡	Orville Kompelien dies @ 103 on July 12.
2011	Aug.	3	➡	Jerome Varpness dies @ 58 on July 17.
2011		10	➡	Bernelda Holmberg dies @ 94 on August 4.
			➡	Stella Weinhold dies @ 90 on July 31.
		31	➡	Ethod Bergeron dies @ 87 on August 21.
			➡	Betty Pentila dies @ 75 on August 22.
2011	Sept.	7	➡	Lila Viola Roti dies @ 102 on August 28.

		28	➡	Gene VanDeVeire dies @ 67 on September 20.
2011	Oct.	19	➡	Henry VanUden dies @ 71 on October 14.
2011	Nov.	2	➡	Bernice Roe dies @ 83 on October 29.
2011		9	➡	Harold "Bud" Lohman dies @ 84 on October 31.
	Dec.	7	➡	Edith Kufus dies @ 79 on November 28.
		14	➡	Patricia Javens dies @ 72 on December 4.
		21	➡	Alma (Todt) Lee dies @ 97 on December 14.
			➡	**Year in Review Issue for 2011 (published Jan. 4, 2012)**
2011		Jan.	➡	Joy Kulow retires after 29 ½ years as Lakeview Librarian.
2011			➡	Greg Isaackson retires after 37 years as Cottonwood City Clerk–Administrator.
2011			➡	Dana Yost publishes book: *The Right Place.*
2011			➡	New business: *Oopsie Daisy Designs* – Heather & Ashtyn Gniffke.
2011		Feb.	➡	Farmer's Co – op Elevator lists Hardware Hank for sale.
2011		Mar.	➡	Mason Schirmer hired as new City Clerk – Administrator.
2011			➡	Hydroswing Doors closes – 17 employees out of work.
2011			➡	Informational meeting on a proposed new City Facilities Building.
2011		April	➡	Litigation by companies against Hydroswing Doors.
2011			➡	New Business: Sandy Dovre and Terry Kempfert: *Defying Gravity Designs.*
2011		May	➡	New Business: Kim Sanders – *Mirror Solutions.*
2011		July	➡	Severe storms in the area, surrounding towns damaged.
2011			➡	Jody Isaackson book published: *On the Cutting Edge* (under the name J. J. Luepke.)
2011		Aug.	➡	Proposed city facilities building still being discussed.
2011		Sept.	➡	10th anniversary of the 911 attacks.
2011			➡	Craig Aamodt participates in the Paris – Brest – Paris *Randonneurs* bicycle event.
2011		Nov.	➡	Lakeview now has 2 cameras in each bus.
2011			➡	Don Shelby at Lakeview for Emilee Olson remembrance.
2011			➡	Article about the old café coming down

2011 ➡ **End Year in Review Issue for 2011**

END 2011

BEGIN 2012

2012	Jan.	11	➡	Wilfred Kockelman dies @ 91 on January 8.
			➡	Florence Gredvig dies @ 92 on January 7.
		18	➡	Remi Doom dies @ 88 on January 10.
2012	Feb.	22	➡	Adeline "Pat" McClain dies @ 87 on February 13.
		29	➡	Belva Timm dies @ 86 on February 23.
			➡	Bradley Stensrud dies @ 55 on February 20.
2012	Mar.	14	➡	Helen Hildebrandt dies @ 93 on March 11.
2012	April	18	➡	Oceanna Knutson dies @ 95 on April 1.
2012	April	25	➡	Howard Midboe dies @ 57 on April 17.
2012	May	2	➡	Cheryl Lund dies @ 57 on April 28.
		30	➡	Dennis Kroger dies @ 75 on May 5.
2012	June	6	➡	Donald N. Rebers dies @ 86 on May 22.
		13	➡	Edna Ericksen dies @ 92 on June 5.
2012	July	4	➡	Alan "AJ" Maag Jr. dies @ 21 on June 25.
		11	➡	Harold "Hal" Loe dies @ 71 on July 5.
2012	Aug.	1	➡	Adeline Timm dies @ 94 on July 23.
		22	➡	James Dahl dies @ 54 on August 19.
2012	Sept.	26	➡	Douglas Wagner dies @ 52 on September 22.
2012	Oct.	3	➡	John VanHeuveln dies @ 76 on September 27.
			➡	Shirley (Harmening) Nelson dies @ 90 on September 22.
		17	➡	Rachel (Caron) Nosbush dies @ 91 on October 12.
2012	Dec.	12	➡	Martin Schmidt dies @ 95 on December 4.
		19	➡	Gordon Colburn dies @ 96 on December 17.
			➡	Harold Schwisow dies @ 91 on December 12.

➡ <u>**Year in Review Issue for 2012 (published Jan. 2, 2013)**</u>

2012	Jan.	➡	Barb Evers retires from North Star after 21 years.
2012		➡	Carol Kompelien retires from Hardware Hank after 19 years.
2012	Feb.	➡	Fire at the city shop – trucks and other equipment lost.
2012	Mar.	➡	Mason Schirmer resigns. Kathy Dahl and Charles Seipel will hold city positions for the interim.
2012	June	➡	Edna Ericksen loses her life in auto accident on Highway 23 and Lyon County Road 9. Alan "AJ" Maag Jr. loses his life in auto accident at Highway 23 and Barstad Road.
2012		➡	Norwegian Mutual Insurance Company begins construction on a new office building on Main Street.
2012		➡	Lyon County and the City of Cottonwood will share a joint public works building in the old truck wash building.
2012	Aug.	➡	Former Lakeview coach Brad Bigler in serious auto accident with his family. Infant son does not survive.
2012		➡	Two more L. E. D. stop signs in the Cottonwood area.
2012	Oct.	➡	City of Cottonwood Maintenance Department moves into the old truck wash building.
2012	Nov.	➡	Old city maintenance shop sold to Farmer's Co – op Elevator.
2012	Dec.	➡	City offices will move to the old Seitz Drugstore building, the city library to be renovated.
2012		➡	**End Year in Review Issue for 2012**

END 2012

BEGIN 2013

2013	Jan.	9	➡	Christ Lutheran members return from mission trip to Tanzania.
2013	Jan.	16	➡	Harriet Velde dies @ 93 on January 10.
			➡	Sandy Turbee, a flight nurse from Wood Lake, publishes

			book "Dear Child of Mine … a Letter From Mom."
		➡	New City Council member Christopher Dahl and re-elected Mayor Ellen Lenz sworn in.
	23	➡	Joseph Haneca dies @ 93 on January 19.
		➡	County supports grant for Cottonwood Library Project.
		➡	North Star Mutual recognizes several employees.
	30	➡	Cottonwood brings back "Fishless Derby" for Feb. 9.
2013	Feb. 6	➡	St. Mary's receives donation from Catholic United Financial.
	13	➡	Fishless Derby is back … several photos.
		➡	Fundraiser at Lakeview for Steve Pottratz.
	20	➡	North Star Insurance contributes $125,000 to Avera Cancer Institute in Marshall.
2013	27	➡	Robert Kompelien dies @ 87 on February 16.
		➡	Lyon County to sell former main garage land in Cottonwood (building was heavily damaged in fire).
2013	Mar. 6	➡	Otis Torke dies @ 95 on February 24.
		➡	Jeff Mauland, president of North Star Mutual Insurance, was elevated to highest state association position (Chairman of the Minnesota Association of Farm Mutual Ins. Companies).
	13	➡	Lois Weseloh dies @ 91 on March 9.
		➡	Lakeview Schools awarded $1,480.66 from Viking Coca-Cola Bottling for a portion of sales of Powerade products.
	20	➡	Lakeview mock trial team places 2nd at state competition.
	27	➡	Cottonwood Ambulance has 2nd annual steak fry.
2013	April 3	➡	Incubator project closed at Village Court on March 31.
2013	April 10	➡	Anton Brusven dies @ 88 on April 8.
		➡	Jean Chandler dies @ 85 on April 7.
		➡	Cottonwood Fire Department's new Danko tanker truck ready for service
	17	➡	Cottonwood couples safe after the Boston Marathon bombings (Chris & Christine Fenske, Phil & Stacie Lienemann, and Terry & Becky Timm).
	24	➡	June Kroger dies @ 79 on April 17.

			➡ County Road 10 from West 5th Street to Highway 59 will be resurfaced with concrete, beginning about May 13.
			➡ Merrill Hanson dies @ 97 on April 16.
2013	May	1	➡ Benefit for Jake Hanson, Lakeview Schools dean of students.
			➡ First-ever Laker Ball held at Lakeview High School last week.
2013	May	8	➡ Reynold E. Baune dies @ 79 on May 4.
			➡ Michael Alness named American Legion Post #503 representative to annual American Legion Boys State.
			➡ Lyon County highway garage land sold in Cottonwood.
2013		15	➡ Melvin Anderson dies @ 90 on May 8.
			➡ Soldier mom returns from duty in time for Mother's Day with her three daughters. She is Ellen Cooley, the daughter and step-daughter of Steve and Gail Gregoire.
2013		22	➡ Clayton Stevens dies @ 90 on May 16.
2013	June	5	➡ Edmon A. Doom dies @ 91 on May 29.

How Cottonwood Voted in Presidential Elections

Since 2000. Source Minnesota Secretary of State's website

2012

Romney 308, Obama 287

2008

McCain 307, Obama 292

2004

Bush 330, Kerry 293

2000

Bush 275, Gore 260, Nader 35

OUR SCHOOLS

Lakeview Public Schools

By Dana Yost

In a remarkable show of inter-community unity, school district voters from Cottonwood and Wood Lake made a decision Dec. 19, 2000, that would vastly change the literal and academic landscapes of both communities.

A decision that showed pride in their schools, a responsibility to their young people, and faith in the future of the place where they live.

Going to the polls on that winter day, voters approved a bond referendum for $12.13 million to build a new pre-school-through-12th-grade public school.

It was a bold move for two small communities to approve a project of that cost. But the Dec. 19, 2000, referendum passed with 838 yes votes and 423 no votes. In other words, 66 percent of voters said yes to the new school.

Photos of the new school by Karen Berg.

On Aug. 20, 2001, the Lakeview School Board certified a bid from Hasslen Construction of Ortonville that was more than $3 million less than the referendum — or $9,011,500.

Efforts by then-Superintendent Palmer Anderson, state Rep. Marty Seifert, R-Marshall, and Sen. Arlene Lesewski, R-Marshall, helped get the state Legislature to approve a debt-equalization bill, which lowered the amount property owners in the Lakeview school district paid in property taxes for the bond.

A little more than a year after the bid was certified, a new school with state-of-the-art science classrooms, a performing arts theater that seats 454, two gymnasiums, two music rooms, a commons area with high ceilings and bright natural lighting, and much more, opened on the north edge of Cottonwood. The date was Sept. 23, 2002.

"My first impression of the new school was that it was very modern and bright," Misty Kuyper, a 2006 Lakeview graduate, recalled in May 2013. "I loved the sky lights in the common area! The new school was very easy to navigate! It is a big school, yet easy to get around, without getting confused!"

The school opened when Kuyper was a freshmen. She and her classmates from the Class of 2006 were the first to attend the new school all four years of high school.

"I had a lot of great memories in the new Lakeview school," she said. "It was very homey and comfortable. I also love the auditorium! It was nice to watch plays, concerts and have speakers come and share in such a nice quiet space."

Kuyper is not unique in her emotions or pride in the school. At an open house before the building opened in 2002, residents and the curious formed long lines before the doors even opened, waiting to get a look inside. The athletic complex has been compared to college facilities, school officials say. People took pride in their schools — the academics, the people who work there and the buildings — in 2000, in 2002, and they still do, said current Lakeview Superintendent Chris Fenske.

"I'd say there's a great sense of pride," Fenske said May 6, 2013, in an interview for this history book. "We had a benefit yesterday for our dean of students, who is battling cancer. It was a Sunday-afternoon type of thing. {And the spring weather was nice, so people could have stayed away, busy outdoors.] But I bet between 800 and 1,000 people showed up for a pork supper and to watch some old guys play basketball! Looking at the numbers, even when we ran the [operating-funds] referendum a couple years ago, which we had to do because state funding has been so flat, it passed 65 percent in favor of, which was unheard of. Since it was a presidential election, the turnout was so high, so you don't always get that [kind of lopsided support for a funding referendum].

"So, yes, there is a sense of pride, and it is as strong as ever. Darlene [Cole] and I try to get down to coffee everyone once in a while, a couple times a month — go visit with people downtown. And when we talk with some of the older gentlemen at coffee, the pride they have in building the school is evident."

As bold as the leap forward was — a $12 million referendum is a big step for rural school districts — school officials and residents had little choice if they wanted to keep their own school building. The existing school buildings in Cottonwood and Wood Lake were both very old, and faced expensive repairs and upgrades merely to meet modern state building codes.

It was possible that the two buildings could be closed, and students left with no options but to enroll in other schools in other cities, such as Marshall, Granite Falls or Minneota.

Mark Vandelanotte was a member of the steering committee that looked into the district's options before the vote in 2000.

"The state of Minnesota wanted the old buildings to get up to code," he recalled. "So we toured different schools that had been remodeled and came back and were asked to get bids to remodel our two old schools. They were talking about a lot of money for an old school, about what it would cost to build a new school."

Vandelanotte credited Palmer Anderson, Lakeview's school superintendent at the time, for urging that the school board and district consider building a new school after leaders heard the costs of remodeling existing buildings.

"Palmer looked into what it would cost to build a new school, and found it would be like $12 million or $13 million," Vandelanotte said. "One of the schools we had toured, someone there said we should make sure we put in a fine-arts theater, which has been great.

"It was a very good experience.

"Palmer did a great job of getting that thing rolling and bringing the two communities together and they really rallied together. I think it turned out excellent."

Former Cottonwood Mayor Tim Fruin also credited Anderson's leadership, saying Anderson unified a wide range of groups around the cause and provided steady communication to keep the whole district informed.

"Palmer Anderson did a great job on those things," Fruin said. "Palmer knew how to do that, knew how to bring things to a critical mass [to get a consensus behind it]."

The school was built with pre-cast concrete panels, ranging from 15 to 30 feet tall. They are supported by structural steel. Helicopters were eventually used to lift and place massive heating and cooling units on the school's roof. The one-level school building occupies 125,000 square feet, a Dec. 21, 2001, Marshall Independent story said.

The athletic field complex was finished in 2006, with a baseball field, softball field, football field and track.

Like Misty Kuyper, Fenske was impressed from the first time he saw the new school, when he came to Cottonwood for a site visit during his job-interview process.

"On my visit, that was an attractive feature — the way they built it, having pre-school through Grade 12 all in one site, really makes it a family-friendly and generally friendly atmosphere. It is nice to have it all in one site."

He speaks not only as the superintendent, but the father of children in school, who knows he can just walk a hall or visit the commons area at lunch and conveniently see his own children.

The design of the building, and the one-site plan, allow for inter-grade bonding and academic work, as well.

"We started a School Buddies program, which coordinates a high school buddy who gets paired up with an elementary buddy," Fenske said. "Those children in the elementary level are kind of handpicked by their teachers, if there is a concern they maybe don't have as many friends, or are new to school. With everybody here in one place, it is easy for the high schoolers to spend time with the elementary students. Also classroom partnerships with high school kids have been rewarding to elementary students. Those kinds of things really make it a family and friendly type of place."

Lakeview isn't just about a new building and new ballfields, of course. There has been academic success and innovations, too.

Lakeview School has received the Bronze Award in 2008, 2009, 2010, 2011 & 2012 as an outstanding High School in the U.S. News and World Report survey of America's best high schools, the school's web site said.

"We've been able to do, I would say, a good job in that area," Fenske said about academics. "We're always evaluating strengths and weaknesses, which is a sign of any good organization."

One example, he said, was the elementary school's literacy program, which is divided into three tiers, depending upon where a student's reading skills are at the beginning of the program. In the second and third tiers, where students may not be as strong of readers as in Tier 1, there are designated, constructive "intervention" steps that are taken if kids fall behind on their ability to read. The program provides a way to track reading levels, and improve them *before* students fall behind, he said.

"Our goal is to have everyone read to grade level by the end of their third-grade year," Fenske said.

The school also changed to a new math curriculum a couple of years ago, and has seen students' math results improve. Another example of advanced teaching methods came in late September 2012 when the school was awarded a $10,000 Monsanto Growing Rural Education grant. It was one of only 176 schools in 35 states to earn the grant. The funds would lead to academic lab work that would cross study disciplines and grade levels.

"The funds will be used for staff development and purchasing of Vernier Probeware," Fenske said in the Sept. 26, 2012, issue of the Marshall Independent. "This equipment allows students hands-on learning opportunities in real-world application settings, like soil testing, working with electrical currents and working with velocities. It's exciting."

It has not only real-world uses, but real-time value, said Fenske, using one of the terms of our digital age. Students can use the probeware to test soil and get immediate results, and apply those results immediately to coursework in science, ag, math classes

"It's across the curriculum" he said in the interview for this book, "and it can be expanded to kindergarten through 12th grade, so kids can do it cross grade-levels [and continue projects or expand projects] into another school year, for instance. Or study using consistent tools and terms from one year to the next].

"The focus is on learning 21st century skills," he told the Independent. "It will allow the kids to collect and analyze data and work collaboratively. They'll also have to communicate about the analyzed results, whether it's a lab report or presentation.

"Technology was important, obviously, when they built the school, and it still is. We have invested a lot in technology. We're using iPads. Right now, we have iPads on carts that can be moved and shared. The board is talking about having every kid in grades 9 through 12 have an iPad next year [the 2013-2014 school year]."

The new facilities and the academic strengths have done exactly what voters hoped back in December 2000: kept their school system relevant, vital for the future.

Student enrollment in 2002 was 564. Student enrollment in 2012-13 was 605, school records said.

"Our enrollment right now is tickling around 600, which is more than when they built the building, so we're full, we're using all our space," Fenske said. "We continue to have a strong number of open enrollees into our district. We offer strong programs, not just the basics like math, science and English. But ag, technology, the fine arts. So our kids do leave here well-rounded and diversified. We have great relationships with Southwest Minnesota State University and Minnesota West [community and technical college], so we are able to expand our [post-secondary-education options which let high school students take college courses] offerings. Our kids are able to leave here with as many as 20 college credits when they graduate. In terms of schools our size, I believe we have the highest in our area in terms of college credits."

Again, some of the success traces back to an interlocking relationship between school and community. In 2010, after several years of the state Legislature holding its school funding at or near a flat level, Lakeview voters approved by a 653-371 margin a referendum to increase per-pupil funding at the local level.

"The Lakeview Public Schools are fortunate to have a very supportive school district community that has provided the needed financial resources to operate excellent programs in great facilities," Fenske's message on the school web site said. "This is not only evident by the building of a new school in 2002, but the recent passage of an $800 per pupil operating levy in 2010. A dedicated staff of teachers, paraprofessionals, administrators, support staff, and Board of Education take pride in the quality and services provided to the students and families within the district."

Fenske likes to see community members active in the school, such as for the fund-raiser for the dean of students in early May 2013. Several residents will use the school halls to exercise by walking, especially in the winters.

"I think we want it to be there for the community, to be a community-center-type thing," he said. "That's important, especially in a smaller town. One of the things we've tried to do and have been pretty successful at it is getting outside groups in here, like the Farmers Co-op Elevator for its annual meeting, and the [Cottonwood Co-op] oil company has some things in here. Getting the facility used that way [is good]. We started having Grandparents Day here for our elementary. We want it to be open to the community, want them to feel they're involved in things that are going on. So it's more than just the academics, the curriculum. There is that social piece as well. I've noticed an increase in that, which is great."

• • •

Before the new school was built, Lakeview elementary and high school students attended school at the old school building in Cottonwood. Middle school students attended the old school building in Wood Lake.

In late 2003, Cottonwood's former school building on Front Street was demolished. A headline in the Dec. 3, 2003, issue of the Tri-County News read: "End of an era: Cottonwood School Building goes down."

In 2004, the city of Cottonwood and its Economic Development Authority purchased the old school building and playground site for residential purposes. Houses have been getting built where the old school and the playground once stood, along the lake.

Bayli Vandelanotte is another member of the Lakeview Class of 2006. She went to elementary school in the old building and high school in the new, and has fond memories of both.

"I remember when talks of a new school first started. If I remember correctly, my Dad [Mark] was on a board that worked to get the referendum passed," she said in May 2013.

"I have good memories of both buildings. I am so thankful for the new school. It was beautifully built and offered students an amazing new gym and theater for concerts and plays. I agree with Misty, I remember walking in on the first day and thinking how modern, bright and clean it was.

"I did however (and still to this day) miss all of the character of the old school (I love older architecture!). [Her sister] Abby and I reminisce every once in awhile about the old school and try to walk through it in our minds. Walking up the stairs to the computer room, going up even farther to the library. Walking up the ramp into the cafeteria. The playground next to the lake (and all the kickballs that are probably at the bottom of the lake). Although we only went there through fifth grade, I have very nice memories of going to school there. It does make me sad that I didn't get the opportunity to go to the same high school as my parents did, but, again, I am so thankful for the new school and all of the opportunities it presented for us. It is cool knowing that our class added our touch of character to the new school for years to come! Lots of good memories in both places!"

• • •

Even with the potential costs, Mark Vandelanotte thought it was time for people of his generation to step forward and get a new building done. He and his wife Jane had two daughters, Abby in 2004 and then Bayli in 2006, graduate from the new school.

"Our parents had come up with the money to build new schools and keep the towns progressing," he said. "And it was our turn then. I didn't seen any reason to spend money on an old school when we could get a new school for the same money.

"My hat's off to the people who voted this in, because they acted in the best interest of the education of the children of the towns. The two communities really came together. Palmer did a lot of work with the legislators. It was quite an undertaking."

And a lasting one. For families relocating to the area, perhaps because a job has brought them to Marshall, when they compare all the neighboring small towns as they decide where to move, learning that Cottonwood has a new school can be a difference-maker in their decision.

"What a positive impact on the town," Vandelanotte said. "You talk to different people who have moved to town. Some had no particular reason to move to Cottonwood – they were moving to the area [for job reasons] and could have moved to anywhere. But the school impressed them. Cottonwood has thriving churches, the new school — these are people with families who have come in, and those things make a difference. That has helped out the community.

"And remember, it's LAKEVIEW. Without Wood Lake, it would never have happened."

Lakeview High School's 2012 Spring Pops music concert. (Tri-County News photo)

Lost, Found & At Home in the New School: Fond Memories

By Angela Yahnka, Lakeview High School Graduate, Class of 2006

Written May 6, 2013, for the 125th Anniversary history book

Since my dad (Tom Yahnka) is a member of the Lakeview faculty I was able to tour the new school while it was in the middle of being built multiple times.

I remember my dad giving me tours every few weeks and while I wandered around, avoiding construction material, I tried to picture what this place would look like completed and full of students and teachers going about their daily routine. I tried to picture what memories I would make there as I began my high school career.

I remember that school started quite late into September 2002 in order to finish construction. I awoke the first day of my freshman year of high school without the typical nerves of an underclassman. We were all in the same boat! Nobody would know where they were going right away and I wouldn't have to worry about ending up in the "Senior Hallway" by accident (no place for a lowly freshman like myself).

My friends and I entered the brand new "Commons" as it would come to be known, with its high ceilings and bright colors, a far cry from the "tunnels" we had become accustomed to. We compared schedules and set off to find our classes, enjoying the smell of fresh paint and the ease of opening and closing brand new lockers (the previous year, in the old Wood Lake Middle School building, I had mastered a complicated combination of jiggles and wiggles that would enable me to open my locker as well as a "slam and lift" method that would allow me to close it and keep it closed).

The first day was going smoothly, and I was navigating the crush of people quite well, due to my "insider" knowledge bestowed upon me during my dad's tours. About the middle of the morning I exited my third or fourth class and took a look at my schedule, "Health" was next up. Hmm….where the heck was that room?? I did a 360 in the hallway, trying to pull my 5-foot-4 self up to full height in a futile attempt to locate the classroom but the entire football team it seemed was blocking my view. I edged my way out into the Commons, thinking it had to be close to the gym, right? All of a sudden, three of my friends ran up to me in a panic: they were looking for the same room. The minutes were ticking down until the second bell, so we started to walk somewhere, anywhere when out of his own office popped my dad. Saved! I quick grabbed his arm, shoved my schedule in his face and asked "Where's this room?" "Down that hallway, to the right!" he said, pointing between the two gyms and we were off again. Crisis adverted!

I spent four years with that building being my second home. Classes during the day, practices at night. Games, concerts, plays, proms and graduation. I remember feeling a sense of pride when visitors would comment on how nice our school was and how lucky we were to get to go there. Since I still live in the area, I have witnessed the evolution of the building. It has begun to look "lived in" but that's a good thing. It shows that students and teachers year after year make their home there and leave their mark at year's end. While the faces in the hallways look different to me now, "Laker Pride" is still evident and the sense of "going home" is still there.

At a fundraiser (the night of May 5, 2013) given for a faculty member fighting a battle with cancer, I saw everyone in the Lakeview community come together at "home" to support him and his family. Alumni, current students, and community members were all in attendance and the building was fairly bursting with support and love. I think all of my favorite memories in that building have been the ones where everyone has come together in support of something or someone and walking around it feels as comfortable as being home with your family.

Photo from Lakeview Public Schools website.

Cottonwood School/Lakeview School Timeline

Compiled by Darlene Cole

Superintendents:

Ralph Brynelson – 1953-Spring of 1991

Palmer Anderson – Spring of 1991-September 2004

Wayne Kazmierczak – January 2005 – December 2007

Chris Fenske – Spring of 2008 until present

Interim Superintendents

Steve Kjorness, Marvin Niedan, Sheldon Johnson

The old school building on Front Street had one gymnasium and one music room. A bond referendum for $12.13 million was passed on Dec. 19, 2000, to provide funds for the acquisition and betterment of school facilities.

We moved to the new school building at 875 Barstad Road N. on the north edge of the city on Sept. 23, 2002. It has two gymnasiums, two music rooms, and a theater that seats 454. The athletic field complex was completed in 2006. Visitors have commented that it's comparable to college athletic complexes. The athletic complex includes a baseball field, softball field, football field and track.

Sports offered in the "olden days" Boys basketball and football. Sports offered now: cross country, volleyball, football, girls and boys basketball, track, girls softball, baseball and golf. Student enrollment in 2002: 564. Student enrollment in 2012-13: 605.

Cottonwood School had a Cooperation/Combination Agreement with Wood Lake from 1991-1994. The two schools consolidated in 1994 and became Lakeview School.

The school and community suffered an unfortunate tragedy on February 19, 2008, when a bus crash took the lives of four of our students: Reed Stevens, Hunter Javens, Jesse Javens and Emilee Olson. There were several students on the bus that incurred injuries. There was a huge outpouring of sympathy from the community and the whole country. Sheldon Johnson was our Interim Superintendent at the time. When he was Superintendent at Monticello School, one of their students was killed in an accident so he had a lot of experience in dealing with a situation like this.

A memorial garden was established in the summer of 2008. It has memory bricks as well as class mottoes for anyone who wishes to purchase a brick. The proceeds go to the Not 4gotten Foundation, which sends Mother's and Father's Day cards to parents in Minnesota who have lost a child.

In 2008, four benches were built and placed around the pond. Each bench has the name of one of the children who died in the bus crash. They were made as an Eagle Scout project by A.J. Maag. In 2010, the Cottonwood Fire Department added a sitting bench.

Also, along on the paved trail that leads to the memorial garden, classmates placed a bench in memory of Lt. Jason Timmerman, who was killed in a bombing in Iraq in 2005. Timmerman was a 1998 graduate of Lakeview High School.

*A tidbit: There has been a descendant of the Paul and Freada Meyer family in the Cottonwood town school every year since Darwin Meyer started school in 1945, and there will be descendants for some years to come. (contributed by Pat Aamodt)

Left: A photo of the old Lakeview School on Front Street used on the cover of invitations to the 2002 All-School Reunion. Below, photos from Joel Dahl show the demolition of the school building to make way for new housing development along the southern shore of Cottonwood Lake.

Cottonwood and Lakeview High School Graduates 1988-2013

Class of 1988

Amy Layne Bockelman

Todd Thomas Bossuyt

Jeffrey Lawrence Caron

Chad Scott Cravens

David Joseph DeSmet

Jodi Lynn Dieken

Michelle Lorraine Dunn

Brandon Daniel Erickson

Ulrike Fiebrandt

Christine Jo Golberg

Jeanette Elaine Johnson

Monica Cecilia Juarez

Brant Eldeen Kompelien

Renae Mary Kompelien

Laura Christine Knudson

Linda Carleen Knudson

Meredith Ann Loe

Catherine Jo Louwagie

Karla Kay Louwagie

Terry Lee Louwagie

Gregory Paul Lund

Wendy Lin Magnuson

Shannon Lori Martin

Gregory Harold Meyer

Lyle Gene Meyer

Lynne Marie Meyer

Christopher Lee Miller

Shawn Edward Myers

Duanna Carol Pederson

Michael John Reishus

Nancy Lee Stoks

Carla Jean Timm

Shelly Marie Timm

Dawn Lynn VanLerberghe

Karen Ann Viane

Douglas Peter Wyffels

Class of 1989

Craig Stanley Aamodt

Kirt Alvin Anderson

Angela Dawn Bockelman

Bruce Jerry Bossuyt

Travis Richard Carothers

Carin Barbara Crouse

Ronda Jo Deuel

Lisa Ann Drummond

Bette Jo Gee

Jeana Nanette Gillispie

Ronda Lea Gregg

Daniel Joseph Hoffman

Kacy David Idso

Troy Jon Javens

Janet ReNae Johnson

Brett Alan Knutson

Bich Ngoc Le

Rhonda May Louwagie

Theresa Ann Louwagie

Paul Raymond Lund Jr.

Susan Rose Mohr

Douglas Wayne Nath

David Allen Nelson

Kyle Isaac Norland

Teresa Ann Olson

Leslie Anne Pederson

Julie Rhodes

Lisa Mae Sanders

Randal Alan Schwartz

Akiko Shiratori

Cory Thomas Sumerfelt

Kari Renee Timmerman

John Marie-Willy Vandehende

Kevin Ernest Viaene

Paul Richard Wambeke

Chad Douglas Warnke

Class of 1990

Lars Alan Anderson

Todd Joseph Baune

Kristian Marie Bjornebo

Brenda Ann Bossuyt

Janel Karen Brockman

Austin Warren Dacey

Daniel John Dahl

Samuel Daniel

Cathryn Ann Devereaux

Kristi Lee DeVries

Christopher Ronald Dieken

Matthew Lane Dosdall

Jamie Marie Engen

Coreen Lee Gee

Bradley John Gregoire

Krisann Lee Huso

Todd David Johnson

Krista Marie Kosen

Shawn Gregory Laleman

David Darrell Loe

Donna Mae Louwagie

Julie Irene Louwagie

Rose Theresa Matthys

Michael James Miller

Michael Lynn Muehler

Sherri Lynn Netjes

John Duane Neuman

Dawn Raschel Neuman

Mona Rebbeng

Amy Lynn Slettedahl

Anthony Davis Schwartz

Shannon Kay Varpness

Kristine Marie Viaene

Paulette Elaine Wambeke

Tara Lee Wisdorf

Class of 1991

Kelly Mac Boe

Chad Donald Bot

Melissa Kristine Breyfogle

Jonathan Jay Brower

Kevin John Brusven

Scott Eric Brusven

Paul Joseph Cravens

Jennifer Jane Dahl

Eric Len Danielson

Jeremy Allen Dieken

Sue Ann Drummond

Bettina Emmerich

Michael Vivian Gould

Michael Roy Gritman

Nicolas Allen Hale

James David Johnson

Shannon Leigh Loe

Divena Daun Loke

Amy Jo Louwagie

Karen Marie Louwagie

Scott Luke Louwagie

John Paul Meyer

Andrew Jon Miller

Heather Maureen O'Reilly

Laura Marie Ozmun

Eric Michael Pederson

Shawn Isadore Peltier

Melissa Emmerson-Reed

Maria Christina Rivas

Monica Duarte Santos

Carol Mae Schwartz

Jason Steven Stensrud

Kristin Ann Sumerfelt

Joy Ann VanLerberghe

Class of 1992

Juan Pablo Arroyo

Diana Crystal Baxter

Michelle Marie Bode

Sandy Jean Bossuyt

Angela Marjorie Caron

Justin Alan Dosdall

Jessica Dayle Engen

Nathan Scott Gillispie

Stacy Ann Haneca

Trudi Ann Hanson

Cory Jay Hubbard

Robbin Sue Knutson

Daryl Jon Kor

Shane William Kroger

Matthew Merle Lenz

Christopher Dale Long

Darin David Louwagie

Daryl Lee Louwagie

Jason Mark Louwagie

Lori Marie Louwagie

Brenda Kay Mahn

Maki Matsumoto

Michael Bruce Meier

April Naomi Meyer

Rhonda Sue Meyer

Jonathan Edward Mohn

Daniel Larry Neuman

Jason Lawrence Neuman

Jennifer Jo Pederson

Susan Marie Pederson

Quinn Patrick Peltier

Travis Wade Peterson

Wiley Conrad Post

Jon Paul Pringle

Leslie Eric Sander

Amy Beth Schmidt

Melissa Dawn Schueler

Amy Kay Slettedahl

Shelly Anne Timm

Sara Ann Timmerman

Sherrie Ann VanUden

Jeremy Jerome Varpness

Gordon Dean Vizecky

Barry Dean Wambeke

Class of 1993

Shanda Charmaine Baune

Michelle Dawn Berres

Amy Marie Bitker

Jill Marie Bortnem

Jill Ann Bot

Brenda Jo Justina Devereaux

Adam Edward Eckstrom

Mitchell Alan Gabbert

Christopher John Gniffke

Amy Marie Golberg

Rachelle JaLae Hagen

Warren David Klein

Brett Raymond Knudson

Bradly Sid Kompelien

Darrin Stanley Kompelien

Robin Joy Kosen

Joyell Faith Kroger

Daniel Joseph Loe

Chris John Louwagie

Curtis Ronald Louwagie

Lewis Oscar Louwagie

Luke Oscar Louwagie

Renae Rose Louwagie

Sheri Marie Louwagie

Jay William Magnuson

Thomas Edward Milner

April Ann Neville

Troy Ryan Nordaune

Rodney James Okeson

Sondra Lee Ozmun

Dawn Renee Persoon

Chastity Lynn Post

Jonathan Verlin Scheer

Amy Lynn Schmidt

Jeffrey Rae Schmidt

Linda Sjodin

Rikki Lee Slettedahl

Ann Margaret Van Maldeghem

Class of 1994

Luke Dixon Anderson

Kevin Michael Bahn

Tim Ryan Bahn

Nicole Lynn Bockelman

Barbara Ann Bossuyt

Shawna Lea Braun

Sarah Charlene Breyfogle

Daniel Paul Busack

Kelly Joanne Caron

Fay Pauline Dacey

Anna Moon Sun Eiler

Ryan Shane Fenger

Stephanie Marie Fischer

Wesley Dennis Grannes

Eric Bradley Grieger

Jessica Leah Hagen

Scott Lee Hall

Brandi Lee Hansen

Tory Jonelle Hansen

Daniel Robert Haugen

Matthew Carl Imes

Greg Allen Jeseritz

Kimberly Sue Knutson

Heather Jo Kissner

Leland Joel Krumrey

Mark Andrew Lancaster

Joseph Lawrence Langer

Mason Mac Loke

Byron Lee Louwagie

Eric John Louwagie

Rebecca Joy Louwagie

Wesley Mark Louwagie

David Michael Mensink

Vicki Lee Netjes

Rebecca Jan Olson

Todd Douglas Olson

Jarrod Ballard Pederson

Joseph William Phinney

Kari Ann M. Pringle

Nathan Eric Emmerson-Reed

Jessica Lea Stensrud

Chad Jeffrey Timm

Cheri Ann Timm

Chad Melvin Torke

Melissa Junette Torke

Chad Thomas VanLerberghe

Ryan Robert Viaene

Steven Andrew Viaene

Michelle Marie Vizecky

Jonathan Jay Wolff

Class of 1995

Annalisa Jane Baumgard

Summer Ann Blomme

Kyle Marc Boe

Jeffrey John Boehne

Jamie Lee Boerboom

Wade Jeseritz Breyfogle

Cory Steven Brockman

Sarah Judith Corder

Emily Jane Cole

Jessica Lee Doom

Jessica Christine Fauteck

Crystal Rae Grannes

Chad Thomas Gregoire

Ryan Lee Hagelstrom

Benjamin Dale Hinz

Michael Scott Hinz

Holly Ann Knutson

Jennifer Ruth Lenz

Paul Nathan Loe

Mark Edwin Loe

Timothy Ryan Loe

Chuck Matthew Louwagie

Jessica Marie Louwagie

Kent Michael Louwagie

Rick Marvin Louwagie

Hazel Marie Matthys

Mark Jason Meier

Michelle Ann Milbradt

Matthew Samuel Mohn

David Ray Neuman

Kristin Ann Rigge

Jamie Paul Slettedahl

Shelly Kay Timm

Eric Andrew Timmerman

Nicole Lynn Van De Veire

Tara Jo VanMaldeghem

Michelle Rosalind Varpness

Jason Allen Wrege

Class of 1996

Kevin Eric Allex

Penny Ellen Anderson

Bjorn Erik Axdahl Arneson

Steven Curtis Bahn

Stacey Kay Bitker

Brian Robert Bode

Staci Lee Brockman

Ina Vel Brusven

Benjamin Christian Dahl

Jason John Danielson

Christine Denise Devereaux

Kelly Marie Devereaux

Siver William Erickson

Jeffrey Charles Fischer

Roxanne Lynn Gee

Aaric Norman Geihl

Joshua Adam Grieger

Gabriela Gutierrez

Steven Robert Hall

Jesse Eric Hoff

Tyler Joseph Juhl

Shannon May Knutson

Gina Elizabeth Kosen

Noelle Delight Lancaster

Jacqueline Jean Louwagie

Wendy Joy Louwagie

Cory Frank Magnuson

Melinda Rose Mohn

Tammy Ann Okeson

David Bradley Parsons

Marita Pedersen

Scott David Pederson

Michelle Delia Peppersack

Ryan Matthew Persoon

Shawna Jone Peterson

Angela Beth Phinney

Michael James Prowatzke

James Thomas Schmidt

Michael Thomas Schuttler

Bruce David Slettedahl

Laura Lee Thompson

Craig Albert Timmerman

Erin Marie Timmerman

Jason David Torke

Kari Undheim

Tabitha Rose VanLerberghe

Shannon Rae VanUden

Marla Jean Wambeke

Daniel James Wrege

Class of 1997

Brandi Jo Aker

Chad Andrew Beckler

Jacquelyn Leah Bednarek

Tanna Marie Benson

Sarah Jean Blomme

Ryan Dean Bortnem

John Paul Caron

David Alan Dahl

Jeremy Douglas DeGier

Timothy Carl Fischer

Courtney Karen Geihl

Jon Patrick Gregoire

Nathan Martin Hagen

Joshua Steven Hawkinson

Rachel Carol Hinz

Angela Marie Hoff

Jennifer Ann Hoff

Shane Adam Hubbard

Jeramiah Jon Javens

Jill Louise Jenkins

Sarah Marie Jenkins

Benjamin Thomas Knight Jensen

Tracey Marie Kissner

James Anthony Kroger

Shane Michael Laleman

Casey Joe Long

Kerry Steven Louwagie

Phillip Daniel Louwagie

Melissa May Meier

Bridget Anna Moore

Sean Michael O'Reilly

Christi Ann Olson

Natalie Rose Ozmun

Colin Wayne Peltier

Mathew Robert Peppersack

Pamela Jean Phinney

Wendy Suzann Rialson

Jonathon Louis Schmidt

Joseph Andrew Schueler

Mindy Lou Van De Veire

Kay Renae VanMaldeghem

Class of 1998

Angelique Alm

David Anderson

Megan Anderson

Hans Arneson

Alynn Baumgard

Jeremy Bjornebo

Heather Boklep

Kari Bortnem

Richard Cole

Joel Dahl

Laura Devereaux

Lisa DeVlieger

Shawn Dieken

Chris Erickson

Justin Erickson

Allison Fischer

Brandon Grieger

Heidi Harris

Aaron Hess

Sarah Hubbard

Adam Isaackson

Jessica Isaackson

Nicholas Jackson

Blair Jones

Jennifer Laleman

Maria Langer

Jennifer Louwagie

Kelly Martin

Hector Matthys

Krystal Mohn

Jeremiah Munson

Alissa Olson

Tanya Ricke

Joshua Scheer

Heather Schmidt

Jeremy Schwisow

Kyle Thompson

Jason Timmerman

Lisa Van Overbeke

Mark Vizecky

Stephanie Javens

(classmate until her death)

Class of 1999

Adam Balding

Steven Bednarek

Michael Bendix

Becky Bitker

Katie Dahl

Bonnie Ellingson

Kyle Fauteck

Hannah Galbraith

Jason Gee

Joshua Girard

Amber Gniffke

Tara Hansen

Marie Hawkinson

Matthew Hoepner

Bryn Jarcho

Derek Jensen

Brandon Jeseritz

Rachel Jeseritz

Corey Juhl

Heather Kelm

Aaron Louwagie

Lacey Louwagie

Mindy Louwagie

Eric Mack

Hazel Mohn

Jason Moonen

Mathew Okeson

Travis Olson

Joshua Onken

Brian Phinney

Alicia Reynolds

Stephanie Rosenau

Tom Rutledge

Mica Schaffran

Andrew Schmidt

Bryan Schrupp

Michelle Schrupp

Carrie Van Overbeke

Blake Vermaat

Delilah Wiesen

Class of 2000

Patrick William Bednarek

Sheila Anne Bengtson

Troy Jonathon Benson

Travis Shane Bockelman

Derik Brian Brewers

Christopher Lee Brown

Megan Sue Busiahn

Tiffany Rai Christensen

Andrew Jeffrey Dahl

Beth Kristen Drager

Katrina Lynn Erickson

Paul Steven Erickson

Dustin Anthony Hagen

Dustin Robert Hanson

Kristen Elizabeth Hoff

David Joel Hokanson

Emmy Anne Isaackson

Damian Marty Javens

Eric Therold Johnson

Brittny Anna Jones

Brent William Kelm

Amber Nicole Kissner

Brittany Kay Knutson

Jessica Rae Knutson

Shaun Gordon Knutson

Lance Matthew Kolhei

Justin Jack Kroger

Adam Wayne Laleman

Ida Elsie Matthys

Janine Jaclyn Milbradt

Andrea Beth Morken

Joshua James Munson

Ryan Scott Naab

Chad Jacob Olson

Zebulon Edward Prairie

Kristi Marie Qunell

Jeremy Ryan Runholt

Brandy Jo Schuttler

Jeremiah Joseph Sumerfelt

Daryn Ross Thompson

Jennifer Lynn Thompson

Christopher Adam Timm

Stacy Lynn Timm

Andrae Trevino

Jinny Dee VanMaldeghem

Class of 2001

Ingrid Christina Arneson

Taylor Michael Benson

Justin Mark Bjornebo

Eric Steven Boerboom

Shalesha Renae Braun

Dennison Drew Brower

Amanda Markell Carlson

Nathan Daniel Cole

Derek John Dahl

Joshuan Gordon Dahl

Steven Francis Devereaux

Erica Jean Dieken

Evan Anthony Doom

Kari DeAnne Eilders

Carrie Anne Erickson

Katie Leigh Fruin

Erin Lynn Galbraith

Nicholas Brady Girard

Christine Noel Gniffke

Dominick James Gregoire

Sean Patrick Hagen

Brent Brien Hansen

Darin B. Hinckley

Heidi Jo Hoepner

Heather June Isaackson

Melanie Carol Jeseritz

Samuel Paul Kremin

Phillip Taylor Lancaster

Ryan Daniel Lange

Teresa Bridget Langer

Stacy Ann Lessman

Emily Rae Long

Amber Jean Louwagie

Kristi Ann Louwagie

Mitchell Sterling McKee

Carmen Marie Mead

Lisa Jean Michalscheck

Jason Eric Munson

Sadie JoAnne Munson

Tamera Jean Nordaune

Tara Kristine Olson

Micah James Peppersack

Christopher Kyle Pesch

Melissa Kay Phinney

Melia Rae Prairie

Corey Dean Rigge

Stacey Jean Schrupp

Benjamin James Schultz

Amanda Marie Sumerfelt

Emily Joy Torke

Mitchell Ryan VanHeuveln

Dustin Bradley VanLerberghe

Susan Kay Viaene

Emily Jane Weidauer

Julianna Marie Wingate

Class of 2002

Margo Anderson

Callista Alm

Tony Bednarek

Jami Brockman

Nikki Darwin

Briana Drager

Ben Elston

Jesse Harris

Quenten Hoehne

Megan Jeseritz

Chad Johnson

Lance Jones

Sarah Kelm

Crystal Kerkvliet

Mandy Kerkvliet

Taylor Kroger

Erin Lange

Kimberly Louwagie

Perry Louwagie

Andrew Mack

Adam Maker

Jeremy Mead

Justin Meyer

Randy Moonen

Jesse Naab

Justin Nelson

Aaron Onken

Brent Padfield

Joel Pine

Katie Qunell

Braden Rosa

Lacey Schmidt

Cassie Schmitt

Kelsi Schultz

Anita Sharkey

Justin Sheets

Levi Shemon

Tami Thompson

Albin Trutna

Desiree Wiesen

Emily Wabeke

Scott Woodbeck

Class of 2003

Robyn Frances Lyn Alu

Chad Darryl Anderson

Christopher Lee Bahn

Roosmarijn Bakker

Benjamin Robert Bentzlin

Russell Emil Bitker

Jennifer Rose Bjornebo

Jacob Allen Busiahn

Alissa Marie Carlson

Aaron James Dahl

Wade David DeVlieger

Andrew Jacob Doom

Bryce Bernard Doom

Aaron Michael Eash

Thomas Kim Falkum

Zachary Kyle Geistfeld

Emily Elizabeth Goodell

Jacob Raymond Gregoire

Laci Lynn Haak

Erin Lynn Hauge

Valerie Marie Hedin

Joshua Michael Helgeson

Joanna Joy Hokanson

Thomas Herbert House

Stephanie Kay Huso

Samantha Jo Javens

Brenton Joseph Johnson

Kristopher Michael Knutson

Tyler Douglas Laleman

Maria Theresa Louwagie

Shawn David Louwagie

Eric Lance Morken

Andrew Joseph Neville

Kassondra Jo Nordmeyer

Denton LeRoy Olson

Jasmine Marie Pine

Adam Daniel Rigge

Ethan David Roe

Cody Lee Runholt

Danielle Marie Schwerin

Codi Charles Shemon

Nathaniel Robert Smith

Shane Douglas Specht

Garret Thomas Thompson

Travis Patrick Timmerman

Jonathan David Vandelanotte

Dustin Duane Warnke

Lee Andrew Weidauer

Dallas Marie Willman

Elsa Christina Zavala

Class of 2004

Tyler Alan Anderson

Stephanie Joy Bahn

Joshua John Bertrand

Heather Emily Bitker

Brittney Ann Boecker

Angela Lea Bonczek

Brandon Justin Bossuyt

Matthew Romain Dahl

Kelsey Marie Dieken

Cody Ray Doom

Sarah Christine Elston

Emily Anne Erickson

Alicia Marie Fjeldheim

Wayne Michael Fjoseide

Erik Steven Gniffke

Ashley Krista Hansen
Anthony James Isaackson
Daniel Glen Isaackson
Brett Gerald Jasperson
Luke David Jeseritz
Tyler Andrew Jeseritz
Jonathan Keith Knutson
Trista Ann Knutson
Candice Rose Kolhei
Katie Ann Kremin
Keisha Lane Kurtzbein
Nathan Terry Lange
Derek Joseph Louwagie
Justin Leonard Louwagie
Krystl Rae Louwagie
Beth Ann Matthys
Jeffery Allen Meier
Ashley Kay Meyer
Tyler Jordan Meyer
Katherine Jo Lynn Muehler
Kenneth Wayne Pesch
Brandon Paul Renken
Michael Scott Rye
Mali Jane Schaffran
Jamie Lee Sheets
Scott Stephan Stefansen
Abby Beth Vandelanotte
Amber Joy VanLerberghe
Jacob A. Warren
Davin David Wiesen
Sean Anthony Woodbeck

Class of 2005

Michael James Bakker
Adam William Carl Blake
Ella Ann Bresson
Eric Richard Dingwall
Benjamin Bruce Drager
Kim Susanne Einerson
Kassidi Robert Fiegen
Jessica Jean Frank
Michael Randy Galbraith
Brooke Jean Geistfeld
Grant Richard Hagen
Bryce Jacob Hansen
Andrew Peter Hellie
Allisa Nicole Hoehne
Kimberly Jo House
Tyler Clinton Isaackson
Tessa Rae Johnson
Robert Allen Johnston
Mally Jo Kerkvliet
Angela Mary Louwagie
Dustin Steven Louwagie
Heidi Jo Louwagie
Kelli Ann Louwagie
Cody James Martin
Samantha Lynn Meyer
Travis Orlean Naab
Evan Lee Paskach
Brian Derek Pehrson
Macon John Peppersack
Brett Alan Pequin
Amanda Jean Redetzke
Tyson Doom Rosa

Kathleen Michelle Rutledge

Megan Ann Schmidt

Richard Howard Schultz

Cindy Rose Sheets

Ciji Rose Shemon

Kody Raymond Smith

Jeremy Gaspard Vandelanotte

Whitney Mae Vandelanotte

Matthew Bryan VanHeuveln

Chelsie Kay Viessman

Class of 2006

Tanner Steven Alm

Terrance Rodney Alm

Shanna Michelle Bahn

Logan David Blake

Jared Gregory Bossuyt

Joshua Paul Brusven

Alyssa Jane Doom

Megan Lee Elston

Cody John Fruin

Randell Jay Girard

Daryl Theodore Gregoire

Sarah Michelle Haak

Cameron Jesse Hauge

Taylor Wescott Hay

Timothy Matthew Helgeson

Alicia Jo Hoff

Lee Thorbjorn Huso

Dana Mae Janachovsky

Christopher Robert Jasperson

Benjamin Joseph Koetters

Misty Lee Kuyper

Courtney Ann Lange

Leiah Joy Louwagie

Robyn Marie Matthys

Heather Lee Meier

Anita Grace Olson

Colby William Post

Zachery Mailen Pringle

Bryce David Renken

Tony Jay Rialson

Abby Jo Schmidt

James Paul Sharkey

Miranda Jo Specht

Kristen Morgan Swope

Bayli Ann Vandelanotte

Kevin Alan VanOverbeke

Jameson John Vermaat

Danielle Lynn Warrick

Derby Joseph Wiesen

Angela Kaye Yahnka

Luke Benjamin Yost

Edgar Andres Zuniga

Class of 2007

Liesl Christine Bahn

Joseph Ray Becker

Sarah Louise Bertrand

Tiffany Elizabeth Boecker

Parry Jared Bossuyt

Keith Richard Brewers

Easton Arvid Doom

Justin Steven Doom

Kendall Leona Doom

Dana Lee Erickson

Karissa Rose Fiegen

Andrew Paul Frank

Jamie Lee Gniffke

Ryan Todd Gniffke

Derek Andrew Golberg

Tonya Lynn Hall

Derek Johan Hansen

Corey Lee Heidebrink

John Daniel Hokanson

Kayla Jean House

Marty Daniel Javens

Joseph Camiel Labat

Tegan Marie Laleman

Gina Marie Louwagie

Zachary Dane Meyer

Brandon Alan Milner

Ashley Ann Morken

Sean Robert Paskach

Alissa Rae Pehrson

Aaron Scott Peterson

Kimberly Ashley Ramos

Austin Russell Rigge

Erica Kristin Roe

Desiree Nicole Schwerin

Ashley Rae Simon

Nicole Rae Sinclair

Joshua Earl Smith

Kristel Steeds

Desiree Maree Tanke

Chase Ian Thompson

Kara Jean Thompson

Caitlin Arlene Vermaat

Shara Kay Weckwerth

Brandon Shane Wee

Class of 2008

Brittany Autumn Anderson

Jeremy Justin Bahn

Joseph Dwayne Bakker

Jeremie James Blondin

Ripley Karen Bresson

Christopher Lowell Dahl

Roisin Lynn Duffy-Gideon

Sheldon Carl Evers

Blake Alan Geistfeld

Torey Jacob Golberg

Rebecca Denise Gregoire

Michelle Catherine Hagen

Steven Richard Heairet

Kaitlin Joy Hellie

Andria Jean Hinz

Karissa Lynne Hyatt

Carl John Janachovsky

Kendra Jade Johnson

Bailey Rose Kissner

Shane Montgomery Kosen

Erin Kate Kroger

Rebecca Kay Krumrey

Brittany Lynn Kurtenbach

Lexie Rae Louwagie

Cory Dean Madison

Sarah Lynn Mauland

Natasha Janice Nordmeyer

Jessica Maria Otts

Christopher Arthur Pequin

Joshua Duane Ramos

Taryn Rae Rosa

Anthony William Ross

Tanya Ann Runholt

Ashley Lynne Schlemmer

Benjamin Jeremiah Schwarz

Brittany Amanda Torgerson

Jance Jerome Vandelanotte

Sara Ellen Vandelanotte

Jessica Marie Wagner

Maria Clara Wilhelm

Derek Edward Willman

Drew Steven Zachow

Class of 2009

Tanner Dean Anderson

Shelby Kristen Bahn

Christopher Brian Bakker

Benjamin Phillip John Blake

Brianne Renae Brusven

Tyler Joseph Dale

Camille Beverly Doom

Dylan Christian Fenger

Dakota Louis Fiene

Lisa Marie Frank

Nathan Jacob Girard

Andrew Raymond Glenn

Chelsey Lynn Gniffke

Alesha Anna Hansen

Kelsey Jo Helgeson

Joshua Virgil Hoff

Analisa Shae Jaspersen

Megan Joy Kremin

Kirsty Lynn Kussatz

Jeremy John Labat

Gavin Tyler Laleman

Kevin Leon Louwagie

Ryan Jonathan Mosch

Mackenzie Jae Nelson

Anna Elizabeth Olson

Isaac Ordell Pehrson

Lisa Erin Petersen

Tyler Daniel Peterson

Katherine Elizabeth Polman

Kyle Jon Redetzke

Alissa Dawn Ricke

Jennifer Ann Rye

Curtis Lee Rykhus

Ethan Kirk Schlemmer

Cody Randall Schmidt

Heidi Marie Sinclair

Miles Nelson Taylor

Kenneth Albert Thompson

Derek Allen Timm

Samantha Kay VanAcker

Morgan Ashley Wee

Matthew Beatty Yahnka

Adriana Zuniga

Class of 2010

Kenneth Michael Becker

Nicholas Raymond Blondin

Dana Elizabeth Boerboom

Joseph Robert Boerboom

Benjamin Justin Bossuyt

Adam Christian Brewers

Kayla Renae Buysse

Carly Christina Doom

Winston Heim Doom

Gavan William Duffy Gideon

Jason Michael Dutcher

Aimee Lynn Falkum

Brandi Diane Geihl

Chase Patrick Geistfeld

Kayla Amber Golberg

Emily June Haak

Keely Jordan Huso

Jose Alberto Jacinto

Dustin Curtis Jones

Kirstan Anne Koetters

Nicholas Jay Kosen

Ryan Douglas Kurtenbach

Levi James Kuyper

Andrew Gene Loken

Tessa LaRae Martin

Chelsey Joy Meyer

Christina Marlene Olson

Sean Todd Pickthorn

Matthew Peter Renken

Brandon Dean Renneke

Maisie Mae Renneke

Trisha Marie Rykhus

Taylor Gregory Schmidt

Jacob Alan Schwarz

Dana Jean Schwerin

Laura Marie Streich

Jesse Harold Timm

Cory Andrew Timmerman

Jessina Marie VanUden

Class of 2011

Ariana Lee Anderson

Jory Gregory Bossuyt

Brady Jordan Enstad

Maverick Roy Fiene

Stetson Steven Herigon

Brandon James Hyatt

Shane Andrew Klein

Parker Daniel Koetters

Caden Mark Laleman

Cassidy Marie Laleman

Gage Daniel Larsen

Ta'Mara Ann Larsen

Bridgette Ann Louwagie

Tristin Marie Louwagie

Nathan Lee Mauland

Steven Jeffrey Meyer

Kaleb Andrew Neu

Bailee Myrtle Olson

Alex Jon Pehrson

Cody David Rykhus

Tami Marie Schmidt

Molly Elizabeth Sinclair

Braden Parker Timm

Derek David Varpness

Samuel Thomas Weston

Class of 2012

Isaac Lee Anderson

Daniel Scott Bakker

Makala Diane Barker

Sarah Lynn Berg

Allison Rae Boehne

Jordan Taylor Breyfogle

Ashlee Marie Busack

Victor Manuel Cerda

Noah Nelson Dovre

Samuel Robert Fenger

Mickel Catherine Goepferich

Jeremy Logan Haack

Bryce Robert Hansen

Daniel James Harraghy

Sydney Marie Horner

Samantha Jane Huizenga

Zachary Taylor Hyatt

Ty Andrew Klocow

Jean Mary Knutson

Tanner Jo Kosen

Kade Michael Lee

Kari Lynn Louwagie

Nicole Ginny Louwagie

Alyssa Jean Lund

Teena Hanna Mattison

Derek Wesley Naab

Shelby Lynn Ness

Erik Richard Nordmeyer

Laura Jean Olson

Lyndsey Renee Peterson

Shawn Michael Polman

Meagan Rose Ramos

Brian Robert Ricke

Cody Devereaux Sleiter

Michael Allen Lee Sowards

Brady Lee St. Aubin

June Elizabeth Stensrud

Melissa Ann Streich

Emily Lauren Swenson

Amber Kristen Taylor

Courtney Renae Taylor

Tyler Knute Thompson

Angela Joy Timm

Jamie Ray Unke

Matthew John VanMoer

Erica Lynn Wagner

Katelyn Rachel Wandersee

Stephanie Nicole Werner

Class of 2013

Kayla Joy Anderson

Alisha Bahma

Kyle Dean Berg

Allison Paige Boerboom

Zack Arthur DuFrane

Quinn Crouse Fenger

Christopher Anthony Hand

Kacie Ann Hartle

Chelsey Jean Johnson

Lydia Rose Johnson

Brody Adam Louwagie

Tyler Jacob Lange

Derek David Larsen

Spencer John Larsen

Jacob Dale Louwagie

Paul Ryan Louwagie

Randy Lee Louwagie

Andrew Lewis Lovsness

Brayden Arthur Meier

Mallory Lynn Meyer

Brandon Roger Moody

Joshua David Myrvik

Hope Krysten Neu

Alicia Suzanne Popowski

Yacqueline Ramirez

Wyatt Edwin Schuster

Steven Lemont Timm

Tegan Jean VanMoer

Lukas Vandelanotte

Justin Stacy Varpness

Damien Keith Wallin

Corbyn Alexandra Wee

Simon James Zwaschka

Reed Stevens and Jesse Javens

(classmates until their deaths)

Lakeview School Bus Crash: February 19, 2008

On the top of a page of a special edition of the Feb. 20, 2008, Marshall Independent, a full-color photo showed a group of Cottonwood firefighters, dressed in their turn-out gear, three of them sitting on the grassy shoulder along state Highway 23. The photo captured the firefighters in a moment of exhaustion, hands on their knees, and perhaps a moment of reflection, too, trying to make sense of one of the most momentous, most bitter and most heartbreaking days in Cottonwood history.

The double-deck headline on the front page of the Independent's special section read "Lakeview's Day of Sorrow." The newspaper's lead story reported that when he was asked at a news conference what the community could do, Cottonwood Fire Chief Dale Louwagie replied simply, "Pray."

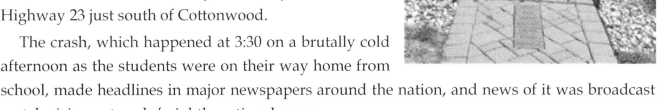

• • •

Four Lakeview Public School students were killed Feb. 19, 2008, and several more students were injured when the school bus they were riding in was struck by a van at the intersection of Lyon County Road 24 and Highway 23 just south of Cottonwood.

The crash, which happened at 3:30 on a brutally cold afternoon as the students were on their way home from school, made headlines in major newspapers around the nation, and news of it was broadcast on television networks' nightly national news.

In the days afterward, there was a massive local, regional and national outpouring of grief and support for Cottonwood, the Lakeview schools and families of the students. Several thousand cupcakes were made for one funeral, so many that the leftovers had to be handed out for mourners to take home. A school in Huntsville, Alabama, sent flowers to the Lakeview school, where the commons area began to overflow with cards, flowers, and other tributes.

The four children who died were: brothers Jesse Javens, 13, and Hunter Javens, 9, the sons of Marty and Rita Javens. Reed Stevens, 12, the son of Daniel and Kandi Stevens. And Emilee Olson, 9, the daughter of Charlie and Traci Olson.

They were among 28 students on the bus. At least 17 other people were hurt, including students, the driver of the van and the driver of a passing pickup truck, who was pinned when the bus rolled partway on top of his truck.

"I lost a lot of innocence that day. This is the kind of thing that isn't supposed to happen," Cottonwood Heidi Beck, a community member and business owner, told the Marshall Independent on the one-year anniversary of the crash. "There was no time to say goodbye. This wasn't where there was a transition time to support the family through an illness. It was (so quick), and they were gone."

• • •

Motorists who came upon the scene on Highway 23 helped bus driver Dennis Devereaux evacuate children from the wrecked bus, passing them to other motorists into the warmth of their cars until rescue workers arrived. Along with the Cottonwood Fire Department and Cottonwood Ambulance Service, units from more than 20 different emergency agencies — including those from neighboring towns, the State Patrol, and North Memorial's air-care — responded to the crash scene, according to the United States Department of Education.

Emilee Olson's funeral was held at Christ Lutheran Church, where her 4-H show horse stood watch outside and a crowd that filled the sanctuary, and rooms in the basement and upstairs of the church mourned inside.

Funerals for Reed Stevens and Hunter and Jesse Javens were held in the school.

Gov. Tim Pawlenty issued a statement calling it "a sad night for Minnesota."

"It is especially heartbreaking when young lives are lost," he said. "Our thoughts and prayers are with the families of those who were killed or injured in this tragic accident."

Interim Lakeview School District Superintendent Sheldon Johnson said: "We lost four beautiful children, and there's nothing in this world that's more devastating than that," he said.

"One of the strengths of a small community is that we're a close-knit community," he said. "When someone hurts, we all hurt. When someone grieves, we all grieve. And we will all rally around one another. We're at rock-bottom right now. ... But we'll put the pieces back together."

The van that struck the bus blew through a stop sign as it traveled east on County Road 24, sailed over a railroad crossing and punched into the bus. The driver of the van, a Guatemalan woman named Olga Franco del Cid, was determined to have been in the U.S. illegally. Her trial was held in Willmar. She was convicted Aug. 6, 2008, of all 24 criminal counts she faced, including four counts of criminal vehicular homicide, 10 felony counts of criminal vehicular operation, seven counts of gross misdemeanor criminal vehicular operation, a charge of giving a false name and date of birth to a peace officer, a charge of having no Minnesota driver's license, and a stop-sign violation, the Marshall Independent reported. She was sentenced to 12-1/2 years in prison.

Rita Javens and other parents spoke to reporters after Franco was sentenced. "There's just not words that can be said about what she's taken away from us," said Javens. "Our hurt will never end, and she needs to realize that. These were our babies, these were our pride and joy."

A memorial garden was later built on the south side of the Lakeview school grounds, with four benches, one each dedicated to the victims who lost their lives.

Bus driver Dennis Devereaux, James Hancock, the driver of the pickup truck who told rescue workers to care for the children first even though he was seriously injured, and Cottonwood's Fire Department and Ambulance Service were later honored for their bravery and efforts at the crash scene.

One of the other positive aspects to emerge from the tragedy was the recovery of student Derek Varpness, who was on the bus and suffered a broken back, severed kidney, four broken ribs, a bruised lung, and had his spleen removed. Varpness was a freshman who wrestled for the Marshall High School team at the time of the crash. He fought back from his injuries to have a successful wrestling career, passing 100 career victories in his senior season.

• • •

Family and friends of the four children who died have created events and organizations to continue to honor and remember them in the year's after the crash. Reed Stevens' family organized an annual Reed's Run road race each fall. Well-known WCCO-TV news anchor Don Shelby gave a motivational speech to students in November 2011.

On the fourth anniversary of the crash, in 2012, a Journey of Hope Day was organized with events at the school. The Marshall Independent wrote that organizers "thought it would be more fitting to plan an event which allows the entire community the opportunity to celebrate the lives of the fallen students, as well as the progression of healing for others who were injured or affected by the crash on Feb. 19, 2008.

"It's definitely better to see smiles and laughter," said Traci Olson, the mother of Emilee. "It's about remembering them, and remembering them in a good way."

Olson was one of the event organizers who helped put together a full day's worth of activities, including a visit from "Crunch," the Minnesota Timberwolves pro basketball team mascot.

Other memorial activities in the years following the crash included a community-wide supper to thank emergency crews, emotional gatherings at the school to celebrate what would have been birthdays for Emilee Olson, and the formation of the Not4gotten organization by families of the victims. The events and memorials have received funding support from local businesses, service clubs and individual donations.

In the Feb. 25, 2009, issue of the Marshall Independent — a year after the bus crash — the Javens, Olson and Stevens families wrote a letter to the editor that said, in part:

"While words are simply not enough, we want to say thank you to so many people for your continued support, prayers, and generous acts of kindness expressed to our families…"

OUR VETERANS

War and Tragedy Strike Home

The war on terror struck home in many ways for Cottonwood residents, sometimes tragically.

Cheryle Sincock, a sister of Cottonwood resident Rhonda Boe, was killed in the Sept. 11, 2001, terrorist attack on the Pentagon, where she worked.

After the 9/11 attacks, dozens of local National Guards troops were called to active duty as part of a larger regional mobilization of the Guard. Many local troops were deployed overseas, to Iraq, Kuwait or Afghanistan, with some deployed multiple times.

One of those local National Guardsmen, 1st Lt. Jason Timmerman, a 1998 graduate of Lakeview High School, lost his life in a bombing Feb. 21, 2005, in Baghdad, Iraq.

Timmerman, 24, was one of three Minnesota Guardsmen killed in the attack. The other two were Staff Sgt. David Day, of St. Louis Park and Sgt. Jesse Lhotka of Appleton. Eight were wounded.

According to a Minnesota Public Radio, the Defense Department said the three soldiers died at around 8 a.m. Feb. 21, when a roadside bomb detonated while an injured soldier was being cared for. That soldier had been injured in a convoy accident caused by a civilian vehicle, the Defense Department said.

The three soldiers who died were all members of the Montevideo-based 151st Field Artillery, which includes units from Marshall, Olivia, Morris, Ortonville, Appleton, and Madison. About 330 members of the 151st mobilized in the fall of 2004 for a deployment set to last 12 months to 18 months, said Guard spokesman Maj. Kevin Olson.

Timmerman, who worked for a time at North Star Insurance, was a graduate of Dakota State University in Madison, S.D., and had been a teacher in Lake Benton. He was promoted within the Guard, and praised by many — in and out of the Guard — for his leadership skills and potential.

The St. Paul Pioneer Press reported:

"A farm kid, Timmerman was part of the large, close-knit Belgian farming community in southwest Minnesota.

" 'We are a small rural community," said the Rev. Paul Hadusek, the priest at the family's Belgian Catholic Church, St. Clotilde's in nearby Green Valley. "Jason was known, liked and admired by so many. It is a great tragedy."

"On the day after the deaths, the rural lane leading to the farm of his parents, Gary and Pat Timmerman, carried a steady procession of cars as dozens of relatives and friends paid their respects. A flag in the windswept yard flew at half-staff in front of a small display that included an antique plow and a sign that read, 'Support Our Troops.'

"Timmerman's younger brother, Travis, also is a member of the 151st Field Artillery in Iraq."

Timmerman joined the National Guard in 1997, the year before he graduated from high school, said Palmer Anderson, former superintendent of schools in Cottonwood. "He was an exemplary type of student," Anderson said. Timmerman was involved in school activities, including the Future Farmers of America and varsity football, where he was a lineman.

"He was part of a class of students who prided themselves in knowledge and clean competition," Anderson said. "It was an impressive class."

Timmerman's funeral was held March 1, 2005, at Holy Redeemer Catholic Church in Marshall, on a day of big, wet, falling snowflakes that melted and darkened the streets around the church as they landed. The church, designed to hold 1,000 people, ran out of room because the crowd of mourners was so large.

People lined up five deep waiting to get in to the church. Space was even tight in a downstairs overflow room as mourners settled for watching the services on closed-circuit TVs.

Among those who attended his funeral were Minnesota Gov. Tim Pawlenty and Minnesota's two U.S. senators, Mark Dayton and Norm Coleman.

Pawlenty, on his way into the church, said he simply wanted "to express our gratitude" to Timmerman's family, according to the Marshall Independent.

Dayton called Timmerman "a true American hero."

Timmerman was not forgotten as time passed. A street near the Marshall National Guard Armory was renamed in his honor. His Lakeview High School classmates placed a bench in his name on the paved hiking and biking path at the new Lakeview school.

Honor Roll of Veterans Who Have Passed Away

MEXICAN WAR

Iver Nelson, Sr.

CIVIL WAR &
INDIAN WARS, G.A.R.

Hugh Chalmers

Henry Frits-Smith

Knut Kjemhus

Olaus L. Lovsness

R. Harrison Price

Olav S. Reishus

Tobias K. Reishus

Hans Samuelson

D. B. York

CIVIL WAR – C.S.A.

Ole Paulson

SPANISH
-AMERICAN WAR

Sven Bjornli

WORLD WAR I

John Aamodt

Alex Anderson

Archie Anderson

Sylfest Anderson

Virgil Anderson

Julius M. Appelthun

Guy Bacon

Olai Barstad

William Beacom, Jr.

Rudolph Belling

John Berg

Augustus Bisbee

Dr. James Bly

Alfred Brenden

John Broughton

C. Christensen

Christ Christensen

Fritz Christensen

James Clark

Phil Desilet

Dr. Sigfrid Engh

Harris Eng

Willie Evers

Emily Frank

John V. Foley

Clarence Garry

Andrew T. Giffen

Thomas A. Gunderson

Adolph Hall

Clarence A. Hatlestad

William Hatlestad

Anton Hoffman

Peter Hoffman

Andrew Hovde

Lloyd Huddleston

Thor Idland

Carl Isaackson

Melvin Johnson

Dr. Joseph Kise

Alfred Kolhei

Carl John Kolhei

Edwin Loe

Tom Loe

Albert Loken

Oscar Loland

Selmer Loland

Gilbert Ludwig

Oscar Mauland

Iver Melling

Leo Molstad

Einar Ness

Dr. A. F. Nellermoe

Lars Oakland

Carl John Olson-
    Hillenbrand

Jordon Olson

Ralph Olson Sr.

Manuel Osness

Simon O. Post

Orville Reishus

Alf Ristvedt

Dr. John B. Robertson

Asa Robinson

Eddie Roti

Oscar Sandbakken

Henry Schlemmer

Irwin Stellmacher

Dr. Thorfinn
    Tharaldson

William Tragesser

Earl Tyler

Oscar Ueland

Camiel VanLerberghe

Arthur VanOverbeke

Lewis Varpness

John Volkmann

George Weinhold

WORLD WAR II

Leroy Alm

Arvid Anderson

W.E. "Bror" Anderson

Robert Anderson

Marvin Belling

Clinton Berg

Oliver Berg

Sanford Berg

Orvin Bergum

Elmer Berre

Arvid Bjornebo

Edwin Bjornebo

Fritz Bjornebo

Harold Bjornebo

Kenneth Bjornebo

Leif Bjornebo

Rolland Boehne

Walter Boerboom

Harry R. Bouressa

Ernest Brusven

Otto Brockmeyer

Carl Carlson

Kermit Carlson

Stanley Christensen

James Cole

Gordon Colburn

Katherine Colburn

Curtis B. Dahl

Edmon Doom

Morton J. Egeland

Harry A. Eckstrom

Douglas Engum

Glen Ericson

Jewel Ericson

Orin Ericson

Albert G. Espeland

Phillip Fauteck

LaVerne Fenger

Raymond Fenger

Duane Fruin

Howard L. Geihl

Oscar Gjervold

Eugene Giffen

Ray Gigstad

Henry Gniffke

Loris Gniffke

Harold Gredvig

Theodore "Twig"
Gregoire

Sanford Gullickson

Thomas Gunderson

Luvern Hanson

Howard Hanson

Jerome Hatlestad

Charles Hellie

Ivan Hill

John Hirmer

Earl Hoff

Harvey O. Hoff

Joe Hoff, Sr.

Kermit Hoiland

Myron Hoiland

Delbert G. "Bud"
Hostetler

Gordon Isaackson

James "Jim" Isaackson

Robert Jaeger

Wilfred Kockelman

Edwin Johnson

Roy B. Johnson

Virgil Johnson

Kermit Johnson

John Kerkvliet

C.B. "Bud" King

Jerule Kise

Kay Knudson

Arden Kremin

John L. Kroger

Leland Krumrey

John "Rollie" Kufus

Edward L. Larson

Virgil Lee

Nalum Lerstad

Milton Lien

John Lines

Robert Lines

Wayne Lines

Raymond Lohman

Garvin Ludwig

Arvid Lund

Clarence Mohn

John Markell

Morris Maland

Burton Mauland

Orton Mauland

Leslie Maxwell

Orville Michaelson

Corellan Michelson

Orphie Miller

Erling Mossige

Burton Nelson

Kenneth Nelson

Morris Nelson

Newell Nelson

Rudolph Nelson

Rudolph Odden

Clarence Oftedahl

Johnny Oftedahl

Elmer Oullette

Paul O. Pearson

Isadore Peltier

Otto Peppersack

Glen Peterson

Dr. Marvin Perrizo

Robert Pfarr

Sylvester Pfarr

Earl Post

M. Wallace Post

Elwood Pringle

Harold Ree

Orrin Reed

Dale Reishus

Irving Reishus

William Reishus

Orin "Curly" Reishus

John Rewerts

Harvey Rigge

Lowell Scarsett

Harold Schwisow

J. Douglas Smith

James Stevens

Orville Stensrud

Vernon Stensrud

Selmer A. Stokke

James Tague

Wallace O. Timgren

Clarence Tritz

George VandeVoorde

Francis VanOverbeke

Harley Varpness

Raymond G. Varpness

Vernon Varpness

Andrew Viaene

Morris Volden

Ervin "Bud" Volkman

Elmer "Pete" Warnke

Vernon Warnke

Rev. Gerhard Weseloh

Robert Wilson

Clifford Wood

Harold Yahnka

KOREAN CONFLICT

Gordon Anderson

Tennes Anderson

Leonard Buysse

Llewellyn Bahn

James Dahl

Marlin Ekstrom

Donald Gniffke

Harland Hanson

Robert L Hanson

Joe Johnson

Gordon Knutson

William Kremin

Dennis Kroger

Donald Joe Nelson

Robert E. Olson

John Pederson

Donald Rosa

Garry Rosa

Bert Ueland

Kenneth Ueland

Bruce Snyder

William Snyder

Norman Swennes

Virgil Thompson

VIETNAM ACTION

Larry Binnebose

Robert Bockelmann

Del Ray Bruss

Wayne Haglund

Leonard Kompelien

John Krumrey

Steven Lovsness

Jerold Reishus

John VanHeuveln

Thelmar Volden

Eddie VanEidie

Edwin Willhite

Willis Wells

GULF WAR

Todd Berg

IRAQ WAR

Jason Timmerman

DECADES OF CHANGE

Cottonwood Post Office

A story from the <u>October 15, 2003</u>, issue of the Tri-County News in which Linda Magnuson, the postmaster at that time, gave the following history of the Cottonwood Post Office:

Magnuson shared its history, which may have been compiled by Mrs. George (Vivian Kelly) Koelz and Gordon T. Colburn. The following is what they wrote, with an update made possible by Margaret Rewerts, a former Cottonwood postmaster.

In the early 1870s mail was brought to our area from Redwood Falls by way of the old town of Yellow Medicine City. From there, it was carried to the Silliards' (now the Harland Sharkey farm) west of Hanley Falls, on to Vineland (the present Kermit and Marvin Johnson farm) three miles north and three miles west of Cottonwood, then to Stavanger (Berre farm), from there to Brenna in Vallers Township (Rolly Lovsness farm) and finally to Marshall. The mail was carried back over the same route.

It arrived at the offices once a week each way and served the people of the area for 16 years. Vineland Post Office, which went out of existence, had the following postmasters: O.S. Reishus (1873-1875), Ole E. Annetti (1875-1878), Sondre Reishus (1878-1886) and Ingeborg O. Reishus (1886-1889).

The Stavanger Post Office had the following postmasters: O.O. Lende, C.J. Bratberg, Rier Swenson, and John P. Berre. The Brenna Post Office had two postmasters: Ole Brenna Sr., and Mrs. Sterk.

When the Great Northern Railroad was constructed (1888), Cottonwood was founded. Vineland Post Office was moved to Cottonwood by Ingeborg O. Reishus. She opened a Book and Stationery Store in connection with the post office.

Christian H. Dahl was appointed on Feb. 15, 1889, to replace Ingeborg Reishus as postmaster. The office was located on the same spot as what became the Huso Fairway Store. This was a two-story frame building with a grocery store and post office downstairs and living quarters above. This building was erected by Christian and Jacob Dahl, who were local contractors in the building business.

207

In November 1890, Jacob Dahl was appointed postmaster and served until October 1894. On Oct. 5, 1894, John Michie became postmaster and held the position for four years. Later, John Michie went into the hardware business in the same building that later housed Nelson Hardware. William D. Lovelace became postmaster in December 1898. He was also editor of the Cottonwood newspaper and the post office was moved into the print shop where Mrs. Fred McLennan (Bessie Reishus) set type by hand. Miss Libbie Mero was the assistant in the Post Office.

In 1903, the first rural route was established with Lars Rassmussen as the first carrier. About this time, the St. Paul Dispatch canvassed the rural area with this attractive offer: A free mail box with each subscription. Many of these boxes were in use until the last few years.

Sarah Dahl became the second postmistress in April 1905. She had purchased the Charles Aamodt building. The Post Office was downstairs and she lived upstairs. She was assisted by her daughters, Selma (Mrs. E.A. Schilling), Hilda (Mrs. Hacket), Mable (Mrs. Sisson) and son, Clarence.

In March 1907, J.V. Kelly took over the rural route. For the first number of years, he drove horses. He will be remembered for his fine, well-trained horses. On cold winter days, he would use a heated soapstone under his feet; covered with a robe, this heat would last for a long time. J.V.'s co-workers remember and comment on his remarkable speed and accuracy in sorting mail.

About this time, Route 2 was established. Richard Napier was the carrier. One of his favorite expressions was, "Who in the world is Gene Del? (General Delivery)!"

In August of 1915, Ernest A. Schilling was appointed postmaster. Gertrude Bly (Mrs. Ludwig Dahl) was his assistant. Upon her resignation, Orion Melvold became the assistant postmaster. Mable Johnson (Mrs. Wilder) also worked in the Post Office. During the 18 years that Mr. Schilling was postmaster, the office was located in three different places. First in the Aamodt building, then across the street from Beth's Variety Store and then to the corner building that became known as the Red Owl store.

Mr. Napier resigned as carrier of Route 2 about 1920. Harry Stephens served this route until the position was filled by J.V. Foley in September of 1921.

Alexander Kolhei replaced Ernest Schilling as postmaster in December of 1933. The office was then moved across the street to its present location. Alex will always be remembered as one the greatest baseball players that Cottonwood ever produced. After Alex passed away, his wife, Evelyn, was appointed the third postmistress in December 1941.

Sanford Gullickson, who started as assistant postmaster in July of 1937, enlisted in the Navy in December of 1942. His position was filled by H.G. Johnson.

J.V. Kelly retired in October of 1943, having served Route 1 faithfully for 36 years. Wayne Peterson took over as temporary carrier until September of 1944 when the two routes were consolidated. J.V. Foley was the carrier for the consolidated route.

In 1945, the Post Office was advanced from third class to second class. Mrs. J.V. Foley was appointed clerk.

H.G. (Jimmy) Johnson retired in 1952. Sandy Gullickson resumed as assistant postmaster. Mrs. J.V. Foley also retired in 1952. She was replaced by Selma Rosvold. J.V. Foley, having served the rural routes for 31 years, also retired in 1952. His first car was a Model T Ford. He drove Ford cars all through the years owned more than 30 in all. He also used horses in the winter and when the roads were muddy. One incident that he would always remember was that, after shoveling out his team of horses from a snow bank, both horses were on the same side of the tongue.

Correlan Michelson transferred from Hanley Falls, replacing Foley on the rural route. On his sudden death in 1957, the route was served by James Cole. The routes were again made into Route 1 with James Cole as the carrier and Route 2 with Gordon Colburn as the carrier.

In 1959, Evelyn Kolhei passed away and Sanford B. Gullickson replaced her as postmaster. Also in 1959, Selma Rosvold resigned and Mildred Wilson filled this vacancy.

Donald Juhl was postmaster from March 1961 to November 1962.

M. Wallace Post was appointed in 1962.

The names dates of the postmasters to this date were taken from the official records of the post office in Washington D.C., and written up by Mrs. George (Vivian Kelly) Koelz and Gordon T. Colburn.

Margaret Rewerts was sworn into the position of Cottonwood postmaster on June 7, 1975, upon the retirement of M. Wallace Post. She served until Linda Magnuson took over on Oct. 19, 1991. Both Rewerts and Magnuson are Cottonwood natives, born and raised here before serving their home town in the postmaster role.

When Magnuson retired, Michele Paskewitz became the new postmaster on April 2, 2005.

"The records of the Post Office Department in our custody show that the Post Office at Cottonwood, Minnesota, was established as Vineland, Yellow Medicine County, on Feb. 10, 1873, with O.P. Reishus as its first postmaster. Its name was changed to Cottonwood Post Office on October 5, 1888." So stated the listing of the postmasters from Washington.

Cottonwood Post Office

Cottonwood, Minnesota, 56229

Postmasters	Dates of Appointment
O.P. Reishus	Feb. 10, 1873
Ole E. Annetti	April 8, 1875
Sondre Reishus	May 16, 1878
Ingeborg O. Reishus	Nov. 9, 1886
Christ H. Dahl	Feb. 15, 1889
Jacob H. Dahl	Nov. 21, 1890
John Michie	Oct. 5, 1894
William D. Lovelace	Dec. 13, 1898
Sarah Dahl	April 5, 1905
Ernest A. Schilling	Aug. 3, 1915
Alex Kolhei	Dec. 3, 1933
Mrs. Alex Kolhei	Dec. 8, 1941
Sanford B. Gullickson	Feb. 19, 1960
Donald W. Juhl	March 17, 1961
M. Wallace Post	Nov. 9, 1962
Margaret Rewerts	June 7, 1975
Linda Magnuson	Oct. 19, 1991
Michele Paskewitz	April 2, 2005

Farming: 25 Years of Big Changes

By Dana Yost

In the summer of 2009, retired local farmers Joe Haneca and Don Rebers sat together at a senior dining table in the Cottonwood Community Center.

As they waited for the noon meal, the two — both since deceased — talked about a newspaper story they'd read that morning about a farm implement dealer's demonstration of the newest high-technology, self-steering tractor.

"Pretty soon," Haneca said, "they are going to get so advanced the farmers won't even have to be in the tractor. They can bring a lawn chair out to their field, and wave as their tractor drives up and down the rows."

That got a good laugh from Rebers. And while agricultural technology is not quite that advanced yet, it has come a long way in the last 25 years — certainly it is much different than the kind of farming Haneca and Rebers were used to. In fact, to say that farming in 2013 is similar to rocket science is actually not that far off.

Satellite-guidance systems, computer-laden, four-wheel-drive tractors that weigh more than the Apollo 11 command module, and science that takes a microscopic look at crop and livestock genetics and even the soil in a field, are among the major developments in agriculture over the last 25 years.

It's all led to bigger farm operations, bigger crop yields (especially in corn), almost no more bean-walking, no more long, hot sweaty days tossing hay bales, but the ability for farmers to do a lot more field and livestock work more quickly than ever.

"The single biggest thing that has changed is technology," said Mark Vandelanotte, who farms south of Cottonwood.

"Twenty-five years ago, I would have laughed if you had told me there would be tractors with auto-steering," he continued as he spoke in an interview for this history book. "But they're here and I use them. While my tractor is steering itself down the field, I can look at the (computer and satellite) monitors in the cab, and constantly compare the numbers [showing how much fertilizer or seed was used] while the tractor is operating. It just goes to show you. It's quite a world."

CENTROL, an agri-science business that started in 1983 by working with farmers on using technology for their fields and had a Cottonwood office until 2010, has a writeup in this 125th anniversary book. It mentions the rapid change in technology. For as much of a breakthrough as field testing was in 1983, today's science is leaps beyond that, the writeup said: "For example, taking one soil sample per acre grew into sophisticated grid sampling to bring global-positioning system (GPS) technology to each acre of the farm."

"You think about those guidance systems and the information we can get from them," Vandelanotte said. "I can put information from my planting into the monitor — which rows used a certain company's seeds, and how much seed — then I can put that monitor back in when we harvest and compare how those rows and that company's see did as far as yield. You can monitor your hogs. You can monitor how rural water does compared to [water from wells or other ground sources], you can track your spraying. It's unbelievable the things you can keep track of.

"In my Dad's age, they never had that. They just went out and worked hard and at the end of the year, they compared their bottom line, and that's how they knew if they had a good year.

"Now, input costs (fertilizer, seed, gas) are so great, you've got to have the output tracking to see where your money is going and to make sure you are getting the best results for your money. You know what works best for your field — if you've got an area where the soil isn't as good and it needs more fertilizer, you know that. You know what it costs to plant in each part of your field, and what the results for each part of your field are. I find that fascinating."

While computers and other high-tech communications devices may be thought of as a young person's field, the average age of farmers has increased, meaning that older farmers have had to adapt to succeed.

"There have been several high impact changes in our industry," said Roger Breyfogle, Al VanOverbeke and John Regnier of the Cottonwood Co-op Oil Co.'s Agronomy Center. "One has been the onslaught of new hardware and software technological advancements, almost all of which have their origins in the earth orbit of a basketball-size sphere called 'Sputnik' more than 50 years ago. Satellites provide navigation and communication for much of this technology and computers control it. When considering the average age of people in our industry, this required a steep, rapid and continuing learning curve for most of the people in the ag industry."

The changes began to take off in the early 1990s, Vandelanotte said, with the beginning of satellite-assisted soil tracking, or "gridding the farm." Fields were meticulously mapped, then, almost inch by inch, were tracked for soil quality, the annual amount of fertilizer needed on each part of the field, how much seed was used, and detailed harvest yields. Farmers could then adjust the amount of fertilizer or seed applied as they went down the field. It means they use less fertilizer, and control its costs more, and maximize yields from each area of the field. It also is protective of the environment, because fertilizer is so closely monitored it's doesn't overlap or build up an excess. "We keep the numbers down," he said.

"We could put fertilizer where it was really needed instead of broadcasting it over the entire field like Dad [Jasper Vandelanotte] did it. We could put fertilizer where it was needed, so it was going to hit the seed to give it a little more [yield].

"We've come a long way with soil conservation, too, because of this. We've learned to do things so soil doesn't erode or blow away. I can remember when (wife) Jane and I started, there'd always be black dirt showing at the end [a season]. Now, we know how to protect the topsoil. I think we conserve soil much more than we used to."

The technology advances have had another big effect in farming: the size of farm operations has gotten larger, while the number of farms has continued to fall. With bigger machinery, soil and field technology, and advances in livestock farming — bigger feedlot operations instead of small cattle or hog set-ups — much more can be done more quickly, and require fewer farmers to do it.

For instance, the advent of genetically-modified seed — such as corn or soybeans that is Roundup ready (not affected by the herbicide Roundup) — means that farmers can quickly spray fields to kill weeds, rather than using the labor-intensive methods of walking bean fields or cultivating.

And, the larger-sized operations are necessary to help farmers get the best efficiency and margins, farmers say. A farmer may have to work double or triple the amount of acres today compared to 25 to 30 years ago. That may make it daunting for young farmers trying to get into farming: how can they afford the land needed to reach those efficiencies? Yet, Vandelanotte sees hope because he knows some young local farmers who are starting out, farming a smaller number of acres and supplementing their income with jobs in construction or carpentry, until they can slowly build up their farm sizes.

Farmers use the Internet and other telecommunications to track grain and livestock prices, and also track how competitors around the globe are faring with their crops, livestock, weather and markets.

"The communication advancements literally brought the world into the farmers' homes, vehicles, equipment cabs, and even their shirt pockets," the Agronomy Center group said. "They are now competing in a world market, versus the 1988 Upper Midwest Corn Belt market, and they have instant access to that market. This technology also allows growers to farm more acres and still micro-manage small individual zones within a particular field for maximum economic yield, using the best agronomic and environmental practices. Improved herbicide programs, especially glyphosate (Roundup), reduced the labor per acre required and allowed growers to farm more acres and to adopt more environmentally favorable minimum-tillage practices."

Another big local change has been the construction of Lone Tree Dairy, which started as a local-investor owned, 1,400-cattle project which opened in the late 1990s just north of Cottonwood. It has had a few different corporate owners since then and now is owned by Alpha Foods.

The last 25 years have changed the landscape. A lot of older farm houses have been abandoned, sometimes bulldozed or burned down and the farm yards themselves converted to farm land. And, sometimes, those that still stand no longer are home to farmers: On an eight-mile stretch of Lyon County Road 10, Pat Aamodt said in May 2013, there are seven or eight farm homes that are occupied now by people who are not farmers.

A lot of numbers show the impact of the changes, not all of them for the better.

• In 1980, Minnesota had between 94,000 and 98,000 farms. In 2007, there were 81,000. That's led to a drop in the population in many rural counties and small towns (but not Lyon County or Cottonwood, which both have grown in population), and had an impact on school enrollments and finances.

• In 1978-82, the average per-acre corn yield was 101 bushels. In 2012, Minnesota's average corn yield was 177 bushels.

• If you sold farm land in 1980 in southwest Minnesota, the average price was $1,760 an acre. In 2013, the *average* value of farmland was at least three times that, according to the United States Department of Agriculture.

Land in or near Lyon County sold at different times for $12,000 or $14,000 an acre, according to various media and ag reporting sources. Land is so valuable, Vandelanotte joked that a farmer of his father's generation could charge more per acre to *rent* out that land in 2013 than what he had paid for it for years ago.

"You think of the building sites and groves that have disappeared since Jane and I started farming," Vandelanotte said. "There's less and less farmers, and we're going to need less and less in the future."

He noted that while planting one day in May 2013 he looked at a square mile of land where there'd been four farm sites at different spots, each with houses, groves and out-buildings when he and Jane started farming. Now, all four are gone, groves and buildings removed and the land converted to farm fields.

Yet higher yields and land values don't automatically translate to higher profits. Crop prices have bobbed up and down but have not changed drastically in the last 25 years. It costs much more to plant and fertilize, and machinery is much more expensive — new top-of-the-line tractors in 1980 could cost between $20,000 to $30,000. The base price on a new John Deere 9430 in 2010 was $261,000. Another way to compare costs to income is that it would have taken about three times as many bushels of corn in 2010 to buy a new pickup than it would have taken in 1980. Inflation on the expense side can be tough for farmers, even with the innovations that help them farm more efficiently.

Yet, agribusiness continues to be a major factor in the local economy, even if there are fewer farm families coming to town to shop, eat or send their kids to school.

"With the value of the land and the taxes that it is bringing in, that's a big factor for the county, [community and school]," Vandelanotte said. He said many skilled tradesmen such as electricians, plumbers and carpenters found steady employment because farmers and agribusinesses continued to expand or build even as other segments of the economy fell after the 2008 financial crisis.

"I think it is a big boost for the local economy," he said.

The same trend has occurred with livestock farmers, where automation, advances in feed quality, and improvements in control of manure and also animal-health environments has led to, often, large operations with concentrations of 1,000 or more head of livestock.

"When Jane and I first started there were a lot of farmers with 40 to 50 cows or 40 to 50 sows," said Vandelanotte, who used to dairy farm but now raises beef cattle along with his grain farming. "When you think of all the farmers milking cows in the Cottonwood, Marshall and Green Valley areas when I started — they've all retired. But the cattle have never left the area. The number of cows are still there, but they are more likely concentrated. Hogs, the same way, there are big concentrations of numbers now."

Scott Dubbelde, general manager of the Farmers Cooperative Elevator, says farming's economic impact is global as well as local.

"Rural America, simply put, feeds the world," he said. "It's pretty much the most important task that an industry could accomplish, and the most important ingredient to a population's survival is food. Agriculture and the related industries are one of America's best assets."

While some worry about the impact of the big farm operations, Vandelanotte believes technology has made for more environmental improvements. While there are still open manure lots, the trend is toward covered and/or underground containments. State and federal pollution control agencies can offer funding assistance to help farmers convert to manure containments. Also, the way manure is applied to fields is much more advanced now, he said — often no longer spread on top of the field, or what could be, depending on the time of year, frozen ground.

"The tendency now is to go for more manure containment and knifing the manure into the field in the fall," Vandelanotte said. "It's more environmentally friendly, and you get most bang for the dollar in terms of how effective it fertilizes."

While some farmers may not like the costs of those changes, Vandelanotte said a big majority understand and believe in the environmental good they bring. It's not only good for the current environment, but will leave better conditions for future generations of farmers — plus cleaner, more comfortable lots are better and healthier for their cattle, too.

Technology and advances in scientific studies don't always mean a switch to large farms with massive grain yields.

West of Cottonwood, Don Bot farms with the no-till practice, which avoids disturbing the soil and can help increase the amount of water and nutrients in the soil, all of which helps fight erosion.

Advances have also allowed a flourishing of organic farming, and farmers who can grow crops specifically for individual customer demand — such as smaller farms in nearby Lac qui Parle County that raise garden-type vegetables.

Jonathan and Carolyn Olson, who farm near the Vandelanottes, raise a lot of organic crops and have won county, state and national farmer of the year recognition for their work.

Among their honors and the farm activities, the Olsons were named the 2008 Lyon County Farm Family of the Year. They were recognized by the University of Minnesota Extension because of their work within the community and commitment to agriculture, said a story in the July 10, 2008 issue of the Marshall Independent.

The Olson family runs an organic farm near Cottonwood, raising corn, soybean, wheat grain and other crops, along with finishing hogs.

"All of our acres are now farmed organically," said Jonathan Olson. "We don't use any prohibited chemicals or commercial fertilizers to raise the crop, we strictly rely on cultivation."

While running an organic farm takes up a lot of time throughout the season, Jonathan Olson, like Mark Vandelanotte, said family is the most important part of their lives.

Jonathan and Carolyn have three daughters, Laura, Christina and Anna. All three graduated from Lakeview High School and went on to college.

"I am very proud of our kids; we raise corn and soybeans, but more importantly we raise our kids," said Jonathan Olson. "It's neat to have them keep their interests on the farm, too."

In April 2011, the Olsons were part of an Ag in the Classroom presentation at the school in Clarkfield. They talked about raising pork, and the variety of meat from pork, and other uses from pork byproducts. They believe it is important to spread the word about agriculture, and especially to encourage young to think about going into various aspects of agribusiness.

"It's cool when you see the little light bulb go on," Carolyn Olson said in the Marshall Independent after the Clarkfield presentation, talking about how students reacted to the information. "It's worth it to present. The kids are asking great questions. They're very receptive to our message. It's always good when you can share your story."

Student Andrew Doyle said he was excited to hear more about pork.

"I love bacon," Doyle said. "I had a bacon-wrapped steak last night and it was really good."

Jonathan Olson said his favorite part of the presentation was informing kids that glycerin, a byproduct of a pig, was in many lipsticks, eye shadows and toothpastes.

"They usually say, 'really?'" Olson said. "Then they tell me they can't wait to tell their moms."

The Agronomy Center and Vandelanotte both say that changes in machinery have made farming more physically comfortable for farmers, and given them more free time to spend with families and recreational pursuits. Mark and Jane Vandelanotte raised two daughters, Abby and Bayli, on their farm. Both daughters graduated from Lakeview High School and went on to earn college degrees.

"The cabs, the machinery we've got now is so much bigger and more comfortable," Vandelanotte said. "There's no dust getting in, it's nice and warm. I know semis were used 25 years ago, but there are a lot more farmers that own semis now for hauling livestock and grain. That saves time. Internet access — there's so much information at your fingertips now.

"Back then, round bales and the larger square bales hadn't been around a long time. They're a lot more prominent now, so that's another big labor-saving thing.

"There is not the hard, long back-breaking days we had when we were younger. You get more family time, and more personal time. And you've got to spend time with your family.

"It's a great way to make a living," he added. "I've thoroughly enjoyed it."

• • •

Later in May, as he was nearing completion of his planting for 2013, Vandelanotte came upon a scene that reinforced how enjoyable it can be. A scene that revealed the beauties of the prairie. A scene many from, say, the Twin Cities or another metro area may never see and, if they do, may never appreciate. Vandelanotte saw wonder, and maybe even beauty:

An early morning, and as he drove, he passed a pasture with cattle spread out, grazing.

"Black cows against that green of the pasture, with the morning sun shining on them," Vandelanotte said. "It looked like a painting."

OUR LAKE

The History of Cottonwood Lake

Adapted from the Jan. 21, 2004, and Feb. 4, 2004, issues of the Tri-County News
By Sue Morton

Thousands of years ago, a glacier of huge proportions crept over west central Minnesota. By the year 9,996 B.C., it had begun to melt. As its power waned, it carved out river valleys and

Photo by Luke Yost

filled the would-be plains with some of the worlds oldest rocks. The moving glacier built ridges and pitted the land with lakes both large and small. As it cut out the Minnesota River Valley, the glacier gouged out a small, rather insignificant 300-acre lake that would someday be named Cottonwood Lake.

It seems only logical that the first visitors to the lake were animals and insects, but eventually man did arrive. There is no recorded history of man's first use of the lake. I can only surmise that man found it to be a valuable natural resource, utilizing it for both survival and recreational needs. Modern technology has eliminated the lake's use as a source of food and water for survival, not to mention ice for cooling food. Yet, Cottonwood Lake has sustained its value as a recreational resource.

"A lake is the landscape's most beautiful and expressive feature. It is the earth's eyes through which the beholder measures the depth of his own nature." These are the words of Henry David Thoreau, one of America's most famous naturalists. Perhaps, in 1871, when William Slater and Harrison Price chose to settle on the northeast side of Cottonwood Lake, they not only saw the depth of their own nature, but also the resourceful value of the lake itself.

Others followed Slater and Harrison's lead. In 1872, more settlers chose to build their dugouts and cabins on the north side of the lake. Some of those names are still familiar in this community on today: Rosvold, Pederson, Nelson, Larson and Reishus are just a few.

It would not have been unusual to name the lake after one of the first settlers. That was common practice, but that is not what happened. Instead, one story suggests that the original surveyors named the lake in 1858, calling it Cottonwood Lake. The name is descriptive. At one time, there was a large clump of cottonwood trees close to the lakeshore. Obviously, they were a distinguishing enough feature to elicit the name of the lake.

When the Northern Railroad extended into Lucas Township in 1888, the station was placed in Cottonwood. It is noted in *A Centennial History of Cottonwood 1888-1898* that an "immense cottonwood tree stood like a tower on the eastern shore of the lake, with smaller cottonwoods also around the lake. The railroad very naturally named its station after these trees and 'Cottonwood' became the name of the village. Whether the great cottonwood trees stood on the east or northeast of the lake, it is a fact that both the lake and the village were appropriately named. "

It is interesting to note that when the township was originally surveyed, almost every low area had natural drainage channels feeding the lake directly. As more and more land was cultivated, these natural ditches disappeared and sloughs began to emerge. Eventually, man-made ditches were dug to help stabilize water flow into the lake.

Fishing and boating are perhaps the most popular sports associated with Cottonwood Lake. The avid fishermen of this area have played an important part in the history of fishing on Cottonwood Lake. In the 1890s, the lake went dry because of a severe drought. By 1907 the local fishermen and boaters had determined the need for ditches to fill the lake and a dam at the outlet to control the water depth.

Between 1907 and today, droughts, rain and man have all played a part in fishing or the lack of fishing on Cottonwood Lake. Drainage from agricultural land contributed to a silt build-up, creating a shallower lake less conducive to fish survival. Between 1938 and 1947, your only Cottonwood Lake catch would mostly likely have been bullhead. With dam and ditch improvements, the help of the Department of Natural Resources, and the concern and help of many local citizens, the lake underwent improvements. Once again in the early 1960s, the lake was stocked with a variety of fingerlings. By 1967, Cottonwood Lake had indeed become "a fishing place." Tourists came with their fishing poles in hand and stood "elbow to elbow" along the shores of the lake. The lake was clear, the water was warm, and the beach was packed with out-of-town visitors.

Cottonwood Lake is a natural run-off lake. Glaciers cut shallow lakes in some parts of the Upper Midwest, and made others much deeper — and often more famous. Cottonwood's has never been too deep, although Joe Amato, the prominent historian and retired Southwest Minnesota State University professor, says evidence shows it was likely deeper than it currently is.

Amato was friends with former North Star Insurance leader Bror Anderson, who lived on the southwest side of the lake. He said Anderson had two documents that showed a sailboat with an 18-foot-high mast sailed the lake in the years before World War I.

"Bror's records indicate the sail boat held 10 to 12 people, which is a fairly significant sail boat. It had been said that the lake was once as deep as 18 feet [it's about 8 feet at its deepest now], and I was dubious about that depth. But Bror had an article or two that confirmed it."

Amato said a sailboat the size of the pre-World War I boat reported on the lake would need water deeper than current levels because it would displace a lot of water, and would need deeper water to turn better — plus its owner likely would not want to bring a boat onto a lake where the mast could end up stuck in the lake bed if the boat capsized. "That there are records of that sailboat, tells you the lake was that deep," Amato said.

Throughout history, the biology of the lake has frequently changed. One study conducted by several local and state agencies discovered the loss of valuable macroscopic life, ... which supported a variety of aquatic animals. This is just one example of a serious loss to the lake's ecosystem. There were many recommendation made to approve the quality of the lake as a result of that study.

Amato lived in Cottonwood from 1969 to the late 1970s. He was involved in that study, which began in 1973. "We were very concerned about the quality of the water, so we set up the study.

"There was some fairly severe erosion. ... Wind erosion raised some real problems. It was kind of a Catch-22. People wanted a lake that [had high water levels]. But if the lake was too high and with the winds we had, it tore apart the banks and caused [a large buildup] of sediment."

Among the other issues the study found or addressed were the effects of a large drainage ditch which Amato believed brought runoff into the lake from a 20-mile square area; and lingering pollution effects from a 1938 mechanical sewage plant. "With a big rain, 380,000 gallons would come through the mechanical plant and [if volume got too high] the plant would shut the water out, and that became a pollution problem."

One of the recommendations from the study was the installation of an aeration system. The Cottonwood Sportsman Club took on that responsibility and maintained the system. The club along with landowners placed riprap along needed shoreline.

The Cottonwood Sportsman Club assisted the DNR with a fish kill in the early 1990s (in an attempt to eliminate rough fish such as bullhead and carp). The following summer, fingerlings were again introduced into the lake. That fall, the first aeration system was established and 80 citizens including Girl Scouts, Cub Scouts, and Boy Scouts cleaned the lakeshore.

Cottonwood Lake has a long and successful history. It remains an important resource to the community.

A history of Cottonwood lake must include the hunters, walkers, birdwatchers, and water skiers. Early in the 20th century, the lake's edges provided good hunting territory. Wolves, fox, ring-necked pheasant, grouse and prairie chickens were all fair game. During the mid-1930s when the Dust Bowl was in fair swing, Cottonwood Lake dried up. It became the habitat of thousands of pheasants. The grass and the weeds provided good cover for both the pheasants and waterfowl. Twice the grasses were set afire to try to quell the bird population.

Walkers now have the pleasure of using a lovely trail on what were, in 2004, undeveloped parts around the lake. The Lions Club created the trail. In 2009 the east side of the lake was included in pedestrian/bike path construction along Barstad Road, funded in part through the state's Safe Routes to School Program.

Birdwatchers have been walking and watching for many years. Cottonwood Lake provides the perfect habitat for waterfowl, woodland birds, and a variety of prairie species.

Boaters dominate the lake on summer weekends. Pontoons, speedboats, canoes, and other watercraft continue to prove the lake lives up to the recreational aspects it has long promised. (For many years, The Point on the northwest shore was also a popular gathering place, especially for young people.)

On summer afternoons, I swim in the lake. In the mornings, I walk around the lake. In the spring and the fall of each year, I watch the birds come and go with the seasons. Someday, before I get too old, I'm going to learn to cross country ski, so I can put the lake to use all year-round! Yes, I swim in that lake, and I love that lake!

And I'm not the only one who loves Cottonwood Lake!

Cottonwood Lake has been a source of joy to many over the years. It's been a source of frustration to some, too, but even the frustrated lake-lovers are just that ... lake lovers! I've heard stories about boating, skiing, fishing, frog legs, mischief, islands, fires, droughts, trash and potatoes. Every word I heard I am sure is God's truth. In the end, all of these memories convinced me of one thing. Cottonwood Lake was an important part of growing up in this small town.

"We kids lived on the lake in summer and winter," retired store manager Bob Molstad told me with a little reminiscent excitement in his voice. "It didn't matter if was 20 below or 80 degrees."

Bob grew up in Cottonwood and his earliest memory of the lake is in the early 1940s when the water was just starting to creep back into the lake after the big drought. "I don't remember the lake ever being completely dry, but I remember there were little islands. We would take wood planks, logs, whatever we could find, and lay them between those little islands." Bob and his friends would spend all day playing games and walking the planks from island to island.

Bob also recalled that there was a big island in the middle of the lake, and on that island was a haystack! Bud Hostetler remembered the haystack, too. As a matter of fact, he claimed there were two big piles of straw. One day he and Jimmy Madison set one of those stacks on fire, "just to see what would happen." According to Bud, "It was so much fun, we set the other one on fire."

That's not all of the mischief that took place on or around the lake. Young Mr. Molstad once "borrowed" a raft without permission. He thinks the raft just might have been built by Bud and Jimmy. It seems little Bob and a friend went paddling all around the lake oblivious to time while their worried parents searched for them. All ended well. The raft was returned to its owner, and the boys returned safely home.

Summer on the lake also meant boating, skiing, and swimming. Every time these topics came up in an interview, the name Wendell Knutson came up, too. Wendall had a big dock. He even put a big diving board on it. Bob Molstad recalls that, "He'd even let us kids use it. He had boats and skis, and he'd put a kid on his shoulders and take him out on the lake! John Smith had a dock, too, and a really good swimming area." Eric Anderson remembers hearing stories of Mr. Knutson pulling skiers, not by boat, but by airplane!

Bob Molstad noted that everyone's parents always knew where they were and what they were up to. Well, except maybe for that raft incident. "That was our pastime," Bob said. "... that lake!"

Bud Hostetler shared other stories about the lake with me, too. A favorite pastime of Cottonwood boys was playing along the lakeshore where they liked to build shacks from discarded lumber. There was also a shack built from an old school bus. Young Mr. Hostetler acquired the lumber for his shack by means of "moonlight requisition," soon after the old hotel was torn down. he also used some of his found lumber to build a boat. Bud and his friends put an old stove in their shack, which they used for frying up frog legs and mourning doves.

Trudy Anderson lived on the lake from the early 1940s until the late 2000s. When she first saw Cottonwood Lake, it was still pretty dry. "People just didn't respect it! They used it for trash." As the water gradually returned to the lake, the Anderson children took on the responsibility of cleaning it. Trudy made them wear tennis shoes into the lake because there was so much glass and many tin cans. Trees and bushes had grown in the lake while it was dry, and the Anderson family had to remove them to make it safe for boating. Trudy said it took some years for the lake to come back, but it did, and along with it came the beautiful sunrises and sunsets that she enjoyed so much.

Taking responsibility for the lake really stuck with the teenaged Eric Anderson, Trudy's son. He and several friends took on the job of ridding the lake of algae. Eric and several friends would drop burlap bags of copper sulfate from their boats into the lake to help clear the water. "I remember swimming through thick green stuff," said Eric. "The copper sulfate really worked!"

Trudy's husband, Bror, enjoyed the lake, too, but it was the winter lake that he favored. Bror was quite the hockey player, and a skilled skater. Trudy remembered that Bror would put on his skates, place their daughter Susan on his shoulders, and glide across the lake.

Amato said "Cottonwood had a pretty extraordinary hockey team in the '40s. Bror played on it and John Lines and six or seven others." The team played and practiced on the Cottonwood Lake ice, but was so good that, one year, it traveled extensively, including to the Canadian border and into North Dakota, playing games against teams from true hockey hot beds, and winning most of them. "They had a very successful hockey team that season," Amato said.

Bror Anderson's Birds
By Joseph A. Amato

In the spring of what Bror knew to be the last year of his life,
He put six goslings on his pond.
He took joy in their growth.

And he spoke to everyone of their certain flight
And possible return.
Their migration became his last parable.

And I, for one, will look for the signs of Bror,
Not in a cemetery, amidst marble inscriptions,
But in the spring, near the horizon,
On the edge of every bird's wing.

Poem first published in Death Book: Terrors, Consolations, Contradictions & Paradoxes (1985, Ellis Press). Reprinted with permission. Bror Anderson, 1915-1973, was a president of North Star Insurance Co., and involved in many aspects of the Cottonwood community and lake.

There were always skating and snowmobile races during the annual Fishless Derby. According to Trudy, if anyone actually caught a fish during the derby, they were required to have Father Becker (who was also Cottonwood's mayor in the 1970s) inspect the fish. It was up to the good Father to determine if the fish was indeed caught in Cottonwood Lake. Bob Molstad recalled that the fire department used to drill holes in the ice to allow fresh water to freeze smoothly. Then they would pile up snow around the holed area to create a skating rink. Another winter sport on the lake was skate sailing. To keep warm between sailing, skating and fishing, everyone would head to one of those nice shacks and warm themselves by the stove! Another sport during the Fishless Derby was broomball. Amato was a goalie on a team that won the Fishless Derby broomball championship in 1977.

Paul Egeland grew up next to Cottonwood Lake. When he was a young boy, there were only two houses between his house and what is now the beach. All the rest of the land was farmland or grove. There was a big grove of trees to the north and west along the lake, "a great place for birds." There were "nesting night herons, screech owls and other birds." When he

Snowmobiling on the lake, February 2013. (Photo from the 125th Anniversary Facebook Page)

was in the ninth grade, Paul started keeping lists of the birds of Cottonwood Lake. He's seen 260 different species of birds in the Egeland backyard alone!

Many times during the hunting season, Paul and his friends would walk out along the lake in the morning before school. "There were a lot more ducks in the [19]50s. Many of the trees around the lake were elms and died when the Dutch elm disease hit. Before the dam was put in the lake, and the big ditches were put in, there was a free flow of fish from the river up to the lake, and there was great diversity of fish. There used to be buffalo fish, but there aren't anymore. When the lake froze out, the amount of dead fish was amazing." Paul recalled that there was an old dirt road that went along the lake out to The Point. "This was a great swimming place."

There's still a road that wanders around the lake, along with the nice path on the west side. Walkers really enjoy this path. Maren Magnuson is a walker. In the early 2000, you could see her walking almost daily around the lake in good weather. "I really miss the walking in the winter," she said. "[Walking] is so peaceful. There's no traffic. I feel safe, too. You get used to seeing all the same people who like to walk the lake, too."

Maren started walking the lake when she returned to Cottonwood to attend Southwest Minnesota State University. Her grandma was a lake walker and invited Maren to join her. They walked together regularly. They would often stop and sit on one of the benches that used to be along the path. They would watch the lake and enjoy each other's company. "Now, when I walk around the lake," said Maren, "I always remember my grandma."

What wonderful memories we have of Cottonwood Lake. Here's one more: In our backyard (on Shoreview Drive), there stands an American elm tree. It stands precariously on the bank and hangs over the lake. When Ordell Lovsness was a boy, he built a fort in that tree. He nailed chicken wire to the trunk to use as a ladder, and hung a rope from the branches so he and his buddies could do Tarzan swings into the lake. Ordell once told us that the tree was full-grown when he played in it. That was more than 90 years ago. Our elm tree is surely a survivor, as are our memories, and our beautiful Cottonwood Lake.

***

Cottonwood Lake has continued to be a busy and popular place in the years between 2004 and 2013.

Many Coming Home Days festival activities take place at the beach on the lake's east end and at C.W. Reishus Park on the east end. The park has been expanded and the shelter house was given a steel roof through the work of the Cottonwood Lions Club.

Large crowds gather around the lake for the fireworks show during Coming Home Days, as well.

The beach and water can be full during the summer, as families, young people and others — either from Cottonwood or from out of town — come to swim, boat, play sand volleyball and picnic. Just like a lot of walkers, kids will take their bicycles on the trail, riding to Lakeview Public School or venturing all the way around the lake. Some young kids in the past 20 years or so would plan most of a summer day around a hike or bike around the lake, bringing picnic lunches to eat when they stopped at the dam on the northwest side.

Jameson Vermaat, who grew up on Front Street on the south side of the lake and is a 2006 Lakeview graduate, became so proficient at wake boarding (similar to snow boarding) that he would compete in tournaments around the state and country.

In February 2013, to help promote the 125th anniversary, there was a busy day of snowmobile racing on the ice-covered lake. And the lake can be dotted with ice-fishing houses during most winters.

There has been extensive housing development on and near Shoreview Drive on the southwest side, and on Northwood Drive on the north side of the lake, both before and after the opening of the new Lakeview Public School in 2002.

In 1999, the city annexed the Northwood First Addition and the final residential plat was approved on the north side of Northwood Drive.

In 2002, Northwood became a paved street and curb and gutter improvements were made.

(Dana Yost contributed information to this story).

OUR CHURCHES

Christt Lutheran Church

From the 2013 Tri-County News Progress Edition

Christ Lutheran Church is a vibrant faith community gathered in ministry to accomplish the mission that God has given to God's church. We are called into God's new creation, gifted by the Holy Spirit, and sent to show the Good News of Jesus Christ for the sake of the world, as

we bring welcome, forgiveness, healing, renewal, and hope to our neighbors locally and in distant places.

The 133-year congregation located at 126 Front Street in Cottonwood is served by full-time ordained pastor, the Rev. Jim Demke, as well as other part-time staff members: Gwen Arneson (lay pastoral assistant), Rhoda Schmidt (administrative

office assistant), and Jon and Jeanette Myrvik (custodians). Our members also find many tasks and areas of ministry where their gifts and talents may be used.

We are open to welcoming all into the work we share in the name of Jesus Christ.

Our Sunday morning faith-growth activities include Sunday Morning Live (9-10 a.m.) for 3-year-olds through high school students. There is also a fellowship opportunity for all ages during that time period. During the school year, our Sunday morning worship service begins at 10:15 a.m. (From Memorial Weekend through Labor Day Weekend, our Sunday morning worship time is changed to 9:30 a.m.) Our worship services normally blend styles of liturgy and music and we are also broadcast on the local cable access channel in Cottonwood for those who wish to worship in that manner.

In addition we have regular youth group events: Bible camp and Vacation Bible School offerings for all ages in the summer; quilting days; a Wednesday evening Bible study for high school students; Bible study groups for adults; choir; and multiple regular opportunities for service in the larger community.

We reach out to the world through our support of missionaries Charles and Anita (Olson) Jackson in Mongolia; the work of the Kikatiti School in Tanzania; and Robin's Nest Orphanage in Jamaica. Anita (Olson) Jackson is a Cottonwood native, the daughter of Ken and Lois Olson.

God is at work in our congregation — in its people and in our space! We recently remodeled three entry and fellowship areas to provide welcome and hospitality, meeting and gathering opportunities. A new Prayer Garden has been created at the rear of our building with a view to the lake. It is hoped that the entire community might find the garden to be a place for solace and prayer in a beautiful lakeside setting.

For more information and photos of our life together, please visit our website at www.christcottonwood.org, or find us on Facebook by searching for Christ Cottonwood.

Iglesia Apolostica

A church serving the area's growing Latino population opened in 1999 at 78 West 1st Street N. The church's pastor is the Rev. Arnoldo Espinoza. In different years at Coming Home Days festivals, church members have provided energetic contemporary music and an authentic ethnic food stand, which has been a popular draw.

English Lutheran Church

The first Lutheran Church in the vicinity of Cottonwood was the Yellow Medicine Norwegian Evangelical Lutheran congregation in 1869. The first settlers of Cottonwood belonged to the Yellow Medicine congregation.

Rev. Thomas Johnson was a traveling missionary and he served until 1871. All Lutheran churches in the area were affiliated with "The Norwegian Synod."

On Nov. 8, 1888, the Cottonwood Norwegian Evangelical church in Lyon and Yellow Medicine counties was organized. The first business meeting of the congregation was Dec. 4, 1888. A constitution was adopted and a call to Rev. N.P. Xavier was extended. He served the congregation until 1889. The first services were held in various school houses and homes of the members.

On Dec. 6, 1891, it was unanimously resolved to build a church in the village of Cottonwood. Construction of the church began on Feb. 15, 1892, the cornerstone was laid in November 1892 and the building was completed. In 1893 the congregation joined with churches in Granite Falls and Hazel Run until 1899. In 1899, the congregation formed a new charge with Dawson and Belview. In 1906, the congregation joined with Ruthton and Florence to form a new charge. This arrangement lasted until 1909, when the congregation merged with a number of German families from the Posen area. On June 6, 1909, a new congregation was organized and given the name of "The Cottonwood English Lutheran Church."

English Lutheran congregation called its first resident pastor in 1941, Rev. Milton Otto, who served until 1946. The church purchased its first parsonage in 1942. In 1955, the congregation voted to build a new church. The groundbreaking ceremony was held on April 15, 1956, and Loris Gniffke was in charge of construction. The cornerstone was laid on July 13, 1956, and placed inside was a copy of the church constitution, Golden Jubilee booklet published in 1938 when the congregation was 50 years old, Luther's catechism, copies of the Marshall Messenger and the Cottonwood Current, and a Bible, and the items from the cornerstone of the old church. Services were held in the new church basement from winter of 1956 to 1957. The cost was $42,000. The church was completed June 1, 1957, and the church dedication was June 23, 1957.

The first organ was donated by Miss Emily Frank and was dedicated on Oct. 20, 1958. From 1958 to 1987, English Lutheran shared its pastor with Zion Lutheran church in Tracy.

In 1966, a new parsonage was discussed and, in 1967, was built and was dedicated in 1968.

In 1970, Pastor Schmidt started a tradition of having an outdoor service to bring the congregation closer to God and nature and have some good fellowship in the congregation. In 1984, a new addition to the church was a canopy and steps in the entrance of the church. In July 1986, the individual cup for communion was voted on and approved to use, along with the common cup.

The church supports Ladies Aid and LYS youth group to this day. It still holds on to the original values established in 1888 and, through the help of Jesus Christ, it will continue to glorify God for many years to come.

Pastors:

1888-1889 N.P. Xavier	1941-1946 Milton Otto
1889-1893 O. Estrem	1946-1955 David Pfeiffer
1893-1896 G.T. Lee	1955 Keith Olmanson
1896-1899 M.C. Aasen	1955-1958 Joseph Peterson
1899-1903 A.O. Aasen	1958-1967 Gerhardt Weseloh
1903-1904 T.S. Reishus	1967-1970 Juul Madson
1904 H. Aanestad	1970-1974 John Schmidt
1906-1909 Axel Bergh	1974-1978 John Krueger
1911-1913 Phil Laux	1978-1986 Gaylin Schmeling
1913-1928 M.F. Mommsen	1987-1993 Daniel Larson
1928-1941 Christian Anderson	1993-2004 John Smith
	2005-present Piet VanKampen

St. Mary's Catholic Parish

By Donna Sanders

St. Mary's Catholic Parish history really began in 1902 when Monsignor James Guillot of Marshall dreamed of beginning a new mission parish in Cottonwood. The parish was born to its legal existence on May 19, 1902, when it was incorporated and the name given was "The Church of St. Mary of Cottonwood, Minnesota." Many problems surfaced and so for the next 50 years St. Mary's existed in name only.

In May of 1953, seven acres of land on the southwestern edge of Cottonwood were purchased for the site of the new church. On June 23, 1953, Father Adalbert Cepress was appointed as the first resident pastor for St. Mary's and, soon after, the building of the new church began. The following four members were appointed to the building committee: Andrew Boerboom, Grant Magnuson, Henry VandeVoorde and Earl LaVoy. Of the four, Earl LaVoy is still living and residing in Marshall.

As no formal building existed at the very beginning, arrangements were made to hold Sunday masses in the American Legion Hall. Marie Fruin (now deceased) used to talk about how she and her husband Duane would walk over to the Legion Hall on Saturday night and set up the altar and chairs for the Mass on Sunday morning. The original church was completed and the first Mass was celebrated in the church Christmas, 1954.

A Parish Center was completed in 1967 under the direction of Father Dennis Becker to provide a home for our resident pastor, parish office space and classrooms for our religious education classes in the basement.

Under the leadership of Father John Pearson, a monument was placed in our cemetery in 1995 and a parish outdoor Mass was held along with the blessing of the monument.

Through the years there have been many physical changes as the need arose. The inside of the church has been repainted several times, carpeting was put in the sanctuary and a new altar and piano was purchased. In 1999 plans began to build an addition to the existing church. A handicapped-accessible ramp was built and completed in 2001 with a parking lot in the back of the church. Plans were made to add a new worship area and use the existing worship area as the gathering area.

A groundbreaking ceremony was held on April 23, 2002 and construction started soon after with the work being completed by late Fall, 2002. Here is our church as it was at Christmas, 2002 (49 years after the start of our parish.)

The Church at Christmas, 2002

50 Years of Faith

1953-2003

The 50th anniversary celebration of the beginning of St. Mary's was held on Sunday, August 10, 2003. Bishop John Nienstedt, Bishop of the Diocese of New Ulm at that time, was present to celebrate the Mass which was followed by a catered dinner and program giving the highlights from the 50 years of its existence.

When St. Mary's began, there were between 60 to 70 households, and currently St. Mary's has approximately 170 households with 105 students registered in our religious education program. Throughout our short history, St. Mary's has been provided wonderful Spiritual Leadership by the different pastors who have been assigned to our parish, currently being served by Father Jack Nordick, sharing him with our neighbor parish, St. Clotilde's in Green Valley.

In the succeeding years, the need for an improved kitchen facility became apparent. A kitchen renovation committee was formed early in 2012 and plans began to remodel the church kitchen. The renovation work was completed by local contractors in time for our Fall

Parish Festival in September of 2012. The church facility as it is today is enjoyed and utilized with many activities continuing to be held during the year.

Lay Leadership has been encouraged through the years and we have seen many men, women and children involved in the St. Mary's parish ministry. St. Mary's Council of Catholic Women (our women's organization) stays active and alive — instrumental in sponsoring many programs and activities, serving funeral luncheons, hosting coffee and rolls after Sunday Masses, bingo nights, potluck meals, nursing home visits, soup and sandwich and salad luncheons. It serves as an action group to help make things happen in the parish, reaching out to the diocese, community, and larger world church where there are needs to be met.

Music has always been a major influence in our parish liturgies and we have been blessed with many talented musicians volunteering their talents during the years of our existence.

Education for our adults and of our young people (as the now deceased Bishop Lucker – the second bishop of the Diocese of New Ulm, so often referred to as "passing on our Catholic faith") continues to be a very important part of parish life. Many men and women accepted the challenge of teaching our religion classes — as our older parishioners retired from teaching, younger members take over the responsibility of teaching our youth.

Along with all of our church activities, our members continue to serve in the community of Cottonwood, helping and serving in many different capacities. We are always proud of our St. Mary's youth throughout the years of our existence who have excelled in the area school functions – in the academic fields, along with the arts (drama, music, speech, etc.) and the various sports.

AND so the Church of St. Mary will continue to exist in this wonderful community and continues to be in the hands of God – With His promise that He will always be with us as we continue to serve Him and do His work here on earth.

St. Lucas Lutheran Church

Eight years before the city of Cottonwood was formally founded, St. Lucas Lutheran Church began in the farm country northwest of town, in Normania Township.

Today, 133 years later, St. Lucas is still very much an active church which, in the last 25 years, has had two major celebrations, invested strongly in building upkeep and upgrades, and was a key player in a decision that brought together a half-dozen small Yellow Medicine County churches under the same organizational umbrella.

"The core group at St. Lucas is still pretty much there," Kirk Lovsness, the congregational president, said in late May 2013.

St. Lucas is a member of the Southwestern Minnesota Synod of the Evangelical Lutheran Church in America (ELCA).

The congregation was formed in 1880. Before then, Norwegian settlers in the Normania Township area worshiped at Yellow Medicine Lutheran Church, which was then west of Hanley Falls, according to the June 10, 2005, issue of the Marshall Independent. The Yellow Medicine parish was divided into three districts, Eastern, Middle and Western. A pastor served all three districts, with services in homes or school houses once a month.

In March 1880, a decision was made for each district to form its own congregation. In May 1880, the Independent said, a congregation of the Western district was organized at Ole Brusven's home in Normania Township and was known as "St. Lucas Norsk Evangeliske Lutherske Menighed." (Norwegian Evangelical Lutheran Church).

The first St. Lucas Church was built in 1887 for $3,564.36. It was dedicated June 2, 1889.

St. Lucas remained connected to Yellow Medicine Lutheran Church until 1893, when it formed a parish with Silo Lutheran (now Christ Lutheran) of Cottonwood.

In 1911, the existing St. Lucas church had become to small to hold the increasing number of parishioners so the church was remodeled, an addition built and a basement added.

On Feb. 4, 1922, the church and its contents, including a pipe organ, were destroyed by fire, the Independent reported in 2005.

Later in 1922, a new church was built at a cost of $14,122.47 and dedicated Sept. 16, 1923.

From the beginning of the church in 1880 until 1921, all services were conducted in Norwegian. From 1921 until 1949, the church had English-language services four times a year.

In 1961, St. Lucas and Christ Lutheran (Silo) discontinued their partnership and St. Lucas formed a parish with Israel Lutheran Church of rural Clarkfield.

The church has had many upgrades through the years, including the addition of air conditioning, a public-address system, new stairway, basement remodeling and the installation of an elevator.

One of the biggest renovation projects was a $100,000, three-year effort begun in 1996 to restore and repair 14 stained-glass windows, along with adding the elevator and residing the church and parsonage. The funds were raised through pledges and donations from congregation members past and present and the work done in phases.

The stained-glass windows, which were more than 70 years old at the time, were and are a source of inspiration for St. Lucas members. The windows which run the length of the east side of the sanctuary will cast a multi-colored hue across pews when the Sunday-morning sun strikes them.

Green pastures and still waters are among the images on an east window, the Tri-County News wrote in 1996. "The window on the western wall depicts Jesus Christ praying while his disciples slept. The images are cast in the golds, blues, greens and reds of the large stained-glass windows. They are windows which in their own fashion dominate, yet compliment, the interior of the church.

"'They are the most beautiful windows I've ever seen in any church,' said Linda Broughton, a member and the church custodian at the time.

"There are days when she is cleaning when the sun shines through the windows and creates prisms throughout the building.

"'I've always admired them,' Myrtle Lovsness said, [adding] that when she thinks of the windows, she thinks of home."

The windows were originally designed by someone from Minneapolis. The 1990s renovation and repair work was done by a company from St. Cloud, which needed five to six weeks to work on each pair of windows.

"A lot of the work in the basement was done by volunteers. The church members were fantastic," late-1990s congregation president Nancy Brusven said in the Sept. 15, 1999, issue of the Tri-County News. "A lot of the labor was done by the members. ... It looks very nice and

I'm proud of our congregation. They've done a fantastic job. It was just a really good old-fashioned concern and care and maintenance of the property that's held in high esteem. The folks are really aware of the need of good care and good stewardship for the building that houses the worshipping community."

That kind of care has been evident in recent years, too.

In April 2012, a new lighted cross was put up, its costs covered fully by Chery Stensrud and her family from memorial funds for her late husband, Brad, who died of cancer Feb. 20, 2012. Brad and Chery were both very active at St. Lucas in many roles. The lighted cross can sometimes look like a beacon to country-road travelers, since St. Lucas sits on a hill along Yellow Medicine County Road 2, not far east of U.S. Highway 59.

Right after that, member Robert Kompelien and the Kompelien family put up a new, large wooden cross below the lighted cross.

And, in 2012, the congregation funded a new roofing project for the church.

The church had large celebrations for its 110th anniversary in 1990, and its 125th anniversary in 2005.

Also, every November, St. Lucas is host to a well-attended Scandinavian meal and baked-goods sale.

In 2004, St. Lucas was one of seven rural congregations in Yellow Medicine County that joined together to form Healing Waters Parishes. The parish was initially served by Rev. Allan Johnson and the Revs. Steve and Evelyn Weston. Currently, Rev. David Wall is the interim pastor for the parish, which now has five member congregations.

With different partners over the years, and in efforts of their own, St. Lucas members continue to strive to make their church a welcoming place where the Christian Gospel is shared and fellowship enjoyed. The strength of St. Lucas, Dieken said in 2005, is in its members: "The grandmas and grandpas, aunts, uncles and cousins all coming together," as the Marshall Independent said, along with an increase in young couples with children. "Everybody cares about each other," Dieken said.

That kind of care was on display May 23, 2013, Kirk Lovsness said, as volunteers mowed lawns and did other groundskeeping in anticipation of what is usually a large number of visitors to the cemetery on Memorial Day Weekend.

"This morning, about seven or eight of us got together to take care of the grounds," he said. "We had three [riding] lawnmowers, a bunch of trimmers … We do it every year to get it ready for Memorial Day. And it didn't take us very long with that many people — we got a lot done in a little time."

The effort did not surprise Lovsness, who has served as a trustee, council president and other roles over the years.

"I think I've been on the council since I was 18," he said. "If you want your church to [survive], you have to participate — in some capacity. You don't have to be on the council to do it. We have a lot members who volunteer. We have a very active church."

St. Lucas Pastors over the last 25 years (not including most interims)

Rev. John Christianson 1979-1989

Rev. Gary Kubly about 10 years

Rev. Mary Dodgson until 2004

Rev. Allan Johnson

Rev. Evelyn Weston

Rev. Steve Weston

Current interim is Rev. David Wall.

Swan Lake Evangelical Free Church

From Swan Lake's web site and information provided by Joan Davis

Swan Lake Evangelical Free Church began sometime prior to 1872 as a gathering of Scottish immigrants in a house on the shore of Swan Lake in rural southwestern Minnesota. These early pioneers organized Argyle Presbyterian Church named after the town in Scotland from where most of them had come. They met in school houses most of the time in those early days. At this time Redwood County extended to the Dakota line and Mankato Presbytery extended to the Pacific Ocean. In July 1890, a church building was erected in the country four miles south of Cottonwood. Rev. Whitney was the first pastor. John D. Smith and James Garry were the first elders.

Throughout its history Swan Lake Church has been known as a "Mother of Churches." It was under the guidance and loan of its pastors that the Presbyterian Church in Marshall, the First Presbyterian Church in Cottonwood and the Clifton and Delhi Presbyterian churches were organized. The family names of Keepers, Brittenham, Gee, Reinboldt, Goplen, Skilling and Pehrson run through later church history.

Among the pastors who served the Swan Lake Presbyterian Church were Rev. Upton, Rev. Watt, Rev. Badger and Rev. Charles Jackson. H.P. Voth and Kermit Velde served as lay-preachers for a number of years. Alan Chalmers, George Smith and John Garry served many years as elders. Charles Craven, Fred McLennan and Jim Christianson were early-day trustees. Ed Snyder served 41 years as trustee.

In 1949, extensive improvements were made to the church building. The church was moved from its original foundation and set over a full basement.

In 1952 the Swan Lake congregation voted to become independent and purchased the church building from the Mankato Presbytery.

Changes were made to the church building in 1963: A new ground-level brick entrance was added and the interior of the sanctuary completely renovated. A great deal of labor was contributed by church members under the able leadership of Larry Cravens, who also designed the building.

The third and fourth generations of Smiths, Snyders, Jensens and Cravens continued to worship at Swan Lake.

In November 1964, the Rev. Robert Lancaster came to Swan Lake. He also worked in the Cottonwood Current news office and, upon the death of the paper's owner, Keith Sisson, bought the paper. Rev. Lancaster continued as full-time pastor until 1972, when he became a ruling elder. Rev. Walter Watt replaced Lancaster as pastor, serving until 1975. He was followed by Rev. Curtis Emerson, who organized a bus ministry, canvassing the town for unchurched children and providing transportation for those who needed it.

Rev. Emerson resigned in 1979 and was followed by the Rev. Edwin Jaeger, who had been a missionary in Iran for 22 years and was forced to leave when the Shah of Iran fell in 1979.

In April 1983 the congregation voted to affiliate with the Evangelical Free Church of America. The first pastor under this affiliation was the Rev. Robert Dunn, who came in May 1983.

In 1985, with youth numbers growing, Swan Lake was given an old vacant building on Main Street in Cottonwood by Loren Ericksen. They renovated the building primarily for use in youth and children's ministries. In 1993 a decision was made to build a new church in Cottonwood that would replace the two facilities that were in use at that time. The congregation moved into the new church building in November of 1994.

At the time that the congregation moved into town average attendance was in the neighborhood of 80 to 85 people. The new church facility had a capacity of about 190 or so. Immediately after moving to town the church began to grow in numbers. By the year 2000 it was becoming evident that an addition was needed to accommodate the numbers that were attending on a regular basis. During 2001, a new 300-seat sanctuary, lobby, and classrooms were built that more than doubled the space available.

In 2003 Swan Lake began once again to be challenged with the idea of planting another church. For several years, Swan Lake members who had been driving to Cottonwood from Granite Falls had been praying about planting an Evangelical Free Church in their community. After consulting with the North Central District, Swan Lake voted to support the core group in planting this new church. In August of 2005, Rock Haven EFC in Granite Falls was launched under the leadership of Pastor John McCosh.

A big part of ensuring an enjoyable experience at Swan Lake Evangelical Free Church involves providing a consistent environment that people can count on week after week, both on Sunday mornings and beyond. Each weekend, you can expect…

• Welcoming hospitality – SLEFC is open to everyone, and will make sure that our guests are warmly welcomed and feel comfortable and relaxed.

- Inspiring music – SLEFC celebrates God's goodness in a style that is energizing, motivating people to appreciate how awesome God is!

- Creative use of multi-media – SLEFC communicates the truths of God to our visual culture in creative and engaging ways.

- Relevant Bible teaching – Our teachers are dedicated to teaching and preaching the Bible in creative ways so that each person can understand and be able to apply it's teachings to our daily lives.

- Sharing Communion– SLEFC participates in The Lord's Supper (Communion—First Sunday of even months). You do not have to be a member of our church to take part. If you are a follower of Jesus Christ you are welcome to share in this simple yet meaningful meal.

- Comfortable dress – SLEFC balances the formality of gathering to be with God with the informality of God's 'come as you are' heart.

- Safe supervision of children – SLEFC ensures that all children and youth workers are trained and screened to protect those entrusted to their care and supervision. We love kids and we want the best for them!

Swan Lake Evangelical Free Church is more than the weekend worship services. Our mission is to help people believe in, belong to, and become like Jesus. Throughout the week we offer different ministries that touch hearts and change lives.

Pastors and leaders at Swan Lake since 1989 include:

1989-1997: Tom Jensen

1998-2000: Eugene Carlson

2001-2005: Craig Cornelius, pastor

2005-2006: David Meinke, interim pastor

2007-present: Raymond Glenn, senior pastor

2008-2010: Christopher Lorentz, first youth pastor

2011-present: Mike Svatek, youth pastor

Present elder board: Pastor Ray Glenn, David Loe, Mark Heuberger, Rod DeGraff, Mark Gustafson, Greg Schwartz and Randy Lindstrom

* On September 23, 2010, the country church south of town, a long-time county landmark, burned down because of an electrical fire.

* Joan (Hirmer) Davis and her daughter, Marissa Davis, are the third and fourth generations of Snyders still worshipping at Swan Lake at the present.

OUR CLUBS & ORGANIZATIONS

American Legion Auxiliary

By Mary Schwisow and Margaret Lund

The American Legion Auxiliary had its beginning on March 20, 1924.

Meetings were held in the council rooms, the school assembly hall or in homes until the past years, when meetings were moved to the Cottonwood Community Center.

We had several special projects that we enjoyed doing through the years. Poppy Day was always exciting for Veterans Day; serving a meal to our local Lions Club at their monthly meetings; sponsoring a noon lunch for the volunteers and medical staff at the local Bloodmobile; furnishing pajamas, etc., for the Veterans Home in Luverne; and serving pie and coffee to our Senior Citizens each November in their honor. Each fall we would hold our annual bazaar. A special honor was to sponsor a high school junior girl to be a representative at Girls State each year when a student was interested in going.

Auxiliary Post #503 disbanded in May 2010 because of not having enough members to continue.

The Cottonwood Country Club

By Sue Morton

The Cottonwood Country Club golf course opened for play on Sunday, May 30, 1976. The first official tee-off group consisted of Susan Anderson Pepin, Bill and Linda Magnuson, Lois and Harold Fratzke, and Marilyn and Norman Geihl.

The 6,846-yard, par-36 course was designed by Martin Johnson, Jr. Although a contractor was hired to build the course, it was volunteers who "spent endless hours picking rocks, planting and watering trees, building sheds and eventually building the clubhouse" which also opened in 1976. Contributions from local businesses and individuals made it possible to establish a tree nursery and build a rest stop off the seventh green.

By 1996 the water irrigation system was updated. Bud Rose Flowers of Marshall donated flowers and plants and again volunteers were important in maintaining the garden areas. Shirley and Donovan Stensrud and Marjorie Reishus were key gardening volunteers. Paved cart paths were established in 1998. Twenty-six trees were added to the course in 2002 and an additional fifteen in 2011. In addition an enclosed patio was completed which added needed room for social events and 19th hole camaraderie. In 2012 the club purchased 13 golf carts in lieu of renting carts annually.

The first Board of Directors consisted of Norman Geihl, President; John Loe, Vice-President; and Greg Isaackson, Secretary-Treasurer. Other original Board Members were Adrian Golberg, Harry Anderson, Trudy Anderson, John Smith, Darris Kompelien and Bill Magnuson. Jerry Heckler was hired as the first groundskeeper. Kathy VanUden and Nancy Laleman both served as Club Managers. The current Board of Directors is Pete Hellie, President; Kyle Boe, Vice-President; Steve Baune, Secretary-Treasurer; and Zeb Prairie, Janelle Bossuyt, Dave Planting, Marlo Moon and Cody Fruin. Tami French is Club Manager and John Geihl is Groundskeeper.

The Cottonwood Golf Club holds an annual fundraiser on Memorial Day each year. Carol and Gene DeSmet play key roles in serving the buffet. Raffle tickets are sold for $50 each. The three big winners of the night walk away with $400, $600 and $1,000 prizes. Other special events held throughout the year have included the Club Championship, a three man best ball tournament, Par Three Fun Tournament, Halloween party, Cinco de Mayo Party and a Ribs and Bibs Cooking Contest and fundraiser.

The traditional Wednesday Ladies Day and Thursday Men's Night continue to be popular. In addition a Monday night league draws participants from not only Cottonwood, but the surrounding communities as well. There are 32 two-man teams that compete in four divisions every Monday night. Larry Nelson started the league and has served as the "Commissioner" for many years. This has created a fun, competitive summer long event for the participants and the Club is very grateful for Larry's contributions and organization.

Rick Rekedal was groundskeeper for thirteen years and played an important role in maintaining a quality course.

The golf club has also played a key part in the success of the Lakeview Schools golf teams by providing a course for local practice and high school competition.

The Cottonwood Country Club continues to provide welcome summer entertainment to our local communities. Our 9-hole course provides a good value and friendly environment for both members and the green-fee paying public.

Hole No. 9. (Photo from swmngolf.com)

Lions Club of Cottonwood

By Larry Isaackson

The Lions Club was organized in May 1953, with 58 charter members. The "Lions" is a service organization working for community and country improvements. Its motto is "We Serve." Internationally, it contributes to help the disabled, schools, clinics, hospitals, the disadvantaged, etc.

One of the first projects of the Lions Club of Cottonwood was fund-raising for a clinic building. The Lions pledged $11,000. The balance was raised from the rest of the community, both town and rural. The clinic was finished in 1955. Dr. Marvin Perrizo, DDS, and M.A. Borgerson, MD, took offices in the building.

The Club has worked on the C.W. Reishus Park, donated land to expand it, put steel on the shelter house and installed plastic/cement parking posts. In 1980-1981 the Lions Club, under the leadership and enthusiasm of President Cliff Hanson, came up with the idea of building a Community Center without the help of a government grant, and the Club helped raise money and provided labor for the building. Over the years, the Lions Club has donated

In 1980-1981, under the leadership of President Cliff Hanson, the Lions Club launched the idea of building a Community Center without help of a government grant. The Lions Club helped raise money and provided labor for the Community Center, located on Main Street.

tables, chairs and carpet to the Community Center as well as help with re-painting the walls.

The Lions Club has built a new shelter house at the City Park and contributed funds for playground equipment there. The Club donated $6,000 to the city of Cottonwood to help pay for sidewalk along Barstad Road.

The Club has donated to the After-Prom Party, summer recreation program, Coming Home Days advertising, Fire Department, Ambulance, Lions Eye Bank, Lions Hearing Foundation and United Way of Southwest Minnesota. It has been a sponsor for the Boy Scouts. It annually holds a "Senior Night" to honor the seniors graduating from high school, plus the giving of two $250 scholarships.

Other activities include: helped serve the meal at the Farmers Co-op Elevator's annual meeting for many years; prepared and served the meal for the Cottonwood Co-op Oil Company's annual meeting for many years; cleaned a two-mile stretch of road ditch along

Highway 23; held fund-raisers at various times for people with health problems; collected used eyeglasses for recycling; patrolled street intersections on Halloween night; picked up Christmas trees in early January; made and served chili for a business showcase & meet-your-neighbor event; and worked on a walking/bike path around the lake where there are no city streets. For a few years, it held a consignment auction as a fund-raiser.

The Cottonwood Area Historical Society

By Pat Aamodt

With several area residents being concerned with preserving Cottonwood history, several informational meetings were held to get input from the community. The Cottonwood Area Historical Society became official on Dec. 16, 1991, when the Articles of Incorporation were signed by the following people: Torgny Anderson, Donna Fratzke, Llewellyn Bahn, Tim Fruin, Pat Aamodt, Al Anderson and Al Smith. The first officers were President Torgny Anderson, Vice President Donna Fratzke, Secretary Pat Aamodt, and Treasurer Al Smith.

An early wish we had was to be able to move the depot to be used as a museum, but there were not enough finances, so that never came to be.

Before the city accepted the Norseth/Larsen House, it approached the CAHS board as to whether there would be interest from the Historical Society in taking over the responsibility of the house.

At a public meeting on April 12, 1993, the CAHS members voted to accept the financial and physical care of the Norseth/Larsen Historical House.

Many different types of fund-raisers were held throughout the years to make this possible.

However, as time went on, interest in the CAHS became less and less. Membership and those willing to give of their time dropped. The board, after many discussions, and a vote taken at the March 19, 2009, Annual Meeting to discontinue our responsibility, attended the city council meeting on April 21, 2009, to relinquish the CAHS responsibility with the Norseth/Larsen House.

The board members at that time were: Pat Aamodt, Al Anderson, Beulah Anderson, John Brower, Barb Crouse, Sue Hanson and Al Smith. Others who have served on the board throughout the years are: Torgny Anderson, Donna Fratzke, Lew Bahn, Tim Fruin, Greg Isaackson, Joy Hellie, Lynn Mauland, Bud Hostetler, Rose Bot, LuAnn Bahn, Al Swennes, Glenda VanLerberghe and Barb Crouse.

Sad to say, the CAHS has been quite inactive since then.

The wonderful part is that the house has been sold to Steve and Robin Alm, who are from right here in Cottonwood and they are taking excellent care of "The House," now known as "Robin's Nest." (see following story)

Norseth/Larsen House

Steve and Robin Alm purchased the historic Norseth/Larsen House in October 2010.

Calling it "Robin's Nest," they plan on keeping the house "era-correct" by refurbishing it to original conditions.

Hosting special events has been fun, and visitors are always welcome. They hope to keep the house a part of Cottonwood history for many years to come.

Cottonwood Senior Citizens

By Margaret Lund and Marge Seitz

The Cottonwood Senior Citizens meet Monday, Wednesday and Friday afternoons from 1:30-4:30. Refreshments are served about 2:45 p.m. and the members take turns bringing goodies.

Towels are embroidered, quilts are stitched on occasion, cards are played and also dominoes, and all enjoy the fellowship.

The center has had good leaders over the years: Elsie Isaackson, Dorothy Severson and Marjorie Seitz, and current leader Margaret Lund. The Senior Citizens hosted a catered chicken dinner the first Wednesday of each month to celebrate birthdays through April 2013.

Senior Dining

By Audrey Hostetler

Since senior dining was first brought to Cottonwood in 1983, meals had been prepared and served at the Cottonwood location. It soon became evident near the end of 2002 that the situation needed to be adjusted because the cost of keeping several small-town sites operating became more expensive. After several meetings, it was decided to consolidate the Cottonwood kitchen with the Marshall kitchen. The meals are prepared in Marshall and transported to the Cottonwood kitchen at the Community Center by someone hired to pick up and serve the meals. Some meals are packaged in the Community Center to be home-delivered by volunteers.

Funding is always a concern for the counties involved in the Senior Dining program, to keep providing nourishing meals . The number of seniors using the site locally has gone down, so the site is open for more people to come to eat and enjoy the fellowship.

Spin-Zone

From the March 2, 2012, Tri-County News

Spin-Zone, owned by Dave Hoff, was established in 2003 as a non-profit, faith-based organization. Spin-Zone's primary purpose is to help people during times of transportation crisis through the temporary use of one of Spin-Zone's vehicles. The operation currently employees three employees and is located at 480 E. 4th St. N. in Cottonwood. In the past year, Spin-Zone has added a couple of wheelchair vans equipped with hydraulic lifts to its fleet of vehicles.

For more information about Spin-Zone, visit its website at www.spin-zone.org, or call 507-423-1000.

Authors of Books with Cottonwood Connections

Joseph Amato: Historian, memoirist, published internationally. Author of approximately 20 books, founder of Crossings Press.

Hugh Curtler: Twelve books on topics from philosophy, ethics, education to modern culture. Earned fellowship from the National Endowment for the Humanities.

Florence Dacey: Four published poetry collections.

Philip Dacey: Twelve full books of poetry, and co-editor of the influential poetry anthology and textbook "Strong Measures." Three-time winner of the national Pushcart Prize, earned a Fulbright Fellowship and National Endowment of the Arts Fellowship.

Austin Dacey: "The Secular Conscience"

Jim Engh: "Slaegten Reishus" (meaning "The Family Reishus")

Lisa (Drummond) Forrest: The poetry collection "To The Eaves."

Erma Huso: "Our Family … Just Recipes and Memories"

Rev. Dr. Kay Jurgenson (granddaughter of the late Ed Elmers): "Hold On, Life is Short"

Daniel Lancaster: "John Beargrease — Legend of Minnesota's North Shore."

Curtis L. Larson: "Memories of a Farm Kid"

J.J. Luepke (aka Jody Isaackson): Four suspense/intrigue novels.

Howard Mohr: Humorist, poet, essayist. Best known for 1987 book "How to Talk Minnesotan," and the Pioneer Public TV special and long-running Plymouth Playhouse musical based on the book. Also author of the books "How to Tell a Tornado (1982), and "A Minnesota Book of Days (and a Few Nights)" (1989). Former writer for the radio show "A Prairie Home Companion."

Sue Morton: A professional storyteller, who has taught classes in storytelling for Senior College and Young Artists workshops at Southwest Minnesota State. Her short story "Soul Light" was published in *Crosstime Science Fiction Anthology Volume VII*. Her poem "Path" was published in *World Treasury of Great Poems Volume II, John Campbell, Editor and Publisher*

Bill Palmer: Five volumes of "To The Colors," books tell the stories of local military veterans.

Marlin B. Reishus: The memoir "If It Is To Be, It's Up To Me."

Susan Runholt: A series of mystery novels for teens.

Dana Yost: Four books, from poetry to local history to essays on rural issues and faith. State and national-award winning daily newspaper editor.

Howard Mohr: Still Talking Minnesotan

Originally published in the May 11, 2013, issue of the Marshall Independent. Reprinted with permission.

By Cindy Votruba

When he wrote his first book, Howard Mohr of Cottonwood tried to make sure he wasn't going to get run out of town.

More than a quarter of a century later, he's still in the same place, but some parts of Mohr's best seller have changed.

A new version of Mohr's classic 1987 book *How To Talk Minnesotan* was scheduled to be released May 28 by Penguin Books.

How the book came about started back in 1985. Mohr had been writing fake commercials and other comedy bits for Garrison Keillor's nationally-broadcast radio program, "A Prairie Home Companion."

It was around that time that Mohr, his wife, Jody, and their daughter were setting off to visit friends in Germany. They were studying phrases in the language and were practicing a few while driving into town for groceries. When they got to a certain one, they kept repeating it and started laughing. In the introduction to the new version, Mohr wrote that "Jody's foot got a little heavy for the patrolman who stopped them. She got a warning for 10 miles per hour over, and I got some material from it: Hey! Why not write a visitor's guide for Minnesota?"

So Mohr wrote Minnesota Language Systems ads for "A Prairie Home Companion" one at a time, with 26 in total.

"After three weeks of study, you think you lived in Minnesota, so would your mom," Mohr said.

Mohr got a call from Ellen Levine, Keillor's agent, who had gotten a call from a publisher wanting Keillor to write a book on the "Minnesota Language Systems." Keillor had said that he hadn't written them, Howard did.

So from 1985 to 1987, Mohr wrote the first version.

"I used the original scripts to write the book," Mohr said. "I always liked the fake commercials. A lot of them were in the book."

From there, Mohr was sent on a book tour all over the country. He remembered such stops as one for public radio in Houston, Texas, and another venue in Dallas that he recalled distinctly.

"I shared a cab with five ladies; they were there for a Mary Kay conference," he said.

The book was also made into a musical by Troupe America back in 1997 and had a five-year run at the Plymouth Playhouse. It was open again in January 2010 for a run through October of that year.

In early 2012, Mohr said his original editor from Viking/Penguin called him out of the blue and said that it's been 25 years and thought he might write an update to *How To Talk Minnesotan.*

"Apparently they had sold 445,000 books," Mohr said. "So I said I would do it."

Mohr said it took him about three months to get started.

"I didn't want to mess up the old book," he said.

He said he was able to convince his editors to take out some of the old stuff, items he thought were too long or didn't care for anymore, and put in the revised parts.

"What I had said is I had not entered the 21st century myself, tell me what should I do?" Mohr said with a laugh.

He's not very kind to Facebook in the new version, Mohr said. He did update a few things, and the hot dish recipe is still being used.

One of the items he changed from the first book, Mohr said, is the percentage of hugs Minnesota men gave their wives without being asked.

"I imagine that has improved over the last 25 years," he said.

Once the book got the way he wanted it, Mohr said writing it became more pleasurable to him. He's particularly glad to get a piece he wrote for the Minneapolis Star Tribune in the book on gambling in the schools. Mohr admits that he writes pretty heavy satire, but the book is mostly light-hearted.

James Dahl: A Gifted Artist

From the Aug. 22, 2012, issue of the Tri-County News of Cottonwood. Reprinted with permission.

By Jessica Stolen

Former Cottonwood artist James Dahl passed away at the age of 54 at Avera McKennan Hospital in Sioux Falls, S.D. [on Aug. 19, 2012], two days after suffering a brain aneurysm.

Dahl was known for his work throughout the area, such as murals painted at Minnesota's Machinery Museum in Hanley Falls, the Marshall bowling alley, a diorama at the Lyon County Museum, a ceiling mural at the Marshall High School cafeteria, and a sculpture on display at Southwest Minnesota State University.

Dahl worked with all media, be it drawing, sculpture or painting. His first exhibit was a show in Chicago in the mid-1980s, and he has also had exhibits at the Minneapolis Institute of Arts.

Dahl also participated in the Lakeview School's Artist in Residence program, teaching elementary students at the school about art during a couple of different school years.

Dahl grew up in Watertown, S.D., and later attended Southwest Minnesota State University from 1979 to 1984.

Dahl was also a seasoned harmonica player and poet.

At the time of his death, he was working on a statue called the Whitney statue, which was being designed to stand near the intersection of 3rd Street and College Drive in downtown Marshall. He had hoped to finish the depiction of Mrs. Mary Whitney, who helped found the city of Marshall, pouring water on the ground in a symbolic baptism of the town of Marshall, by late August or early September 2012. [After Dahl's death, another Cottonwood artist, John Sterner, was engaged to finish the statue, giving Cottonwood artists leading roles in one of the most significant works of public art in the region in many years.]

***

In a 2009 story in the Marshall Independent, Dahl talked about the diversity of the types of art he created and media he used:

While he considers drawing to be the backbone of his art, Dahl works in all media. His work varies widely from chainsaw sculpture to rock balancing. When asked about his working process, he says he collects ideas and items to use. He never knows for sure what he will do with them or when he will use them, "but when it clicks, it clicks," he said.

His ideas for subject matter are taken from everyday life and can vary widely from religion to social commentary. While he does not do political art, if there is a war, he'll do a piece about that. If there is an earthquake or tsunami, you'll find him working on an artwork which expresses his feelings.

All of his work is based on his strong faith.

"The basis for all that I do is more about God than anything. God has given me a lot of talent and shown me so many things. I wouldn't have this talent if there wasn't a reason for it," he said.

… Art professor Jim Swartz said, "Jim is a true artist in every sense of the word."

Local Sculptors and Painters

James Dahl

John Sterner

Local Inventors

Einar Oftedal

Harold Fratzke

OUR MEMORIES

Memories of some of the buildings/businesses

that were once on Main Street

By Karen (Dahl) Klein

HENRY TAKLE HARDWARE STORE

In 1933, Henry Takle bought the hardware store in Cottonwood from Fred McLennan and moved his family to town from Revere, Minn. His family consisted of wife Josie, daughter Maxine and son Everett.

The store was located on the corner of Main and W. 1st Street. The new Norwegian Mutual Insurance building is now located on that site.

The extra clerks in the store were his daughter Maxine and Kermit Lien.

Henry sold everything, from any type of item used in the house, to anything for shops or farms.

In 1945, his son-in-law Norman Dahl, with his wife Maxine and daughters Cynthia and Karen, moved into the apartment over the store. Norman was the main repair man and delivered bottled gas.

In 1955, Henry sold the business to Kenneth Nelson. Norman and family continued to live upstairs.

In 1968, Maxine started a Variety Store in the front part, with the Library being in the back portion.

Because of health issues, Maxine sold the building to Loren Erickson about 1974.

On May 29, 1985, the Fire Department burned the building as a fire practice.

There was an empty lot to the east of the store, which was used for rolle bolle lanes in the back. In the front, there was a popcorn stand.

FORMER BUILDINGS/BUSINESSES WHERE THE UNITED SOUTHWEST BANK NOW STANDS, AT 111 W. MAIN

On the corner was the <u>Red Owl Store,</u> owned by James and Evelyn Flor. They, with their sons James Jr. (Jimmy) and Robert (Bobby) lived in the apartment above.

In the back, the office was upstairs above the "big red owl." You could see everything from there. In the back store room, the supplies were kept on full platforms. Wonderful places for hide-and-seek.

In the basement, there was an opening in the next store's basement. This, too, made for great hiding.

The store next door, to the west, was a clothing store owned by Ev and Judy Vermilyea. It was called Skogmo's. They and their children, Cheryl, Susan and Bruce, lived in the front apartment and they rented out the back apartment.

The next building, to the west of Skogmo's, was the movie theater, owned by Mr. and Mrs. Wayne Peterson. There were shows every Tuesday and Thursday, plus a Sunday matinee. Sunday and Monday showed the same movie. Wednesday was a different movie, and Friday and Saturday had the same show.

ROY NEAL HATCHERY

Where the TNT store, at 108 W. Main Street (formerly Ericksen Furniture), was until recently, there was a hatchery. In the early 1950s, it was owned by Roy Neal, his wife and daughters, Jean and Carol.

It was a wonderful place to use for roller skating in the winter, as it had to be kept so warm for the eggs to hatch. It was all concrete flooring, which was really terrific for smooth "sailing" and speed.

It was a sad day when they sold and went to Granite Falls to operate a variety store.

BEN and STELLA SLETTE CAFÉ

For 25 years, Ben and Stella (Dahl) Slette had a restaurant on Main Street. First, it was located where Kirk Lovsness has his insurance business, at 68 W. Main, and then where the city office/library was at 86 W. Main.

Ben would be up to the café at 5 a.m. to get things started before Stella came to do the baking. She made 15 to 20 pies a day, plus doughnuts, long johns, bismarcks, cookies, etc.

They were open until 9 p.m. and it was the best place to go for ice cream after a show.

Larson's Cafe

From Memories of a Farm Kid by Curtis L. Larson, whose parents were Leslie and Ruth Larson, and brother of Donna Mae Reishus, all former residents of Cottonwood. Used by permission from Mark Larson, son of Curtis Larson.

Sometime in 1939 or 1940, Dad and Mom bought the restaurant [located where Kirk Lovsness' Insurance Service Agency is now] in Cottonwood. It was the only restaurant in town, known as Nelson's Café, and was doing a very good business. It [then] became Larson's Café, open for business from 6:30 a.m. to 11 p.m. seven days a week. It had about 12 booths, a dining counter for about 10 people and near the entrance a counter for selling ice cream, cigarettes, etc., as well as the cash register.

Running the restaurant was a major undertaking. Mom became the chief cook for three meals per day. Dad was the dining counter server, cashier and business operator. There was a cook to help Mom and a special cook who made 12 or more pies every day. They had four waitresses on shifts throughout the day and evening. Mom and Dad both worked every day eight to 12 hours. Both Mom and Dad did their jobs very well, but it was hard work with long days, especially Saturdays. On Saturday evening the farm families congregated on Main Street to do their weekly shopping and to socialize.

It was Dad's idea to buy the restaurant. He saw it, I'm sure, as a way to prepare themselves financially for the future. He and Mom were both a year or two past 40 and, because of The Depression and the drought years, they had no savings. All they had was their relatively small equity in the farm, purchased three years earlier, and the value of their livestock and farm equipment. Mom saw it as a lot of hard work for both of them and worried that it might not work out so well. I don't know the purchase price, but it no doubt required a loan in addition to the farm mortgage. But this was a commercial venture, and economic conditions were on the upswing. If all went well for five or more years in the restaurant, it would give them a "nest egg" for retirement about 20 years off.

• • •

On Saturday evenings in town during the summer, Main Street was crowded with people, mostly farm families, from 7 until 10 p.m. We all worked that evening, busy serving hamburgers, pie and coffee, ice cream sundaes, malted milks and hundreds of ice cream cones, so it seemed, at five cents each. Dad worked non-stop dishing up cones, with about a dozen flavors to offer. If asked, he would reel off all the flavors. Mom was in the kitchen doing hamburgers and other sandwiches and dishing up cuts of pie.

254

After working a full day on the farm, I served customers at the counter on Saturday nights and made up a lot of sundaes and malts. After closing we had to clean up, including mopping the floors, so we didn't get away until almost midnight. This was because a few guys would come in from the pool hall five minutes before our closing time and order hamburgers. I was really bushed those nights, but so was everyone in our crew.

Restaurant dinners then were served at noon every day, Monday through Saturday. It was roast beef every other day and roast pork on the alternate days as the standard fare. Mashed potatoes and gravy went with it, also two slices of white bread and butter as well as coffee or milk. No vegetables as I recall. Some would have a piece of pie with more coffee. The weekday dinner customers were nearly all men who had jobs in town. Some of them did physical work, which burned up lots of calories.

I remember very little about the evening meals, only that "short orders," were always available and, if left over from noon, roast beef or pork as a sandwich, either plain or with potatoes and gravy. Most of the school teachers came for their main meal at supper time, so the restaurant crew got to know them quite well. Breakfast was a busy time, too, with some teachers included. The teachers were mostly women, young and single, with several new ones coming each fall. The single guys in town took a special interest in the teachers, who occasionally ended up marrying a local man. I remember three women teachers who did so while I was in college.

• • •

Every Sunday noon, we served baked chicken dinners with the usual trimmings. It was always very good. As times got better, a few farm families would eat out Sunday after church. If so, it would be chicken dinner at Larson's Café. They would be warmly greeted by Dad as well as waitresses. If Dad didn't know them, he would by the time they left.

The restaurant and the pool hall were also quite busy on Saturday night. The pool hall had customers other evenings as well and a few daytime customers. As teenagers we could go there to play pool or play snooker, which required more skill. I went with a friend or two once in a while, but never on Saturday night. Prohibition had ended a few years before, so 3.2 beer was sold there at the bar. Nothing stronger was sold in town until years later. There were tables, which were used mostly for card games — no gambling that I ever saw. Only men were seen there, except for a few upper-teenage boys — no women.

For the most part, farm families and others were happy to socialize in the restaurant and on the main street sidewalks. The grocery, hardware, and other stores were, of course, open all evening. Moms and dads were also doing their weekly shopping. This provided additional opportunities to visit with neighbors and friends. Unless you were new in town, you knew everyone you saw uptown and could take time to visit a bit while shopping.

The café was swarming with pheasant hunters for several weekends in October. Most of them came from the Twin Cities. Some of them had farmer friends or relatives that would welcome them for hunting in their corn fields. Others had to scout around for fields that were not posted with "No Hunting" signs. I don't know where they stayed overnight — perhaps at motels in Marshall or Granite Falls — but they turned up at our restaurant for many of their meals. After tramping through corn fields for hours, they had big appetites. And of course talk of pheasant hunting experiences filled the air in Larson's Café. It was a busy place.

Larson's Café, circa 1942: Ruth, Leslie, servers and cooks. (From the book *Memories of a Farm Kid*. Reprinted with permission)

Fondly Remembering Andy's Place

By Fran Viane

In January of 2001, Andy Viaene closed the door of the much-loved establishment called Andy's Place after 43 years of business.

We moved from our farm by Hendricks, Minn., to Cottonwood in 1958, when Andy injured his back and couldn't farm anymore.

He bought the Southside Pool Hall from his dad, Cyriel Viaene, in 1958.

In 1966, Andy purchased the Northside Pool Hall, which he named Andy's Place.

Andy loved people and made many friends, from young to old.

The young people loved him as he made them feel very special, and let them play video games or shoot pool for little to nothing — he knew they didn't have much money to spend.

Andy was active in our community with 20 years on the fire department, five years on ambulance; involvement in the Sportsmen's Club, bowling league and softball league.

Andy passed away on Nov. 4, 2007.

We were proud to call Cottonwood our home, with memories and many wonderful friends. It was a great place to raise our family of five children.

P.S. When Andy closed, some of his friends wanted a meeting place for cards and pool. He sold the building to them and it was reopened. Some time later, they moved the business a few doors to the west. Now the old pool building is empty.

Cottonwood in 1893: "The Town Is Most Beautiful"

This was originally published in the March 25, 1893, edition of the Cottonwood Current newspaper, just five years after the city was founded. It was reprinted in 1963 in the 75th Anniversary celebration booklet, which described the particular issue of the Current as very rare. "This is perhaps the only extant copy of this Current, as the establishment was destroyed by fire shortly thereafter." editors wrote in the 1963 booklet. "Our thanks go to Mr. Arvid F. Wall of San Francisco, California, son of one of Cottonwood's pioneer businessmen, who has preserved this issue of the Current through the many years and now makes it available for presenting this priceless excerpt.

MAIN STREET AND THE LAKE, LOOKING NORTH.

This drawing of Cottonwood, with the lake in the background, appeared in the March 25, 1893, edition of the Cottonwood Current and was reprinted with the following story in the city's 75th anniversary book in 1963.

"As we read, let us place ourselves in the midst of that pioneer year, and in the stead of J.F. Paige, editor, who wrote ...."

COTTONWOOD: A YOUNG AND THRIFTY TOWN

Somewhere about the year 1860 Uncle Sam sent his henchmen into this section of his grand domain, to run parallel lines by which he might be able to more accurately designate his belongings and at the same time get such topographical knowledge as was necessary to have, in order that he might fulfill his promise to "give everyone a farm." At that time a different scene presented itself to the gazer's eye from that of today. The critic's eye, from certain standpoints, might have considered the view much more beautiful than that of today, and no doubt the hunters of those days, who followed their game over these flower bedecked prairies, deemed themselves as near heaven or the Garden of Eden, as was possible for mortal man to get. Instead of beautiful fields of waving grain extending as far as the eye could reach, with magnificent farm houses surrounded by large and comfortable stables and granaries, he would have beheld a scene of such exquisite loveliness, that he would have thought himself in "Fairy Land."

A broad expanse of land over which he could travel for days and even months without the slightest change or interruption, topographically speaking, with the exception of now and then a shallow stream, which, with the help of his trusty horse, he could readily ford. A slightly undulating prairie, covered by the richest of verdure, with now and then a lake of the purest water glittering in the sun, whose bosom was never disturbed except by the wild geese and ducks which made these waters their home, or by the Indian canoe, propelled by its dusky inmate in quest of game, both the lakes and the prairie furnished in such liberal quantities. What a contrast between then and now. Could that lone hunter, who pitched his tent on these broad prairies, wherever night overtook him, be made to believe that in these few years such changes could have taken place? We doubt if an angel from heaven could have convinced him of such a possibility. But what can have caused these great changes? The answer comes voluntarily: civilization. The white man, with his manifold implements of agriculture, appeared on the scene of future beauty. And lo! The whole is changed, and all this grand prairie, which, at that time, yielded nothing to man save sustenance to the vast herds of buffalo, deer and Indians, now yields produce sufficient to support the people of the whole United States, while millions of acres yet remain unclaimed.

Up to the year 1871, very few whites had visited this section of the country and with the exception of a few straggling hunters, who were attracted here by the large herds of buffalo, which roamed at will over the prairies, perhaps no white person had visited it with any idea of settlement. But during the summer of '71, a few hardy pioneers, attracted by the apparent fertility of the soil, and the beauty of its many lakes scattered about in just the right proportion to furnish water as it might be needed, ventured to break up a small piece of prairie and establish homes, though rude and temporary, and sending for their families, spent the winter of 1871-72 here. We gather from statistics that W.H. Slater and John Moe were the first settlers to arrive.

Later on, somewhere about the middle of June, came E.T. Hamre, Pete Eliason and Irving Egoness and a short time after Allend Christian and Harrison Price put in an appearance. E.T. Hamre, Pete Eliason, Allend Christian and Harrison Price still remain here and are classed among our thriftiest and most prosperous farmers. At a later period came another installment of equally hardy sons of toil among whom was our townsman, O.H. Dahl. Mr. Dahl early realized the nice future in store for those who remained to fight out the battle of life and the result is he is still here, hale and hearty, one of our most respected and wealthy citizens.

The breaking plow once started it was never allowed to stop. Others soon learned of this rich granary of the west and were not slow to follow. The settlers soon found that their numbers would warrant an organization and, in July, 1873, the town was organized. It was named Canton at first, but for some reason that was not satisfactory and the name of the town was changed to Lisbon and again to Moe, but finally the name of Lucas was settled upon, which it still retains. The first town meeting was held on the 5th of August, 1873, and resulted in the election of James Wardrop as chairman with O.H. Dahl and John Moe as side supervisors; Harrison Price, clerk; N.H. Dahl, assessor and treasurer; T.S. Norgaard and R.H. Dahl, justices; R.J. Benjamin and Geo. Anderson, constables. The first school was taught by Miss Williams the same year of the organization in a building owned by Harrison Price on section 2.

The Great Northern railroad, a map of which appears in this issue, was built through this town in 1888, up to which time very little material advancement had taken place. But the impetus which that grand road gave to the whole country we felt in no small degree in this immediate vicinity and the fact remains indelibly stamped upon the reasoning faculties of every individual of this great growing west, that to the railroads, in a great degree, we owe our prosperity. To such men as James J. Hill, whose stubborn persistency in the future prosperity and grandure (sic) of this great west, more than any other one man, do the people of these rich prairies owe their present prosperity. Such men achieve popularity and wealth and it is right that they should. Who that knows the history of the Great Northern railroad, and his many other great undertakings, does not venerate the man? In our ardor for the Great Northern and its more than great projector, we had nearly forgotten our subject matter. Immediately upon the completion of the railroad, the boom for Cottonwood took place. The church, which stands on the shore of Lake Cottonwood, was the first building. The building now occupied by the post office and Dahl Bros. general merchandise, was built the same fall by C.H. and J.H. Dahl. Martin Ness built the building now occupied by himself as a furniture store and Bomstad's saloon. The same fall several other buildings were in different stages of completion. The same fall Uncle Sam gave us post office facilities and A.S. Reishus for postmaster, who held the office but a short time, resigning in favor of C.H. Dahl, who, November 1st, resigned in favor of his brother J.H. Dahl, who is still holding the same position. The village of Cottonwood had made such rapid progress that in the year 1891, serious thoughts of organization finally culminated in the incorporation of the village, the 12th day of January, 1892. On the 1st of February, 1892, the following officers were elected: M. Norseth, Mayor; Thos. McKinley, J.H. Dahl, and George Russell, Councilmen; C.T. Hansen, Recorder; Chas. Wall, Treasurer; J.P. Krog and O.H. Dahl, Justices; D.B. York and O. Johnson, Constables.

On the 9th of March the regular election took place resulting in the election of the following officers: Thomas McKinley, Mayor; George Russell, J.L. Otis and L. Larson, Councilmen; C.T. Hansen, Recorder; Chas. Wall, Treasurer; J. Bell and O.A. Brenna, Justices; D.B. York and O. Johnson, Constables.

Soon after being incorporated the citizens, with that spirit of go-aheaditiveness, which is peculiar in all western men, prepared to establish, grade and build sidewalks and crossings upon the main thoroughfares; street lamps were erected, a jail was built and the general welfare of the inhabitants carefully looked after. The town is most beautiful, located on the southeast bank of Lake Cottonwood, thirteen miles northeast of Marshall, the county seat, and has a population of between four and five hundred. We have an excellent city government and the laws are all good and well enforced. Life and property are secure. Values are well established and maintained and with the good society, healthy and delightful climate, handsome and eligible location of the city as to drainage, etc., railroad, telegraph and mail facilities all parts of the world, make all the conditions of life here pleasant and agreeable.

J.F. Paige, editor

March 25, 1893

Downtown Saturday Nights

From the book "If It Is To Be, It Is Up To Me," the personal memoirs of Marlin B. Reishus. Reprinted with permission from the author.

When I was fourteen, I started working summers with my dad as a carpenter's helper in his construction company. I earned forty cents an hour, and thought that was a lot of money. Most of the time, he and his crew would work ten-hour days, six days a week. So did I. Occasionally on a Saturday, the crew would quit work at four o'clock, after working eight hours. I liked when that happened because Saturday night was a big night in Cottonwood. There were more people downtown Saturday night than any other time during the week. The high school band would set up on the street corner in front of the bank, and former high school band members brought their instruments and joined in for a one-hour concert. Chairs and music stands were literally on the street. The area was roped off, so people knew not to park in those four or five parking places. After every piece, people in the cars would honk their horns, which was their version of applause.

The Overhead Bridge

By Pat Aamodt

Have you ever wondered when the overhead bridge — which leads into Cottonwood from the south off Highway 23 — was constructed?

Some time ago, Nancy Meyer gave me some pictures that had been in her Grandma Clara Nelson's photo book. They were pictures of the overhead bridge at different stages of construction, but there were no dates. That triggered a hunt to find some dates and information.

Reading in one of our town history books, I found out that old Highway 23 (now Barstad Road) was constructed in 1936, so that was a starting point.

In visiting with Steve Lee, I learned that he, too, was interested and had actually written to the Minnesota Department of Transportation back in January 2010 to find the same information.

This information was included in MnDOT's reply: "Dear Mr. Lee ... you also requested some information on the overhead structure (bridge) that brings the old Highway 23 roadway from east side of the BNSF Railroad to the west side of the railroad, just south of Cottonwood. This roadway belongs to Lyon County and is called Lyon County State Aid Highway 32 (CSAH 32). The State of Minnesota officially turned that roadway over to Lyon County in 1972 when the present-day alignment of State Highway 23 was constructed on the east side of BNSF railroad tracks. The bridge you are inquiring about was originally constructed in 1936. In 1999 Lyon County completed a bridge reconditioning project on the structure and everything on the bridge was built new except for the piers.

"With the original bridge constructed in 1936, there is essentially no information on who sponsored the project, why it was constructed, or what funding source was used in Mn/DOT's records. Please contact Lyon County regarding information regarding the original design of the bridge. All files pertaining to the roadway were turned over to Lyon County when the roadway was given to Lyon County in 1972."

Going through issues of the 1936 Cottonwood Current, I was able to find the following short articles:

• May 8, 1936: "Equipment Arrives to Begin Work on TH 17: A large shipment of road building equipment arrived here the first of the week and was moved to the old baseball field on the Reishus farm north of town, which the contractor, H.P. Englund, has chosen for a permanent site while building the new road from Cottonwood to Hanley Falls. All heavy equipment was shipped here by rail from Glasgow, Montana, while a fleet of some 50 trucks made the journey overland.

"Work on the new road we are informed will begin today, the crew dividing into two units, one starting at the St. Louis bridge in Hanley Falls and other at a point south of Cottonwood where the overhead bridge will be built. The route of the new highway, now under construction, will follow the Great Northern railroad tracks on the west side of the right-of-way.

"Three concrete bridges will be built between here and Hanley Falls and material for the purpose arrived here this week. These bridges will be built by a bridge contractor, Mr. Englund having nothing to do with bridge construction.

"Judging from the large amount of road machinery and the large force of men employed, the new road will be pushed to completion in a hurry. Mr. Englund has hired a number of local men, who will have work with the road crew until the project is finished."

• May 8, 1936: "Chambers and Spencer have moved to new camping grounds north of town and will commence today on the work of building the state road thru the village limits. The work will require twelve or fifteen days."

• June 4, 1936: "Grading for the new highway has been completed from the south up to the village limits, and all that yet remains to be done on this portion of the road is the construction of the overhead bridge crossing the Great Northern railway track. The contract for this bridge has been let to the Ernest M. Ganley Co., Inc., of Minneapolis for $38,584."

• July 10, 1936: "Sharp Detour Causes Automobile Accident: Morris Stevens, about 22 years old, son of Mrs. Chas. Stevens living north and west of Cottonwood, met with a serious automobile accident at a point just north of Cottonwood where the detour of old No. 17 joins the newly constructed highway. Coming along at a fast clip about 10 o'clock last Saturday night he failed to make the turn and his car plunged forward into the ditch and turned over what was considered three and a half times, breaking down the top and otherwise damaging the car. The young man was brought to town in a semi-conscious condition, where an examination revealed that he hadn't been seriously injured. It seems strange that immense sums of money are expended to build over-head bridges to conserve human life, while negligently leaving a death trap like the one north of town. Those who observed the demolished car could not conceive how one could come through it without meeting death."

• Aug. 21, 1936: "A maintenance crew of the state highway department this week blacktopped the street from the west railroad crossing through main street to Dahl & Laingen's corner, and the new highway also from the same point of beginning to the Henry Arneson home. This was done for the convenience of traffic until the new overhead bridge south of Cottonwood is completed, opening up travel on the new T.H. No. 17. This is a sample of how Cottonwood streets will appear, should the voters at the special election August 25 vote to bond the municipality for $4,000."

• Sept. 18, 1936: "Bids will be opened by the State Highway department on October 2 for grading and gravel surfacing of T.H. No. 17 between Cottonwood and Hanley Falls, 8.2 miles, comprising 7,500 cubic yards of excavation and 7,050 cubic yards of gravel surfacing."

• Nov. 20, 1936: "With the completion of the work of gravelling the new highway, Ed Bathers and his group of engineers and office help, who have made Cottonwood their headquarters since last April, will pack up their belongings and leave Monday for other fields of labor in the services of the state highway department. We understand Mr. and Mrs. Harold Cook and family will locate in Marshall for the winter."

Popcorn Stand

A long-standing summer favorite, the Popcorn Stand in downtown Cottonwood, came to an end when it closed after the summer of 1999. Cliff and Sue Hanson owned it for several years and their four daughters operated it over 13 summers. Dave Wiesen then bought it and his daughters operated it for six years. It was so busy during the 1988 Cottonwood Centennial that the stand ran out of 700 home-made lollipops. There had been at least two other stands that preceded the one that the Hansons and Wiesens owned. Before the Hansons bought it, the current stand was owned, in succession, by Harlen and Dori Gniffke (who built it in 1948), Lloyd and Ruby Kroger, Ray and Marge Gigstad, Steve and then Jerry Rekedal, then Jeff and Todd Lewis.

It could be found next to the old Takle Hardware Store and former Snooks/Jim's Café, where the new Norwegian Mutual building has since been constructed.

From the July 2, 1997, issue of the Tri-County News
By Karen Berg

If you want a bag of popcorn in Cottonwood, it's not hard to find one. You just drive down Main Street and talk to Desiree Wiesen. She is the current owner of the Popcorn Stand. Wiesen's sister, Delilah, became the owner in 1993, buying it from Cliff Hanson. This is Desiree's first year.

You can buy ice cream treats, popcorn and candy. Popcorn now sells for 50 cents a bag. Because of government regulations they are not able to sell lollipops; they would be required to make them at the stand and it is not set up for that.

Wiesen likes the business end of it, getting the loan, ordering supplies and depositing the money. "It just pays for itself and is a great place to hang out," Wiesen said.

She also enjoys it when the former owners of the Popcorn Stand stop by and reminisce.

Wiesen could reminisce back quite a few years.

Years ago there was a man named George Davis, otherwise known as "Popcorn Davis," who pulled his cart selling popcorn on the main street in Cottonwood.

Stella Slette remembers him as being a friendly man, with a slight bend in his back as he walked. Myrtle Loland said, "George was pushing popcorn 100 years ago." But of course it was actually in the 1920s that you could buy a bag of popcorn from Davis for 5 cents.

Davis wasn't the only traveling popcorn man. Paul Lund looks back on the Saturday nights when he was a kid in the late 1930s and 1940s. "Each of us kids got a nickel, with that nickel you could buy either a Cherrio, popsicle, package of gum or a bag of popcorn from Ed Ringsven," Lund said.

Ringsven had a gas portable popcorn machine on a cart that he pushed along. "In those days, on Saturday nights, the town was full, stores were open and the folks were sitting on their car fenders on Main Street. Back when you could sit on fenders and not bend them," Lund said.

It was the same when Victor Lien ran the popcorn stand. Lien said, "The popcorn stand was a place for young kids to hang around, kids folks sitting in cars, gawking at people, eating popcorn, listening to the band." Lien was a young kid at the time Pat Davis used to have a popcorn machine in the old theater. Lien bought it and kept it in the hardware store. Lien would drag out the machine and sell popcorn.

In 1931, Lien "built the little shack," with the help of Wendell Knudson. Lien would open on Wednesday and Saturday evenings and summer holidays. In 1933, he expanded and, along with selling popcorn, he sold hamburgers, Lien said. "Everything was a nickel."

Rachel Knudson recalls the little popcorn shack, built by her brother Victor and husband Wendell. It was on the property owned by [Henry] Takle, who also had the hardware store next door. After Lien graduated in 1934, he left town and Amanda (Nordli) Madison ran it for awhile. Rachel Knudson said, "her hamburgers and pie were so popular. It would sit about six people."

The building was eventually moved off the Takle land. Since the building was like a little house, it was eventually moved across the railroad tracks near the elevator and Ole Pearson lived in it. The move left an empty spot on Main Street.

It did not take long for popcorn to return to the spot on the Takle property. In 1948, Harlen and Dori Gniffke built the popcorn stand as it now sits today. Gniffke answered an ad to buy a popcorn machine. Dori added lollipops. Dori, being from Wood Lake, remembered the lollipops being sold at the drugstore as a kid, so she started making them and selling them at the popcorn stand. "It was horrid to make them. You had to work fast to scoop the ice cream and dip them in chocolate with no air conditioning at home," where she made them, she said. It was a special treat if you got a free lollipop. The Gniffkes would put one free stick to every 10 to 15 [that were sold].

The concept of making money selling popcorn and lollipops continued when Lloyd and Ruby Kroger bought the stand from the Gniffkes around 1956. Sharnie Fischer, their daughter, said, "I opened at 6:30 p.m. and then, later on, when my folks came up, I was free to go. It was nice. I also remember making the lollipops. Dad scooped and I dipped."

Marge Gigstad also recalled the scooping and the dipping of the lollipops. She made 1,000 in advance at one time when she was not going to be available to work. Ray and Marge

Gigstad ran the stand for about nine years after 1957. The Gigstads owned two popcorn machines. During those years the school did not own a machine so the oldest son took the machine to the school for games and out to the softball games. "We sold a lot of popcorn. We would buy 400 to 500 pounds of popcorn every month," Gigstad said.

Steve Rekedal continued running the popcorn machine at the school and at football games after he bought it from the Gigstads in 1967. He would open when it got nice in the spring and close it before school started. "Talk about a job," Rekedal said, but he also said it was a good experience. Steve sold it to his brother Jerry in 1970 and Jerry ran it until 1973.

During the 1960s and 1970s, the kids who came to the popcorn stand had a great advantage. They could sit in front of the café next door on the slab of cement and, while they visited, they could watch the older "cool" guys drive by in their "hot" cars, or wait for the football players to stop by after practice. Not only was it a good place to meet up with friends, but as Dave Berg said, "It was a great place to meet chicks."

Starting with Rekedal, a younger generation kept the stand going. When Jeff Lewis bought the stand in 1973 he was selling lollipops for 15 cents and two for a quarter. Lori Fruin (Jeff and Todd's sister) remembered helping make lollipops and getting paid a penny for each one. The popcorn bags went up from a nickel to 15 cents for a small bag and 35 cents for a large bag. Fruin said, "Another hot item to sell was the 'Red Hot Dollar Licorice' pieces, which were sold for a penny each. Twenty-five cents would fill a bag.

The family continued the operation with Todd running it from 1976-1979.

When the stand was sold, another family started a tradition. When the Cliff and Sue Hansons owned the stand, their four children ran it, starting with Heidi, Kris, Sonya and Trudy. Trudy did not even want to open up the stand if the lollipops weren't made, since people came from all over to buy a lollipop at the price of 25 cents and later 40 cents. Sue recalled keeping count one year and found out they sold 5,000 lollipops. Sue said, "Kids learned a lot, how to deal with people, make change, ordering supplies." The Hansons sold the stand to Delilah Wiesen in 1993.

After many years near the corner on Main Street, the Popcorn Stand is showing its years. Desiree Wiesen said she is thinking of replacing the stand because she plans to operate it for a few more years. "I like talking with people so I will be here for a couple of more years." Now, to find 5 cents to buy a bag of popcorn, maybe 50 cents.

Cottonwood Sports Highlights 1988-2013

• Cottonwood won the 1989 Class A state high school girls golf team championship, and Cottonwood-Wood Lake won the 1991 Class A state high school girls golf team championship. Both teams were coached by Mike O'Reilly.

• Other Cottonwood or Lakeview High School conference and postseason champions:

— Football: Buffalo Ridge Conference champions 1987, 1988; Southwest Ridge Conference champions 2003. Section champions 1987.

— Girls golf: Camden Conference champions 1992, 1998, 2003, 2005. Sub-section champions 1992, 1993, 1997, 1998, 2001, 2003. Section champions: 2000, 2008.

— Boys golf: Camden Conference champions 2002, 2006. Sub-section champions 1993, 1994, 1996, 1997, 1999, 2000, 2001. Section champions: 1991, 1996, 1999.

— Girls basketball: Camden Conference champions 1993, 1999, 2000, 2006, 2007, 2009.

— Boys basketball: Camden Conference champions 1996, 2006, 2007.

— Baseball: Camden Conference champions 2003, 2005.

• LeRoy Jolstad of rural Cottonwood was inducted into the Minnesota Softball Hall of Fame in 2008, 44 years after he played his first competitive league softball game with the Cottonwood Knights.

Jolstad was a star fast-pitch softball pitcher, first in Cottonwood, then the Twin Cities, before playing for more than 20 years with teams from Mankato.

It was with the Mettler's Bar team and then the Happy Chef team of Mankato that Jolstad achieved his greatest success. He led Happy Chef to eight consecutive Class AA state tournaments from 1982-1989, and played on seven national championship teams, including in 2007 as a member of a team from Memphis, Tenn.

• Hugh Curtler, a resident of Cottonwood since 1969, enjoyed great success as the women's tennis coach at Southwest State University from 1979-1992. His teams won nine consecutive conference tournaments and were ranked in the top 10 in the nation in the NAIA division six times. Curtler was named the 1990 national NAIA women's tennis coach of the year, was chosen for the Southwest State athletic Hall of Honor in 1992 and inducted into the Northern Sun Intercollegiate Conference Hall of Fame in 2000.

• Cottonwood resident Murl Fischer was the manager and his son Jason Fischer was the star player for the Granite Falls amateur (town-team) baseball team that won the Class C Minnesota state title in 1993. Jason Fischer also starred for the Granite Falls team that won the 2002 Class C state championship. Jay Magnuson of Cottonwood also played for the 1993 team.

• Construction of the athletic field complex at the new Lakeview High School was completed in 2006. The athletic complex includes a baseball field, softball field, football field and track.

• Jeff Dahl of Cottonwood was inducted into the Augsburg College athletic Hall of Fame Oct. 11, 2007. He played basketball at Augsburg, in Minneapolis, and graduated in 1974. Dahl, 6-foot-4, was a starter in his junior and senior seasons, and held the school record for rebounds-per-game average at the time he graduated. The record was not broken for 25 years. Before Augsburg, Dahl starred in three sports at Cottonwood High School, where the basketball team posted a 19-1 record his senior year of 1970 and the football team had a 7-1-1 record.

• Annual Cottonwood Country Club golf course club champions

2008 was the last year that the Club Championship was held.

MEN

1976 — Mike O'Reilly

1977 — Mike O'Reilly

1978 — Wynston Boe

1979 — Mike O'Reilly

1980 — Adrian Golberg

1981 — Del Lange

1982 — Curt Hanson

1983 — Allen Jaeger

1984 — Allen Jaeger

1985 — Neil Kroger

1986 — Curt Hanson

1987 — Allen Jaeger

1988 — Steve Hawkinson

1989 — Jason Fischer

1990 — Jason Fischer

1991 — Jason Fischer

1992 — Jason Fischer

1993 — Jason Fischer

1994 — Jason Fischer

1995 — Jason Fischer

1996 — Jason Fischer

1997 — Jason Fischer

1998 — Cory Hendrickson

1999 — Josh Hawkinson

2000 — Josh Hawkinson

2001 — Ryan Lange

2002 — Stuart Scott

2003 — Kyle Boe

2004, 2005, 2006 not held

2008 — Ryan Lange

WOMEN:

1976 — Donna Sanders

1977 — Donna Sanders

1978 — Donna Sanders

1979 — Donna Sanders

1980 — Donna Sanders

1981 — Candy Gniffke

1982 — Scotty Mogenson

1983 — Helen Pearson

1984 — Scotty Mogenson

1985 — Scotty Mogenson

1986 — Kathy Johnson

1987 — Sharon Dahl

1988 — Sharon Dahl

1989 — Sharon Dahl

1990 — Leslie Anderson

1991 — Judy Van Maldeghem

1992 — none

1993 — Nancy Kremin

1994 — Sharon Dahl

1995 — Judy Van Maldeghem

1996 — Judy Van Maldeghem

1997 — Candice Kater

1998 — Judy Van Maldeghem

1999 — Judy Van Maldeghem

2000 — Judy Golberg

2001 — Judy Van Maldeghem

2002 — Judy Van Maldeghem

2003 — Dallas Willman

None after 2003

Compiled by Sue Morton

THE NEWBORN TOWN

Giving Cottonwood its Name

From the Nov. 12, 1874, issue of the Redwood Gazette newspaper

Lyon County: This county has a newborn town, the innocent young hopeful being named Lucas, after Capt. J.R. Lucas, the chief clerk in the state auditor's office.

From the book Minnesota Place Names by Warren Upham

COTTONWOOD: "A city in Lucas Township, section 9, platted in July 1888, received its name from the adjacent lake, which has cottonwood trees on its shore. The city was first settled about 1871 on a townsite of 372 acres and was incorporated as a village January 12, 1892. The mail was first received at Vineland, Yellow Medicine County, 1873-88, where Ole S. Reishus was postmaster on his homestead; when Reishus moved to the Cottonwood site in 1888, the post office also moved and changed its name; his wife, Igebor O. Reishus, became postmaster; it had a Great Northern Railway station."

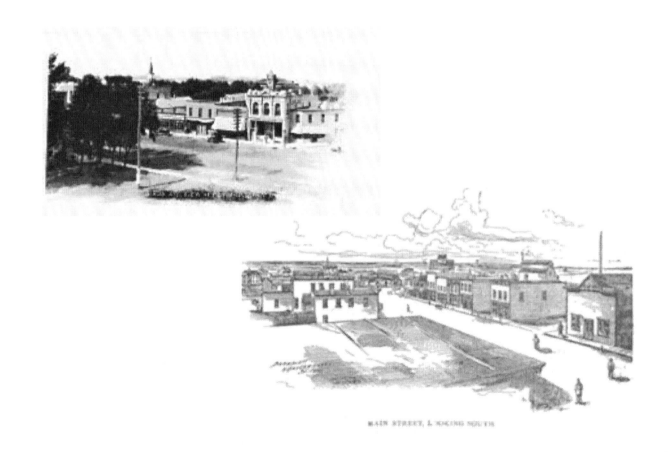

MAIN STREET, LOOKING SOUTH

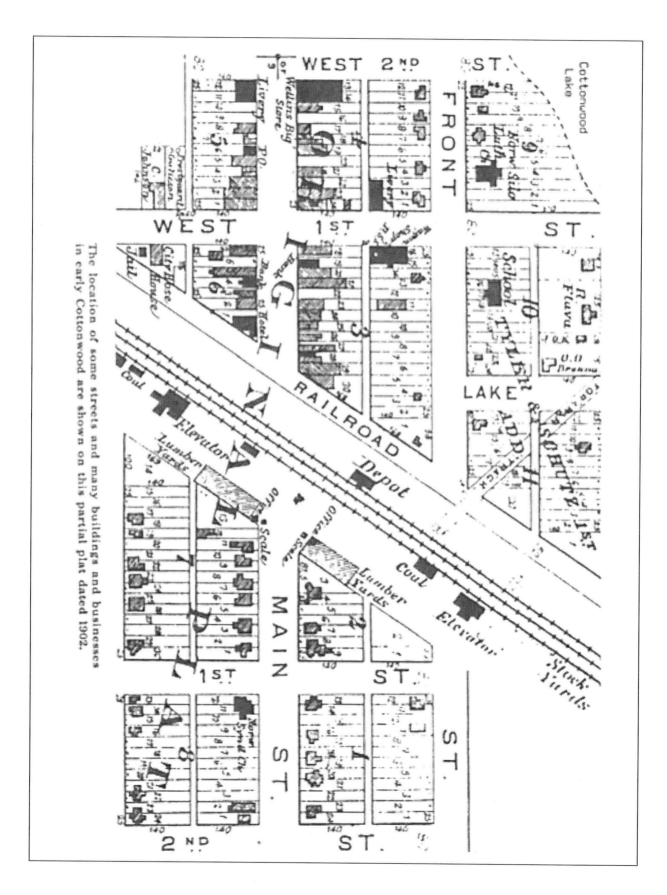

The location of some streets and many buildings and businesses in early Cottonwood are shown on this partial plat dated 1902.

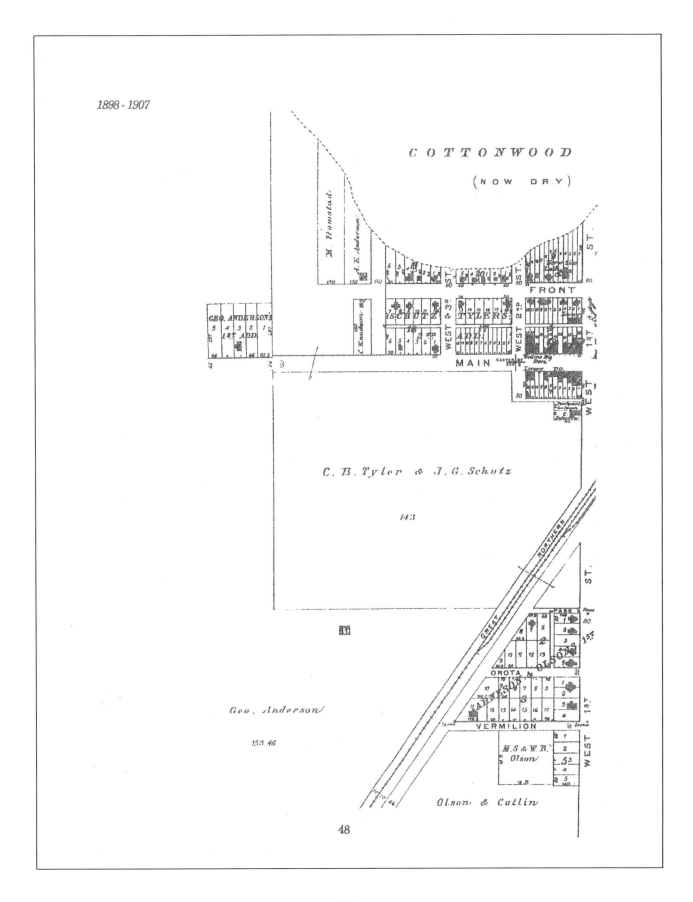

1898 - 1907

COTTONWOOD
(NOW DRY)

C. B. Tyler & J. G. Schutz

143

Geo. Anderson

153.46

Olson & Catlin

48

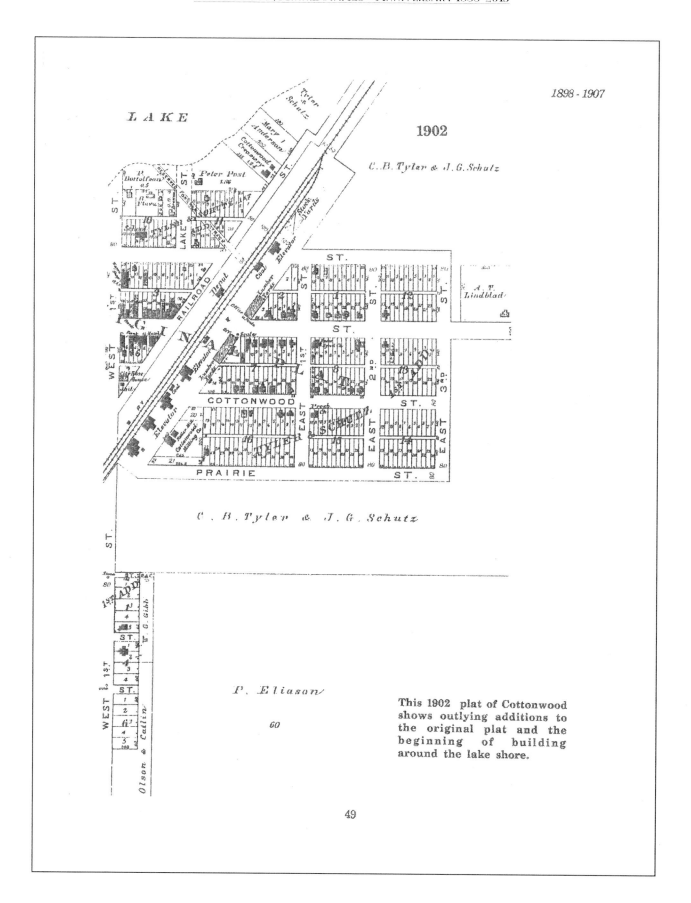

1898 - 1907

1902

This 1902 plat of Cottonwood shows outlying additions to the original plat and the beginning of building around the lake shore.

49

The former jail building was demolished in 2012

ABOVE: Shelly Meyer is shown receiving a check for $35 for her winning design for the 125th Anniversary Logo. She is pictured with members of the anniversary celebration steering committee Tim Fruin, left, and Joel Dahl. LEFT: A time capsule was opened and resealed during the Centennial celebration in 1988, with instructions not to open it again until the 150th anniversary of Cottonwood in 2038. The time capsule is located in Legion Memorial Park on Main Street.

THE WIDE VIEW

OUR WINTERS

Cottonwood not spared in memorable winter of 1996-97

One of the worst winters on record happened within the last 25 years, and Cottonwood found itself in the middle of it.

It was the winter of 1996-1997, when much of Minnesota and the eastern Dakotas received record snowfall amounts and at least nine full-blown blizzards. And much of it came early: By the end of January 2007, according to the Minnesota Department of Natural Resources, most communities in the western third of Minnesota already had been hit with 100 to 200 percent of their snowfall totals for the whole winter. The area around Cottonwood got between 56 to 64 inches of snow from October 1996-March 2007, which was less than places like Fargo, N.D., which got about 100 inches of snow. On a scale of 0 to 100, with 100 being the highest, Cottonwood's snowfall totals scored a 90 when compared to winters from 1931 to 1991, the DNR said.

Deep snow is everywhere on both sides of the driveway at the Jerry and Pat Aamodt farm just west of Cottonwood in this photo taken in early January 1997.

In December 2006, the National Weather Service reporting station in Marshall recorded 23.1 inches of snow, or about 125 percent more than the previous three Decembers combined. The next month, January 2007, the Marshall station recorded 15 inches of snow — for a total of 38 inches in just those two months alone. Marshall's *average annual* snowfall is 39.8 inches.

Headlines in the Tri-County News reflect the winter's impact on Cottonwood, starting with a story in the Nov. 20, 1996, issue about a power outage caused by an ice storm. Schools were closed by a storm Dec. 18, 1996.

According to notes from Pat Aamodt, on Jan. 4, 1997, ice and rain turned to snow. By Jan. 5, it had become a blizzard that closed Christ Lutheran Church — there was no Sunday worship.

On Jan. 9, another blizzard shut down the Lakeview Schools again, and on Jan. 12, yet another blizzard led to the cancelling of Sunday school at Christ Lutheran, but there was worship service.

The Jan. 8, 1997, issue of the Tri-County News reported that a "snowstorm strands people in Cottonwood," and a headline in the issue of the following week said, "snow removal taking its toll on area budgets."

On Jan. 22, 1997, came a headline that revealed the serious toll of the winter: President Clinton acted by signing a declaration that would release federal funds to help — "Area declared a snow disaster," said the Tri-County News.

Yet, even as spring drew near, snow continued. The March 5 issue of the newspaper bore a headline that said, "School closes again."

The winter became the topic of science studies and books, especially those looking at the causes of the spring flooding that followed the heavy snowfalls.

"December, 1996, featured freezing rain events, snow storms and blizzards throughout the month," a DNR report from the spring of 1997 said. "Hardest hit was the western third of Minnesota, where the prairie landscape did little to slow the arctic winds. Schools and offices closed in mid- December, foreshadowing additional closures in January. Christmas Day was the coldest and most snow-covered on record for many communities.

Another major storm began to influence Minnesota late in the afternoon of January 3, with freezing rain in western sections of the state. The precipitation continued as a mix of rain, freezing rain, ice pellets and snow in the south and east on January 4, but changed over to all snow across western, central and northern Minnesota. Some west central and central areas received over two feet of snow, making this one of the larger snowfalls on record.

"The precipitation ended early January 5, but high winds throughout the day caused extensive blowing and drifting, which hampered travel. Frequent occurrences of snow and blowing snow continued throughout the state during January. While none of the storms matched the snowfall totals recorded during the early-January event, moderate snowfall and high winds redistributed the snow pack. In the prairie terrain of southern, western, and northwestern Minnesota, the frequent blizzard or near-blizzard conditions closed roads, schools, government offices and businesses."

When the snow melted in early spring, it caused severe flooding in the neighboring communities of Granite Falls and Montevideo in early April, and Cottonwood residents went to the aid of those towns, helping to fill sandbags and other work to fight rising river levels, and provide other assistance to flood victims. Even in April, as rivers flooded, the long winter still had a grasp on the area: on April 5-6, 1997, as residents and volunteers fought the flooding, they were pounded with one last two-day blizzard, too.

• • •

There were plenty of severe winters before 1996-97, too, and plenty of bad winter storms.

Case's History of Lyon County (1884) writes that the winter of 1872-73 was the "most terrible ever recorded, before or since," said the Cottonwood Centennial history book of 1988. The Centennial book also cites the winter of 1880 as being severe, and worse because it lasted so long.

The Centennial book said the earlier pioneers of 1872-73 may have actually handled their harsh winter better than later settlers because they lived in sod dugout homes — houses dug into the ground.

"There was a basic difference in local perception," the Centennial book says. "In [1872-73], people were living in sod dugouts, the best of all protection from weather extremes. By 1880, most were living in log or frame houses, neither of which were noted for comfort. Besides, this was prairie country and there were no groves as yet to mellow the howling winds. Further, settlers were scattered and far between, and road construction had not begun. And so it was that many lost their way and froze to death."

The winter of 1935-36 was called the harshest winter in living memory by the Centennial book in 1988. "It began with heavy snowfall and persistent winds. Roads were kept open with great difficulty, the only recourse for township-road travelers being the scoop shovel and neighbors' horses to pull the automobiles through the drifts. By January motor travel on the highways and byways had come to a halt. When supplies of food and fuel ran out, farmers hitched their horses to bobsleds and threaded their way around the highest drifts, cutting fences when necessary. But snowfall continued, the winds increased and the temperatures kept falling. There ensued two months of extraordinary cold, temperatures remaining at 20 or

At left: Snow drifts on Main Street in this photo from 1913. Above: There was both snow *and* cold in this photo taken Feb. 2, 1917. The temperature was 20-below-zero at noon that day in Cottonwood.

more below zero. On February 16, 1936, a reliable thermometer registered 39 degrees below zero. Two factors helped avoid disaster. Most people kept generous supplies of potatoes, flour, meat and fuel (farmers usually had supplies of corn cobs and wood for fuel). Nobody starved or froze to death."

Four years later, the infamous Armistice Day blizzard of Nov. 11, 1940, roared through Minnesota like an invasion, "so severe as to almost blot out memories of any other storms." It wasn't just Minnesota that got hit — the storm cut a path 1,000 miles wide from Kansas to Michigan — but Minnesota bore the brunt. Temperatures were unseasonably warm in early

afternoon at about 60 degrees, but soon dropped by 50 degrees to well below freezing. Snowfalls of up to 27 inches and winds of between 50 to 80 mph were recorded in Minnesota. The storm killed a total of 145 people, 49 in Minnesota. No one was killed in the Cottonwood area, but the storm rattled people all the same. "Here, a phenomenon occurred which distinguished this storm from all but the most rare. A powerful wind, with great quantities of loose snow into a dust so fine and so thick as to make free breathing all but impossible. And the truth was that at times a person could not see his own hand a foot in front of his face. For brutal ferocity, this storm has had few if any equals."

Some other memorable winters and storms, with information gleaned from the Cottonwood Centennial book, Tri-County News or the Internet:

• Advances in meteorology, technology and communications since World War II have allowed weather forecasters to give earlier and better warnings of expected storms, and that has helped reduce death tolls from blizzards. Yet, some storms still sneak up on us all. One of those was an Alberta Clipper blizzard which, bringing cold air and strong winds from Canada, caught thousands of people unprepared on Feb. 4, 1984. With winds up to 80 mph causing a wall of white, even though snowfall totals were only a few inches, the storm brought death and shock to southern Minnesota, according to a University of Minnesota report. The storm hit Cottonwood around 7 p.m. with 75 mph winds and a roar "like a freight train," which "made visibility non-existent instantly." About 30 people stayed overnight at the Cottonwood Community Center. There were severe windchills, many people stranded in vehicles or fish houses, even in the gym at Southwest State when college basketball fans there watching a game were ordered to stay inside. Depending on the source, between 16 to 23 deaths were blamed on the Clipper in Minnesota.

- In 1951, there were four blizzards in three weeks.
- The blizzard of Jan. 11-13, 1975, was said by many to have been the worst of the century. The blizzard dealt a deadly blow to the area's pheasant population.
- Another bad storm hit March 23-25, 1975, bringing snow, rain, sleet, thunder, lightning and high winds. Cottonwood area farms were without power for 24 hours.
- Cottonwood was included in the swath of the Halloween Blizzard of 1991 that dropped up to 28 inches of snow on the region.
- On Jan. 19, 1994, Cottonwood's low temperature was 30-degrees-below-zero.

A more pleasant scene from the winter of 2012-13: The Anundson family won the 125th Anniversary celebration's snow-sculpture contest in February 2013 with this birthday-cake sculpture at the Rose Wisdorf home.

From left, a crew of terrific Cottonwood baseball players in the mid-1950s: Harold Yahnka ,Rolly Lovsness, Wynston Boe, Reed Lovsness and Mike Michelson.

Tidbits

• Did you know that Julius T. Knudson (Wendell Knudson's father) sold lumber, posts and shingles from his home site on Front Street? There is an advertisement in the Sept. 18, 1936, issue of the Cottonwood Current. He was still in business in 1940 when Fred Aamodt (Stan and Jerry Aamodt's father) built their chicken coop. J.T. was also an agent for Baker Brothers Studebaker cars in Montevideo.

• Bart Fauteck taught 31 years at Cottonwood and Lakeview schools without taking a sick day. His streak passed 5,000 days in 1995.

• There are no longer Boy Scouts or Girl Scouts groups in Cottonwood.

• The Presbyterian Church on East Cottonwood Street, since converted into a house, had its last service in 1990. The steeple was removed in 2000. The church was erected in 1898.

• Ground was broken for a Habitat for Humanity House on Cottonwood's east side on July 21, 2004.

• The oldest living graduate of Cottonwood, as of May 18, 2013, was Ardith (Aamodt) Sween, right, born June 15, 1913.

• The oldest living former business owner in Cottonwood is Marge Seitz.

• Brothers Stan and Jerry Aamodt, who farm west of town, are believed to be Cottonwood's oldest full-time farmers. They started farming their father's land when they were teen-agers. They do not rent out their land, or help their children farm on a part-time basis but continue to farm their own land full-time.

• In 1976, at the first Memorial Day drawing at the new Cottonwood Country Club, Lois Fratzke won the pick-up.

• Old Highway 17 goes to the current city burning site.

• In the falls of 2007 and 2008, two junior high girls, Mallory Meyer and Corbyn Wee, were members of the junior high football team, a first in Cottonwood.

• Does anyone know when the clock on top of Murph's coffee shop/pool hall was removed?

• There are still wagon tracks near the old Swan Lake Church site, south of Cottonwood on County Road 9, from when the "Red River Express" went from New Ulm to Ortonville. (Information from Erv Schwartz and Jim Runholt. Information originally came from John Smith.)

• Two men from the Cottonwood area who fulfilled their military duty through the National Guard were John Reishus, who passed away in 1999 and Harold "Hal" Loe, who passed away in 2012.

• The Lyon County Highway Shop, which was located on the west edge of Cottonwood along County Road 10, was severely damaged by fire on Feb. 4, 2012. It was later demolished. The county and city of Cottonwood came to an agreement later on that the city would buy the building at 300 East 4th Street N., which had been the former Truckers Pride Truck Wash, and least part of it to the county for its maintenance garage.

• In the mid-1970s, historian and former Cottonwood resident Joe Amato got the help of two city employees, Clinton Berg and John Hirmer, to create a smooth skating/hockey surface on the ice of Cottonwood Lake. As he worked with the two, Amato visited with them. Both Berg and Hirmer were veterans of World War II. Hirmer fought in the Battle of the Bulge in Europe in the winter of 1944-45, and Berg fought in the Pacific. It was bitterly cold at the lengthy Battle of the Bulge, and many soldiers suffered frostbite and other injuries to their feet. Hirmer told Amato that a big reason he survived the battle was that, every morning, he would dry his socks before putting them back on and putting on his boots— something he learned while farming near Cottonwood. Amato asked Berg how he survived the Pacific. "I wanted to go crazy," Berg said as he described some of the intense warfare he endured. "But none of the guys around me were going crazy, so I couldn't either."

• There are a couple of Cottonwood ties to the nationally famous public radio variety program "A Prairie Home Companion," hosted by Garrison Keillor:

— In 1982, humorist and author Howard Mohr, who lives south of Cottonwood, began a stint of several years as a regular guest on the program. The famous country music guitarist Chet Atkins made his first guest appearance on "A Prairie Home Companion" that same year.

— In 1985, "A Prairie Home Companion" toured nationally and gave live performances in the summer and fall from such places as Atlanta, Baton Route, La., Laramie, Wyo., Seattle, Claremont, Calif., and Hawaii. The show returned to Minnesota for a nationally-broadcast live performance from Cottonwood that winter — and a blizzard hit.

• Several business owners seemed to move their businesses around to different buildings, a trend throughout Cottonwood history. Sometimes, their businesses occupied more than one building at a time, other times they would move from one location to another. If you read the history of business and building ownership earlier in this book, you may at first be confused to see a store or store owner listed in more than one place, but that is the reason why: In some cases, they were often on the move.

• The jail, a small building on 1st Street (pictured on Page 278) was demolished in 2012 to make room for a parking lot for the new Norwegian Mutual Insurance office.

Acknowledgements

There are so many to thank for the publication of this history book. Our special thanks go to Kathy Dahl and Charlie Seipel at City Hall for going above and beyond in so many ways. Thank you to those who wrote new articles or stories or contributed new photos. Also, thanks to all those who consented to interviews, provided information of any kind (dates, photos, old stories, documents, remembered a name, etc.). You were all very gracious of your time, memories and thoughts about Cottonwood. Another special thank you to the Tri-County News, Marshall Independent and Joe Amato for granting permission for us to reprint in their entirety various stories and a poem. To anyone who in any way helped make this book a reality, we are grateful. And we hope that coming generations will be grateful, too.